CORPORATE AND EXECUTIVE TAX SHELTERED INVESTMENTS

CORPORATE AND EXECUTIVE TAX SHELTERED INVESTMENTS

edited by
Peter C. Reid

tax consultant
Gustave Simons

Presidents Publishing House, Inc. • New York • New York • 1972

Book Designed by GEORGE H. BUEHLER

Library of Congress Catalog No. 78–180228

ISBN 0–87856013–0

Copyright © 1972 by **PRESIDENTS PUBLISHING HOUSE**, Inc.
Printed in the United States of America by
HADDON CRAFTSMEN

FIRST PRINTING

CONTENTS

Commentary
Depending on a Batting Average—The Promoter's Investment—Exchanging an Oil Interest For Common Stock

INTRODUCTION

Faced with constantly rising taxes, corporations and individuals alike are actively seeking effective ways by which to shelter their income. It is no easy task to comprehend the intricacies and complexities of today's tax laws—laws which have been made even more unfathomable by the Tax Reform Act of 1969. Yet the opportunities for tax-sheltered investments are there for the individual or company knowing where to look. This book is intended to help them in their quest. It will tell them when a sheltered investment is possible, what investment areas can be sheltered, how to evaluate specific shelters in terms of specific needs, how the transaction can be made, the legal and accounting procedures—and how to evaluate the impact of the 1969 Act.

In addition, this book will alert the reader to the many potential booby traps with which the tax shelter field is strewn. The authors of these chapters do not ignore the pitfalls inherent in many tax shelters. Instead, they frankly point them out and suggest possible ways to avoid them.

The book does not pretend to be a complete treatment of what is a vast subject. That would be impossible in a volume ten times as long. The chapters do offer, however, basic guidelines which can lead the reader to areas which he may want to explore further with his tax counsel.

Most of the book's chapters are based on material presented in a series of informal talks at workshop programs held by Corporate Seminars, Inc. These talks were given by the foremost practitioners in the field of tax-shelter investments. In some instances, question and answer periods have been included for their additional contributions to the subject.

In adapting the extensive material, the aim has been to avoid the academic, the overtechnical, and the theoretical. Rather than comprising an incomprehensible treatise, the book offers practical guidance in terms the layman can understand. Although it can be of help to the accountant and the attorney, it is primarily aimed at the investor, whether he be a corporation executive or a self-employed professional.

The chapters fall naturally into two major sections: first, aspects of tax shelters in general, and second, specific types of tax shelter investment. Thus, by the end of the book, the reader should have a comprehensive, substantial knowledge of the tax shelter field in its many aspects.

I am indebted to Gustave Simons for his authoritative overview tying the many chapters neatly together, and for his perceptive comments following individual chapters.

Peter C. Reid
January, 1972

SECTION I:

OPPORTUNITIES AND PROBLEMS IN TAX SHELTER INVESTMENT

1

THE COMPLEXITIES OF TAX SHELTERS: AN OVERVIEW

By Gustave Simons

The book you are about to read contains over 20 authoritative articles on various aspects of tax shelter investments and the specific types of investments available to the taxpayer. Why, then, you well may ask, is this overview article necessary in addition to these articles?

There are several answers to that question. First, many of the principles underlying tax shelter investments—as well as changes in

Mr. Simons is senior partner, Gustave Simons and Associates; president, American Management Counsel those principles made by the 1969 Tax Reform Act—apply generally to every tax shelter. To deal with them in each separate article would inflict burdensome repetition on the reader. An author, discussing a specific tax shelter investment, such as real estate, cannot be expected to deal in depth with changes in the capital gains tax, the minimum tax, the maximum tax, and other important general factors that affect all tax shelter investments. Thus a need is created for a comprehensive overview going beyond the confines of any specific tax shelter.

Moreover, the effect of certain tax provisions applicable to a specific type of tax shelter investment can vary greatly according to the investor's overall financial and tax situation. For example, in real estate investment, there are new recapture provisions for accelerated depreciation that, although burdensome, do not in *most* cases lessen the attractiveness of real estate as a tax haven. But in situations in which an investor must pay a high capital gains tax plus the new minimum preference tax because of his overall tax situation, a real estate deal will no longer provide a tax shelter.

Here is a brief example: Assume that the investor acquires a structure for $100,000. It is depreciated down to $40,000. This $60,000 of depreciation reflects $30,000 of straight line depreciation and $30,000 of accelerated depreciation. The depreciation reduces the basis of the property to $40,000. Thus, everything in excess of $40,000 is taken as taxable gain. If the property is sold for $140,000, how is the "gain" of $100,000 treated?

Thirty thousand would be treated as ordinary income, reflecting the accelerated depreciation taken. Thirty thousand would be treated as capital gain, reflecting the straight line depreciation taken; and $40,000, representing the increase in the value of the property over its original price, is also taxed as capital gain. This could still represent a very attractive tax situation. Even with the $30,000 of accelerated depreciation that is recaptured, the taxpayer-investor has enjoyed a tax holiday measured by the time between the tax savings attributable to the reduction of his ordinary income tax in the years when the accelerated depreciation was taken, and his payment of ordinary income tax for the year in which the property is sold. He has had the use of the money during this interval. Moreover, the sale might take place in a year of lower tax brackets, or proceeds might even be stretched out over many years by means of an installment sale.

However, these depreciation recapture provisions of the 1969 Act can appear very different if the $70,000 capital gain in this case was taxed not at the old 25 percent rate, but rather at a 60 percent rate. *(See Chapter 9.)* Moreover, the accelerated depreciation might have been taxed at a 10 percent additional rate during the years that it was taken, because it became an item of tax preference. Such a contingency could create a complete reversal of the deal's attractiveness.

Variables of this kind cannot be treated easily in each article on a specific tax shelter. Instead they must be included in a general overview.

Furthermore, only an overview article can specify which tax shelters are best for each type of investor who may be reading this book—and the range will be great, from salaried executive to self-employed professional to the individual with unearned income.

DEFINING A TAX SHELTER

Basically, a tax shelter is any investment that affords the investor relatively large deductions; permits the realization of income tax at lower tax levels; or provides protection from other taxes such as the estate tax or the tax on unreasonable accumulation of surplus.

Under this broad definition, many types of investment qualify as tax shelters. No single volume could describe every form of investment that has some tax advantages. Nor could any book in fairness restrict itself only to the traditional tax shelters such as oil and real estate. Therefore, this book has aimed at a middle road: it includes articles on traditional investments, but it also deals with investments which, although not ordinarily considered as tax shelters, nevertheless are endowed with very potent tax sheltering capabilities. Two examples are pension plans and minimum deposit insurance, either of which can often be used in conjunction with such investments as oil or real estate to offset some of the difficulties encountered with these more traditional shelters.

Here is an illustration of how this might be done. Suppose an individual wants not only immediate tax savings, plus a means to provide insurance to protect his family, but especially a way to ease the liquidation of the primary tax shelter at his death.

He could first go into an accelerated depreciation program which would throw off a substantial after-tax income in the first five years of ownership. Simultaneously, he could acquire some life insurance policies. IRC-264 provides that only three out of the first seven years premiums may be borrowed. In the eighth year, a large portion of the premiums paid without borrowing can be recaptured by a large loan, so that eventually the only investment in the policy is the payment of deductible interest on the loans. Some of the tax-free income thrown off in the early years by the accelerated depreciation investment could then be used to pay the first four annual premiums in cash. He would then borrow the next three premiums, paying only minimal and deductible interest, and in the eighth year borrow back the major part of the premiums paid in the first four years. In this type of tandem operation, as one of the investments loses favor from a tax point of view, the other gains it—and the net result is excellent.

COMPARING A SHELTER WITH A NONSHELTER

It is easily seen from this example alone that our broad, simplified definition of a tax shelter covers a multitude of complexities. Evaluating specific tax shelters is no easy task because of the challenging number of variables and factors that must be considered. This can be illustrated by comparing the features of a completely non-sheltered tax situation with a bona fide tax shelter investment.

Suppose an investor buys a brand name from a company and then licenses its use—in exchange for royalties—for limited periods of time such as ten years. This is a completely unsheltered arrangement because, according to the tax laws, not only is his outlay for the brand name nondeductible, but the royalties he receives will be taxed as ordinary income.

Compare this with a situation in which the same investor forms a partnership with another individual to do research and development work. Their resulting patents are licensed in exchange for royalties. But in this case, the investment in research costs is tax deductible and the royalties are taxed at capital gains rates. The investor has put his money into a bona fide tax shelter.

The striking impact of this on his income can be shown with some hypothetical figures. Assume, for example, that in the first case the brand name was purchased by a corporation in which the investor invested $500,000. Also assume that his other income put him into the 70 percent individual income tax bracket, while the corporation had other income of $25,000 a year.

Assuming that he is getting a 10 percent return on his investment, the $50,000 coming on top of the $25,000 would be subject to a full federal corporate tax. If this rate is 50 percent, the investor will be left with $250,000 after ten years of royalties. If this amount were distributed as dividends in the 70 percent bracket, he would retain only $75,000. Thus, with an after-tax investment of $500,000, and an after-tax yield of $7,500 a year, his annual conversion ratio is a meager 1.5 percent.

But suppose the investor had chosen instead to invest $500,-000 in the tax-sheltered research and development business? Let us say he patents an invention which yields the same annual $50,000 in royalties for ten years. Because his investment is deductible, his after-tax investment would cost him only 30 percent of his actual outlay: $150,000. Assuming he had no other capital gains or tax preference items, his $50,000 royalty would be taxed at only the 25 percent federal rate, netting him an annual return of $37,500 for a robust conversion ratio of 25 percent.

The conclusion might seem undebatable: between a tax-sheltered investment and an unsheltered investment, the shelter is always the right choice. But it is not that simple. There are too many variables involved. For example, the royalty on the brand name, although it would provide a low return, might be a sure thing, whereas the research and development effort might be a total failure. Or, the investor might acquire the brand name as an individual so that even if the royalty came in at the 70 percent federal level it would still yield twice as much after-tax income as would be available by siphoning it through a personal holding company. Or, the brand name royalty might go on forever while the patent royalties presumably would last for only seventeen years.

EVALUATING DIFFERENT TYPES OF SHELTERS

These are but a few of the simpler variables involved—there are others of a more complex nature. The point is, however, that merely comparing a sheltered situation with a non-sheltered situation is a tricky problem. And obviously, comparing and evaluating different types of tax shelters can be even trickier. There are some general guidelines, however, that may help the prospective investor to know what to look for:

Always Compare Alternative Shelters

It is important always to compare any specific tax shelter with one or more alternative tax shelters—or, as has just been done, with an unsheltered investment that has economic potential. In addition, the investor should consider the possibility of making a sheltered investment in tandem with a non-sheltered investment. For example, the corporation which acquired and licensed the brand name might also try to develop other products by spending the royalties for research and development.

Consider All Possible Taxes

In evaluating a tax shelter, *all* the types of taxes which might be involved must be considered. There are, of course, federal corporate taxes, federal individual taxes on unearned income, personal holding company taxes, and capital gains taxes. Then, still within the federal area, there is the minimum tax on tax preference income. In many cases this last tax can hit an investor three times on a tax shelter. It can hit him at the deduction point as in the case of accelerated depreciation on real estate. Moreover, if the real estate is heavily mortgaged, the *excess investment* interest on the tax preference may be *totally* disallowed to the extent that it exceeds certain exemptions and credits. Then, when the property is sold, as indicated earlier, part of the proceeds will probably be treated as ordinary income through the recapture provisions. Even that portion which is a capital gain can create a tax preference which not only adds the minimum tax to what may be an increased capital gains rate, but also may "infect" earned income by reducing the amount subject to the maximum taxable ceiling—60 percent in 1971 and 50 percent thereafter (IRC–1348). This infection can last for five years.

Still another tax which must be considered is the estate tax. Some shelters are particularly vulnerable to estate taxes, while others are particularly favored in this respect. If the investor died, whether he owned the invention directly or through a corporation, the Internal Revenue Service might apply a very high evaluation by capitalizing the income. Thus, even with a time discount, a high estate tax could result. Yet the invention might not be a liquid asset and many years might be required to collect the royalties necessary to pay the estate tax. Of course, the impact of the estate tax can be greatly eased by freezing values through cross purchase agreements—particularly if such agreements are tied in with tax deductible, tax exempt, minimum deposit insurance. In any case, the estate tax must never be disregarded when a tax shelter is being evaluated.

The tax on unreasonable accumulation of surplus (IRC–531) is another federal tax to be considered. Some tax shelters increase exposure to this tax, while others decrease the exposure or even eliminate the income subject to the tax altogether.

In the case of a foreign investment, the interest equalization tax must be considered. This tax should be kept in mind in connection with Mr. Martin's chapter (Ch. 24) on Curacao as a tax haven.

Evaluate Shelters in Context

The investor should also examine a potential investment in the context of all other tax shelters in which he is involved. Repeatedly, the chapters which follow say that a given tax shelter is attractive only in a given tax bracket. But whether a particular investor is in a given bracket depends on what other deductions or tax sheltered investments he might have in that year—or even in earlier or later years if carry-backs or carry-overs result, as sometimes is the case with a tax sheltered investment.

Moreover, both in the year of investment and in the year of liquidation, the investor must consider other items of tax preference, not only in the specific year involved but in the four preceding years plus the four following years. Such caution is necessary because the minimum tax on tax preferences can, by itself, directly dilute the benefit of many tax shelters. This circumstance applies, however, only if a tax preference exceeds various levels (one level is used in imposing the minimum tax under IRC-57, and another level in disqualifying income as earned income entitled to the benefit of the ceiling on maximum tax. IRC-1348). Much depends on whether a tax preference brings the investor into the danger zone under IRC-57 or IRC-1348, or both. He should always bear in mind that, because of tax preferences, the disqualification of income from the protection of the ceiling on maximum tax under IRC-1348 can apply not only to the particular year, but also on the basis of the average excess in that year and the four preceding years.

Assume that between 1971 and 1979 there are items of tax preference in 1975 only. That year may then be averaged out over 1971 through 1975. However, if the ceiling is applicable in 1976, 1977, 1978 or 1979, the year in question, 1975, could alternatively be used for averaging out tax preference items for 1976 and the four preceding years, and similarly for 1977, 1978 or 1979. This means that the tax preferences may have an impact over a nine-year period. For example, a long-term capital gain of $600,000 creates $300,000 of tax preference. If this occurs in 1975, it can mean, even if there were no prior tax preferences, that the average excess over $30,000 for the taxable year and the four preceding years (the period used in IRC-1348) is $30,000 a year. Thus, income sheltered by IRC-1348 is reduced by $30,000 (the average) or by the entire $300,000 for 1975, if there is that much income.

On the other hand, assume that there is no earned income in 1975 or in any year until 1979, and that there are no items of tax preference during this period other than the one capital gain in 1975.

It still holds that the average tax preference for 1979 and the four preceding years exceeds $30,000 a year by an equal amount, resulting in the disqualification of $30,000 of earned income in 1979. Although the formula used is slightly more complicated than presented here, the example does make the point that the investor must consider tax preferences not only upon undertaking an investment, but during the entire period the investment will be held. Accelerated depreciation and percentage depletion on petroleum, for instance, are tax preference items in every year they are taken.

Consider Timing of Benefits

The investor should evaluate the timing element of different tax shelters with great care. For example, two of the most effective tax shelters are employee trusts and minimum deposit insurance. Yet neither one provides immediate benefits in terms of after-tax income. In both shelters, the increment value over the years is not taxed until final distribution. With employee trusts, the distribution can be maneuvered so that it is favorable as far as income tax is concerned. Moreover, if the employee dies, the proceeds are free from estate tax. With minimum deposit insurance, the proceeds are entirely free from income tax, and through proper use of trusts can be kept free of estate taxes as well.

These benefits, however, are not immediate, and the investor who needs a quick increase in his after-tax income should be aware of this. What he might do is provide security for himself and his family by means of an employee trust and some form of insurance or variable annuity program. Then for immediate benefits, he should cast around for another kind of tax shelter. (He should understand, however, that quick tax shelter results usually involve taking a deduction larger than the cash investment, which can eventually result in a more serious exposure in legal terms, or a mere deferment of the tax burden to a later time, or even a lesser return in proportion to the after-tax cost.)

Evaluate Legal Vulnerability of Shelters

Another important aspect for the investor to consider is a tax shelter's vulnerability to attack through legislative changes, judicial interpretation, or administrative mandate.

The legal vulnerability of a tax shelter is based on several factors. One is the shelter's degree of social usefulness, as explained in Chapter 2. Examples of socially useful tax shelters are petroleum, research and development, insurance, and employee trusts. Ordinarily, the more socially useful a tax shelter is, the less vulnerable it is to attack. But it does not always work out this way, as can be gathered from my comments following Chapter 2. Other factors can weaken the protection provided by the social usefulness of a tax shelter.

One such factor is popularity. A tax shelter that gains popularity with the financial elite of Wall Street can also gain in vulnerability. This happens because the financial elite are sufficiently numerous to invite Congressional attention, but not to be politically potent. For example, prior to November, 1968, a popular shelter on Wall Street was the acquisition of capital growth assets on a highly leveraged basis with interest paid for five or more years in advance. This shelter was protected by a revenue ruling explicitly permitting a cash-basis taxpayer to take five years of interest in advance as a deduction. But as more and more specialists in this type of investment sprang up, the Internal Revenue Service became concerned—and in November, 1968, it announced that *prospectively* future payments of interest in advance would be allowed only under certain very limited circumstances. Precisely the same thing happened with equipment leasing, also a very popular shelter in the past because of the accelerated depreciation on airplanes, computers, and the like, which exceed the cash payer's investment by a large multiple.

In both of these cases, the beneficiaries of these shelters lacked the political clout to preserve them. As a result, both shelters were severely clobbered by the Treasury Department and Congress.

On the other hand, there are examples of shelters which are not only socially useful, but whose beneficiaries have ample political power to protect them. One is insurance. Backing up its social usefulness is the considerable influence of large insurance companies with their tens of millions of policy holders. As a result, insurance companies have fared far more favorably in the developing pattern of tax law than has equipment leasing.

Oil is another example. Not only is petroleum more socially useful than many other forms of tax shelter investment, but the oil lobby is one of the best organized and financed in Washington. It was not surprising, then, that oil was affected by the 1969 Tax Reform Act only by having the percentage depreciation reduced to a still healthy 22 percent and having it treated as a tax preference. The major benefit of this tax shelter—the deductibility of drilling expenses— was left untouched.

Still another factor affecting the vulnerability of a tax shelter is the degree to which it is merely a legal gimmick. For example, investors in agribusiness can now avoid the Excess Deduction Account (which treats the recapture of deductions in excess of $25,000 a year as ordinary income) by making their investments through a Subchapter S corporation. This strategy, however, is such a transparent legal gimmick—made possible through a technical oversight of Congress—that it undoubtedly will be eliminated by legislative action.

If a tax shelter offers solid benefits but is vulnerable to legal attack, any investor using it should be certain he can cash in on the benefits rapidly. If he wants to lock himself into a tax shelter for the long haul, he should invest in one that is relatively invulnerable to future change by legislative action. Minimum deposit insurance is such a shelter. This is true because only very minor limitations have been placed on it in the past by Congress, and even these were applied only to policies acquired after widespread warnings had been given to the public. Accordingly, even though a long time is required to realize the tremendous tax benefits in insurance, the man who invests in such a program can be certain that those benefits will not be taken away from him by Congressional action.

Be Wary of Need for Constant Escalation

In considering a tax shelter, the investor must also ask himself whether or not he might end up its slave instead of its master. With some types of tax shelters, constant escalation of investment is needed to continue enjoying the benefits and offsetting the disadvantages. For example, tax shelters that depend on accelerated depreciation reverse themselves after a few years and instead of giving the taxpayer more deductions than his cash layout, they begin to saddle him with more taxable income than his net cash flow can handle. Many investors have answered this problem by buying more airplanes or more shopping centers whose accelerated depreciation would offset the excess income from prior acquisitions. By 1970, however, not only had business conditions made these roll-over deals harder to find, but the tax benefits themselves had been severely hit by the 1969 Tax Reform Act.

Another hazard involved in a tax shelter requiring constant escalation is the possibility of what can happen if the investor dies. One brilliant businessman with an income of several hundred thousand dollars in 1970 paid not one cent of income tax and only $16,000 of minimum tax on tax preferences. He accomplished this through accelerated depreciation on real estate investments. He was confident that he could continue to enjoy these tax benefits by simply escalating his investments. What he did not consider was that if he died, estate tax liabilities would force liquidation of the real estate properties, and no executor would have the capacity or willingness to take the business risk inherent in continuing to pursue this type of transaction. This particular businessman would have been even more astute if, while continuing his accelerated depreciation ventures, he had also directed some of his sheltered income into minimum deposit insurance so that upon his death there would have accrued some large gains without either income tax or estate tax.

Consider the Program's Integrity

Finally, in evaluating tax shelters, the investor must investigate the integrity of the program he is considering. Most programs in all types of tax shelters are ethically sound. However, certain types of tax shelters lend themselves more readily to unscrupulous promotion than others. For example, although petroleum is theoretically one of the best tax shelters, it is a highly esoteric and speculative one. Therefore, the unwary investor may find himself in the hands of a promoter who is not really looking out for his best interests. Needless to say, the credentials of the authors of the petroleum chapters in this book are above question.

Investment in cattle is another tax shelter area that lends itself to unethical practices, since the investor seldom sees the substance of his investment. Indeed, some cattle program promoters have been known to sell the same cow twenty times over. Actually, most programs in this field are legitimate, but the investor must be wary that he does not put his money into one of the rare ones that is not.

This problem is not quite so sensitive in other tax shelter areas. Pension plans and insurance, for example, are in fields that have been closely regulated for many years. While there is no guarantee that a few programs in these fields may not be unethical, the investor will usually find himself dealing with either a large trust company or insurance company with a well established reputation for integrity.

The flux of legislative, judicial and administrative determinations is so great that any aspect of this volume or any one similar to it, should be checked out with counsel before being activated. For example, Chapter 22 deals with pension trusts. On August 15, 1971, President Nixon promulgated his wage freeze. Did this apply to pension trusts?

In World War II, qualified pension and profit sharing trusts were exempt from salary stabilization. Far from having an inflationary tendency, they had a stabilizing tendency.

The guidelines, published on August 23, 1971, under the President's order, included pension trusts in the prohibited category. On reading this, the author challenged it for the reasons stated above. On August 25, he was advised from authoritative sources that pension trusts were to be exempt notwithstanding the August 23rd publication.

In footnoting the various chapters, we have indicated past or present political vulnerability to the extent possible, but we cannot pretend to omniscience.

CHOOSING THE BEST TAX SHELTER FOR SPECIFIC NEEDS

Because of the wide variety of tax shelters, each with its unique benefits and drawbacks, it is not an easy task for the investor to know which is best for his particular situation. Indeed, there is often no *one* type of shelter that will meet his needs completely. In such a case the best solution is to choose two types that complement each other. For example, he might invest in one tax shelter with short-term benefits but long-term problems and another where there are no immediate tax advantages but definite long-range benefits.

Let us examine now the tax shelter needs of five different types of investors—some fairly common, some rare—and suggest shelter programs that would fill those needs.

The High-Paid Executive

The executive with a high salary—often in six figures—is frequently in search of a tax shelter for his earned income. This, despite the attempt of Congress to lure the executive away from tax shelters by imposing a ceiling (60 percent in 1971 and 50 percent thereafter) on the tax on earned income. This, Congress reasoned, would eliminate the executive's need for a tax shelter. The fallacy of this theory is brilliantly explained by Sol J. Upbin in Chapter 3. In one example he shows that a man earning $125,000 saves only $3,240 in taxes by reason of the ceiling. The same man, if he has in addition to his salary a long-term capital gain of another $125,000, saves only $3,075 because of the ceiling. This example demonstrates how in certain situations the tax impact on capital gains has been almost doubled by the 1969 Tax Reform Act, a point discussed at length in Chapter 8.

Moreover, the salaried executive may have other such unearned income as rents, dividends, or royalties. This income is completely unsheltered.

Most salaried executives, then, still need tax shelters. The question is: What kind? The answer depends to a large extent on his particular circumstances. If his security requirements are already covered by a vested pension or profit-sharing trust participation, by adequate deductible insurance programs or by family trusts, then the emphasis should be on shelters that provide more immediate tax benefits, such as oil, real estate, or cattle.

On the other hand, if he can live comfortably on his salary after deducting taxes, but is concerned about future security because his employer provides an inadequate employee benefit program, then he needs other types of tax shelters. He might try to persuade his employer to provide him with a selective salary continuance program that will give him both security requirements and death protection for him and his family (as illustrated in the second part of Chapter 8.) If this is not feasible, the employer might incorporate the executive and then lease his services rather than pay him directly as an employee. The employee's own company could then install an adequate pension plan providing both the retirement and insurance protection he needs.

Incorporating the Executive As an example, take the case of an electronics executive in his early fifties, earning $200,000 a year, who cannot persuade his employer to put in either an adequate pension and insurance program for the company's employees or a salary continuance plan for him. But he does persuade the company to engage his own corporation under a consulting contract at the same annual cost to the company. Indeed, the employer actually saves money, because he no longer has to expend any funds for the former employee's benefits.

Here is the way it works: the executive's corporation pays him $125,000 a year and deposits approximately $45,000 into a qualified pension trust. This trust fund can be invested tax free and will provide immediate life insurance protection (free of estate tax) of over $600,000 plus a pension at age 65 of over $6,000 a month, or a lump sum available in cash at retirement of almost a million dollars. The executive can retire before sixty-five at a reduced pension. Even if the contract is terminated, several hundred thousand dollars will have accrued in the pension fund after a few years.

This arrangement does create one problem for the executive. The $125,000 salary plus the $45,000 pension contribution leaves his corporation with $30,000 of taxable income. This amount would be subject to corporate federal taxes of about $8,000 and state taxes of about $2,000, leaving $20,000. Since the corporation is controlled by less than five people and earns all its income from the services of its one stockholder, it is a personal holding company and therefore subject to the personal holding company tax on the retained $20,000.

What is the solution? One approach would be to eliminate the $30,000 corporate income so that it would be excluded from personal holding company treatment. If the $30,000 were drilled away in an oil program, for example, no taxable income would be left in the corporation. Then, as soon as the income from oil was two-thirds as great as the adjusted gross income attributable to the services of the stockholder-executive, the corporation would cease to be in the personal holding company category.

If no qualified oil program can be found, the corporation could turn to a cattle feeding operation as described in Chapter 18. In addition to minimal business risk, this operation has three tax virtues: it gives immediate deductions; the income comes in the following year and may again be sheltered; and it is ordinary business income that can help take the corporation out of the personal holding company category.

Another approach might have the corporation pay the tax on the $30,000 and then distribute the remaining $20,000 as a dividend to the executive. However, unless the executive has personal deductions to offset the dividend, it must be sheltered. One reason is that, even though his $125,000 salary is sheltered by the ceiling, the dividend, as unearned income, is taxed in the same bracket as though it came on top of the $125,000.

The dividend can be sheltered through an oil investment, a real estate investment, or a good agricultural investment, including cattle breeding. The last mentioned, as pointed out in Chapters 18 and 19, can to some extent provide capital gains as opposed to cattle feeding which merely defers income or changes personal holding company income to business income.

Other Alternatives for the Executive What alternatives does the executive have if he cannot persuade his employer either to install a decent pension plan or salary continuance plan or contract for his services through his own corporation? One alternative is to find another employer who will provide either of these shelters. However, if the executive is harnessed to a long-term contract with an intransigent employer, his only alternative is to seek his own tax shelters. His selection, of course, again depends on his needs and goals. He may well find that they can be met by integrating short- and long-term shelter operations, such as combining minimum deposit insurance and real estate, cattle, or oil. (Oil, in some cases, can provide both short- *and* long-term advantages, since any long-term income from producing wells is sheltered by the percentage depletion allowance.)

The Self-Employed Professional

The tax shelter approach for a professional—be he lawyer, accountant, physician, dentist, veterinarian, architect, engineer, or entertainer—is similar to that for the salaried executive. Like the salaried executive, the professional's first choice might be to incorporate. Through recent legislation, this is possible now even for those in the so-called learned professions such as medicine and law.

One such case involved a 55-year-old physician with two 30-year-old junior physicians and five younger nursing assistants associated with him. The older physician was earning about $50,000 a year; the two younger ones about $15,000 each.

The group was formed into a professional corporation. The senior physician received a salary of about $1,600 a month and a pension plan providing for 40 percent of compensation less social security benefits. The plan's total annual pre-tax cost was slightly over $26,000, of which almost $23,000 was allocated to the physician. Assuming earnings of 4 percent, this provided a monthly pension of over $1,500, insurance protection of approximately $150,000, and cash available at retirement of almost $300,000. The net result of this plan was that almost $23,000 a year of the physician's earnings were sheltered, at a cost to him for his associates of only $2,000 a year after taxes.

Each of the younger physicians received $750 a month, pension of over $600, insurance of over $60,000, and cash at retirement of almost $100,000. Because the junior physicians had 28 years in which to accumulate the necessary funds at retirement, the annual cost for each physician was only about $1,200.

The Taxpayer with Unearned Income

If a man's income is comprised of dividends on securities or rent from land which he owns outright, his tax sheltering capacities are great because he may invest hard dollars—that is, after-tax dollars along with his taxable dollars. Such a situation makes it far easier to shelter the taxable dollars. The job could be done, for example, by a sound real estate program without accelerated depreciation. The investor should especially consider low rental rehabilitation projects as described in Chapters 14 & 16. In addition, he should consider the private annuity transaction described in Chapter 8.

The Trust Fund Beneficiary

If an individual is the beneficiary of a large trust fund, a pension plan will do him no good because his income is wholly unearned. His tax shelter approach would depend on his particular circumstances. If his children are the remaindermen of the trust, he must provide security for his wife in the event of his death, unless he wants her to be dependent on the generosity of her children. On the other hand, if he has no children or they are not remaindermen of the trust, it becomes even more urgent to provide security for his wife or his children.

In such cases, the beneficiary could turn to minimum deposit insurance, but only in tandem with real estate providing depreciation. This can be done in two ways. Either the beneficiary can buy real estate or cattle with accelerated depreciation, integrated into his minimum deposit insurance program, or he can ask the trustee to buy ordinary improved real estate with straight line depreciation sheltering the rental income in whole or part.

The advantage of the latter approach derives from the fact that the trustee can use some of the trust capital as a down payment for real estate rather than using substantial leverage. Moreover, the beneficiary receives the rental and the shelter of the depreciation deduction without having to set aside a sinking fund to offset the depreciation. Finally, if there is a mortgage, its amortization comes out of the trust capital.

The Taxpayer with Short-Term High Income

An example of this category might be an athlete who has a very high income for limited number of years. His best bet in tax shelters would be, as in the case of the salaried executive, to incorporate. He could then put together a combination of pension plan or profit-sharing plan or both. This approach would shelter 25 percent of his earned income.

The Taxpayer with a One-Shot Large Unearned Income.

An example of this type might be an individual who wins a large lottery. The best shelter for him would be a highly leveraged program where the deductions exceed the cash outlay. Such a program might be in cattle feeding, highly leveraged real estate, or the occasional oil program where deductions twice as large as the cash investment are available.

There are other types of taxpayers with tax shelter needs, of course. There is the man whose principal problem is shelter from an estate tax. There is the corporation with high taxable earnings which it wants to shelter without unduly reducing its reportable earnings. There is the corporation with the problem of unreasonable accumulation of earnings and a possible IRC-531 tax. All of these problems will be discussed later in individual commentaries that will follow each chapter of the book.

2

HOW TAX SHELTERS PROMOTE OUR NATIONAL GOALS

Milton A. Dauber

Far too often, the laws that make tax shelters possible are described as "loopholes" or "gimmicks." Nothing could be farther from the truth. Congress adopted these laws after careful deliberation, with the purpose of serving some major social or economic goal. Therefore, when an individual or corporate investor is utilizing these techniques, he is, in addition to improving his own financial position, furthering a legitimate, national economic goal.

MR. DAUBER IS CHAIRMAN OF GEO DYNAMICS, INC., AN INDEPENDENT OIL AND GAS EXPLORATION AND OPERATIONS FIRM. HE IS ALSO PRESIDENT OF INTRAMERICAN MANAGEMENT CORPORATION.

BENEFITS OF TAX-EXEMPT BONDS

This fact is perhaps most obvious in the case of tax-exempt municipal bonds. There, the clear, overriding social goal is to enable state and municipal governments to carry out their capital expanison programs at the lowest possible cost. This goal is achieved by conferring a tax benefit upon the purchaser of the municipal bond.

As so often happens in a progressive tax rate system, the higher the bracket, the larger the benefit to the taxpayer from such an investment. But the benefit also aids the low-bracket taxpayer indirectly. If it were not for this particular exemption, the cities and the states would be forced to pay a higher rate of interest in the marketplace in order to achieve their capital budgets. This would mean higher taxes, and very frequently, regressive taxes—such as the sales tax, flat-rate wage or income tax, or gross-receipts tax—inflicted upon the vast majority of the country's citizens.

Ironically, the high-bracket investor would not really suffer, because the higher coupon interest would compensate him for the tax that he would have to pay on municipal bonds.

DEPLETION ALLOWANCES: OIL AND OTHER MINERALS

It can be similarly shown that other forms of tax shelter investment also serve legitimate national goals. Consider, for example, the allowance of percentage depletion for oil—and for at least 100 other minerals—which is probably the most discussed deduction made available in American business. Its effectiveness as an incentive to increased petroleum production has been well proven in the forty years or more that it has been a part of our tax laws.

However, there are some well-meaning, if uninformed, critics who say that this advantage should be available only to full-time participants in the petroleum industry, not to high-bracket individuals or other relatively passive petroleum investors.

Most assuredly, the depletion allowance and other special tax rules are an incentive to passive investment in oil and gas exploration and discovery. But the critics have failed to ask why it is that the petroleum industry permits outsiders to join in the exploration and development of new sources of oil. After all, if the tax benefits are so tremendous, why do not the professionals simply keep it all for themselves?

The answer is clear: participation by private investors is desirable—in fact, necessary—because such investors provide the risk capital needed to bring into production many useful sources of petroleum which would otherwise go untapped.

Although the oil industry is dominated by several giant firms, it also includes many small and medium-sized firms that serve a useful role. It is these companies which derive the greatest benefit from joint-venture exploration and development with private risk capital—and the protection of this segment of the oil industry is definitely in the national interest. Those who would seek to limit the number of players in the oil game must face up to the possibility that such limitations could cripple this part of the oil industry and significantly harm the economy of at least a dozen states.

EQUIPMENT LEASING BENEFITS

Tax benefits for equipment leasing also serve a national goal. Why, one might ask, should it be possible for a private investor to purchase a railroad car and lease it to a railroad? For one reason, the railroad might be incapable of purchasing the equipment itself, either with its own funds or through long-term bank financing. By giving the high-bracket private investor the benefits of special amortization, the law enables him to shoulder the risk of and keep up the efficiency of the transportation system.

Such competition in financing is a major governmental policy that has received much attention from the Supreme Court and from federal regulatory agencies. Accelerated depreciation was put into the statutes specifically to encourage investment in additional equipment.

TAX SHELTER THROUGH REAL ESTATE

Real estate is another example of how national policy is served by our tax shelter laws. In 1966, tremors ran through our economy as the credit crunch caused a severe cutback in real estate construction. If tax benefits can induce private investors to pump risk capital into new construction, then certainly the country as a whole stands to benefit as well.

Further, Congress has explicitly recognized that this tax shelter plays a vital role in evoking the private capital needed to provide improved housing for the underprivileged segment of society.

THE INVESTOR AND AGRICULTURE

Last, but by no means least, consider the role of individual and corporate investors in the agricultural sector of the economy. The tax rules benefiting the agricultural investor include the cash method of accounting and the equating of investment in cattle to investment in any other form of productive property. These rules certainly induce substantial cattle investment. The deductibility of various expenses involved in the acquisition and operation of farm land similarly encourages long-term investment in this form of property.

These private investments exert a stabilizing force in the agricultural economy. Because the markets for cattle and land are thus expanded, the farmer can obtain increased mobility of capital. He is more readily able to liquidate his own investment whenever he desires to do so. In addition, agricultural employment is increased and profit opportunities for local businesses, such as feed mill operators, are expanded. Finally, leasing of investor-owned agricultural land to farmers permits easier entry into the agricultural industry and removes the crushing burden of land ownership from the small or under-capitalized farmer.

CONCLUSION

These then, are some of the ways in which the tax-sheltered investor—often to his own surprise—plays an important role in adding to the productive capabilities of that complex miracle, the United States economy.

COMMENTARY

This thoughtful contribution makes a sound point: the long-term survival of most tax shelters depends either on their social usefulness or on the fact that they are so rarely used that they escape attention.

RESTRICTIONS ON SOCIALLY USEFUL SHELTERS

However, a reservation must be added: even socially useful investments can be subjected to legislative restrictions on their tax benefits. For example, Mr. Dauber points out that real estate and agriculture are tax sheltered in order to prime those two areas of our economy. Yet serious limitations have now been placed on both of these tax shelters. How did this come about? One answer lies in the fact that by the late 1960's many wealthy people had started jumping on the real estate and agriculture tax shelter bandwagon. In Hollywood, these shelters were used by motion picture and television stars who were burdened with six-figure incomes. In Florida, they helped many beneficiaries of multi-million dollar trust funds. Finally, Wall Street got into the act, with some Stock Exchange firms tying into enterprises dealing both in real estate and agricultural shelters. The problem was that when the more aggressive Wall Street firms put on crash promotion programs, not only did the SEC attempt to monitor these programs, but by the fall of 1969 Congress became extremely interested in them as well. As a result, the 1969 Tax Reform Act included provisions that seriously hurt the very two examples used by Mr. Dauber to illustrate socially useful tax shelters.

Restrictions on Real Estate

Real estate, for example, suffered the following blows:

1. A sharp reduction occurred in the amount of accelerated depreciation allowed.

2. On the sale of real estate, the provisions treating the recapture of excessive depreciation over straight line were toughened.

3. Capital gains taxes were subject to increases in many instances of from 60 to 140 percent from the old 25 percent level.

4. The accelerated depreciation was treated as an item of tax preference (IRC-57).

5. Interest in excess of the income attributable to the borrowed money would be treated as a tax preference through 1971.

6. Beginning in 1972, interest on an investment debt of an individual which exceeds the net income from such investment by more than $25,000 annually would be partially disallowed under a complicated formula detailed in IRC-163 (d).

All of these provisions damaged what was previously a particularly favored tax shelter area. The only area of real estate that received certain immunities was the rehabilitation of low-rental residential property—a type of real estate investment whose social usefulness far outweighs its present popularity.

Restrictions on Agriculture

Agriculture was similarly hard hit. Among the damaging blows were the following:

1. Under IRC-1245, as amended by the 1969 Act, all depreciation taken on cattle or livestock was treated as

ordinary income when the depreciated animal itself was sold at more than its depreciated cost.

2. The accelerated depreciation was treated as a tax preference, subjecting the taxpayer to a possible minimum tax which could even infect his shelter on earned income for a period up to five years (IRC-1348).

3. Even where capital gains might be achieved, the holding period was lengthened and the cumulative tax burden of the capital gains was substantially enlarged in certain cases.

4. A new hobby loss rule (IRC-183) disallowed deductions in an activity not carried on for profit. This rule applies to investments in which the individual plays a passive role and which he apparently makes to produce losses rather than income. Only if the income exceeds the deductions in two out of five years will the presumption of a profit motive be allowed.

The conclusion to be drawn from what has happened to these two tax shelters is not that Mr. Dauber's theme is unwarranted, but rather that even a socially useful tax shelter can become too popular for its own good.

3

THREE KEY CHANGES IN THE 1969 TAX ACT

Sol J. Upbin

At first reading, the Tax Reform Act of 1969 seems to have struck a severe blow not only at specific tax shelters, but at the very concept of tax-sheltered investments. But a closer look at the finer points in this complex piece of legislation indicates that many of the adverse effects can be minimized through proper planning.

In support of this position, the following discussion will focus on three key changes made by the 1969 Reform Act. It will also demonstrate with specific examples how the Act has affected the

MR. UPBIN IS A C.P.A., AND TAX MANAGER OF ARTHUR ANDERSEN & CO.

individual investor, and in some cases how a certain amount of sheltered investment has been encouraged. The changes to be discussed are in the following areas:

1. The minimum tax on preference items

2. Excess investment interest

3. The maximum tax on earned income

THE MINIMUM TAX ON PREFERENCE ITEMS

One of the major Tax Reform Act changes imposes a new 10 percent minimum tax on total "tax preference" items in excess of the allowable exemptions. The new tax was to apply to nine preferential items through 1971. Then only eight of these items were to be affected, since excess investment interest moved out of the preference category and into the disallowance category. Of the nine preference items affected by the new tax, the following six items specifically relate to shelters.

1. Excess investment interest. As pointed out above, excess investment interest would be a preferential item only through 1971. This item can be defined as the amount by which the interest expense to carry investment property for taxable years beginning before 1972 exceeds net investment income. Note that this preference relates only to investment property. Consequently, a mortgage on a private home would be excluded. Moreover, the item applies only to individuals not to corporations (with the exception of Subchapter S corporations and personal holding companies).

2. Excess of acclerated depreciation on real property over that which would have been claimed with straight-line depreciation. The investor should not fall into the common error of thinking that he can take all his real estate investments and lump them together to calculate this item. It must be done on a property by property basis. Thus, those older properties which have straight line depreciation higher than that computed under an accelerated method produce no benefit in determining this preference.

3. Excess of accelerated depreciation on personal property subject to a net lease over that which would have been claimed with

straight-line depreciation. To understand this preference item, it is important to know exactly what "net lease" means. A net lease exists if (a) the lessor is guaranteed a specific return or is guaranteed against loss in whole or in part, or (b) the trade or business expenses related to the lease total less than 15 percent of the rental income. The latter is the more important of the two conditions. Trade or business expenses include such items as insurance, repairs, and maintenance. They do not include interest or depreciation. This preference item applies only to personal property and not to real property. Keep in mind, that, just as with excess investment interest, corporations are not covered by this preference item.

4. Amortization of railroad rolling stock in excess of the accelerated depreciation rate otherwise allowed. This item, intended as an incentive to the railroad industry, was an important plus that came out of the Tax Reform Act. It is now possible to write off railroad equipment on a straight-line basis over sixty months, at 20 percent a year, for five years. Previously, an investor had to write it off over a fourteen-year period, which meant that, even if he took double declining balance depreciation on the railroad equipment, the best he could get on the first year was 14 percent. Now he can amortize the railroad stock on a sixty-month basis and compare the write-off with what he could have taken on an accelerated basis. The spread represents his preference.

The impact of this item has been somewhat minimized by the new business depreciation rules announced by the Treasury Department on January 11, 1971, which, among other things, shortened the guideline life of equipment acquired after 1970 by 20 percent.

5. Excess of the depletion deduction over the adjusted basis of the property. With this item, the investor does not enter into the preference category until his percentage depletion exceeds the adjusted cost of the property.

6. Untaxed portion of long-term capital gains. For individuals this is merely 50 percent of the excess of net long-term capital gains over net short-term capital losses. For corporations, under existing tax rates, the preference for 1971 and later years is three-eighths of net long-term capital gain.

The 10 percent minimum tax on these preference items will

not affect the tax-shelter investor as much as might be expected. The investor will seldom have a problem with any one preference item since only a combination of such items will bring the minimum tax into play. The exemption of $30,000, plus his regular income tax otherwise payable, will in many cases serve to eliminate the amount of minimum tax due. For example, a taxpayer with $100,000 of ordinary taxable income who had no other preference items, would need $435,000 of long-term capital gains before he would have to pay a dollar of minimum tax.

As a result of a recent amendment to the minimum tax provisions, investors will be able to carry forward for seven years as an additional exemption the amount by which the regular income taxes for a tax year exceed total tax preferences over $30,000. Thus, the 10 percent minimum tax provision, like others in the Tax Reform Act, gives the impression of being damaging to the tax sheltered investor, but in actual practice it is relatively easy to live with. That is, of course, if the investor plans carefully.

INVESTMENT INTEREST EXPENSE

As discussed above, excess investment interest would no longer be a tax preference item in 1972. Limits will be placed on the deduction for interest paid or incurred to carry investments. The investor will have no problem, however, if his expense is under $25,000, since there is an automatic allowance of that amount. And even investment interest expense over $25,000 will be allowed to the extent the investor has net investment income composed of such items as dividends and interest. Moreover, he also gets an allowance for investment interest to the extent of his net, long-term capital gains. And if he still has some excess investment interest expense beyond the combination of the $25,000 allowance plus the other two allowances, a further allowance is made of one-half of such an excess. The remaining one-half can be carried over to future years. Practically speaking, then, the shift of excess investment interest from the preference list to the disallowance list should not cause much distress for the typical tax sheltered investor.

This can be illustrated easily with the brief example of a taxpayer whose $100,000 of gross income is made up of $95,000 in salary and $5,000 in dividends. Assume that he incurs $50,000 in investment interest expense and that all his other deductions and exemptions are offset by the other items of income.

How would the disallowance be determined? He gets his $25,000 basic allowance for investment interest expense. His dividend income gives him an allowance of $5,000 more. One-half of the remaining $20,000 is allowed, while the other $10,000, which is not deductible, can be a carry over to the next year. It should be observed that $50,000 of interest expense indicates a very substantial loan, since at 9 percent interest, the loan would have to be in the area of $555,000.

THE MAXIMUM TAX ON EARNED INCOME

The maximum marginal rate on earned taxable income was reduced from 70 percent to 60 percent in 1971, with a further reduction to 50 percent in 1972. There is no doubt of what the Congress was trying to achieve with this major provision of the 1969 Tax Reform Act. The aim of the legislators was to discourage the use of tax shelters by reducing the taxpayer's need for them. Why, they reasoned, should businessmen and other taxpayers spend time and energy seeking tax shelters when the most that the IRS can now take of their income is 50 percent in 1972 (60 percent in 1971)?

Congress seems to have overlooked some very sound reasons why those seeking to save on taxes should still continue to utilize tax shelters. For example, executives at the earnings level which produces some benefit under maximum tax rules, also frequently realize some unearned income, that is, capital gains on sale of option stock.

To clarify this point, let us consider the example of a married taxpayer filing a joint return for 1972. As shown in Example 1, he made $125,000 and had $24,000 in deductions—giving him earned taxable income of $101,000 (since he only has salary income, his taxable income is considered to be all earned taxable income).

How much will he save through the 50 percent maximum tax

LIMITATION OF TAX ON EARNED INCOME
Example 1

Salary	$125,000
Personal Deductions/Exemptions	24,000
Earned Taxable Income	$101,000

Calculation of Tax

Tier 1 Normal tax on $52,000 of Earned Taxable Income	$18,060
Tier 2 Limited tax on balance of Earned Taxable Income ($101,000–52,000) x 50%	24,500
TAX	$42,560

* * * *

Tax if there were no limitation provision	$45,800
Tax with limitation provision	42,560
SAVINGS	$3,240

provision? His tax on the first $52,000—before the ceiling takes effect —is $18,060. Now that the ceiling has come into play, the tax on the remaining $49,000 is $24,500, making his total tax $42,560. Without the maximum tax provision, he would have paid $45,800—thus he has saved $3,240.

A Variation—With the Same Results

A variation of this example shows the interplay of tax preferences and the maximum tax computation. In Example 2, our executive has still made $125,000 in salary, but he has also realized capital gains of $125,000. He still has the same amount of personal deductions and exemptions.

After separating the items of adjusted gross income between the earned category and the unearned category, he ends up with a total adjusted gross income of $187,500. This figure is arrived at after allowing the exclusion of one-half of the long-term capital gains. Since the ratio between earned income and total income is two-thirds, then two-thirds of his taxable income is considered earned taxable income.

However, since part of this income is a tax preference item,

LIMITATION OF TAX ON EARNED INCOME
Example 2

	Salary	$125,000
	Long Term Capital Gain	125,000
	Personal Deductions/Exemptions	24,000

	Earned Income	Unearned Income	Total Income
Gross Incomes	$125,000	$125,000	$250,000
Deductions *for*			
Adjusted Gross Incomes	0	62,500 (1)	62,500
ADJUSTED GROSS INCOMES	$125,000	$62,500	$187,500
Deductions/Exemptions			
from Adj. Gross Incomes	16,000	8,000	24,000
TAXABLE INCOMES	$109,000	$54,500	$163,500

(1) One-half of long term gain shown as deduction for adjusted gross income for illustration purposes.

Calculation of Tax

	Earned Income	Unearned Income	Total Income
TAXABLE INCOMES	$109,000	$54,000	$163,500
Adjustment for tax pre-ferences in excess of $30,000:			
1/2 of long term gain			
$62,500–30,000	(32,500)	32,500	0
ADJUSTED TAXABLE INCOMES	$76,500	$87,000	$163,500

* * * *

Tax if there were no limitation provision	$85,960
Tax with limitation provision	82,255
Savings from Limitation Provision	$3,705

the computation will be somewhat different. Our taxpayer generated tax preference income equal to one-half of the long-term capital gain, or $62,500. Since he gets a $30,000 allowance on this, the adjustment to earned taxable income for preferences applies only to the last $32,500, a figure which moves into the unearned income column.

After considering the effect of the alternative tax on capital gains and the maximum tax on earned income, the executive ends up with a total tax of $82,255. He has avoided the minimum tax on preference items on his capital gains because he has an exclusion of $30,000 which, when added to his tax of $82,255, exceeds the excluded portion of capital gains, that is, $62,500.

But the important point here is that his capital gains have created significant unearned taxable income which can be sheltered at the individual's top bracket.

Why Tax Shelters Are Still Needed

Here is a third example to show that tax shelters are still very much needed. In this example, as you will see from *Example 3,* the executive has incurred a $50,000 tax-shelter loss. We are assuming that this shelter does not produce a tax preference—it could be, for instance, an intangible drilling deduction.

The $50,000 loss plus the exclusion for one-half of the net long-term capital gain reduces the unearned income column. The ratio of earned income to total income is now approximately 91 percent—thus, 91 percent of the total income constitutes his earned taxable income.

It can easily be seen that the executive has achieved gratifying results with his $50,000 tax-shelter loss. His savings amount to $29,665—or a 59.3 percent tax benefit on the shelter loss. Possible savings on state taxes could increase this percentage.

The point that these examples makes is clear: despite the 50 percent maximum ceiling on earned income, if unearned income exists—as, for example, through capital gains—the taxpayer still needs a tax shelter. It is not unusual, of course, to find significant unearned income among our highly paid executive group.

This brief look at three key changes in the 1969 Tax Reform Act is not a study in depth, nor is it intended to be one. However, it does—we hope—put across the reassuring view that although these changes may not be lovable, they can be lived with.

LIMITATION OF TAX ON EARNED INCOME
Example 3

Salary		$125,000
Long Term Capital Gain		125,000
"Tax Shelter" Loss		50,000(1)
Personal Deductions/Exemptions		24,000

	Earned Income	Unearned Income	Total Income
Gross Incomes	$125,000	$125,000	$250,000
Deductions *for* Adjusted Gross Income:			
1/2 long term gain		62,500 (2)	
tax shelter		50,000	112,500
ADJUSTED GROSS INCOMES	$125,000	$12,500	$137,500
Deductions/Exemptions			
from Adjusted Gross Incomes	21,820	2,180	24,000
TAXABLE INCOMES	$103,180	$10,320	$113,500

Calculation of Tax

	Earned Income	Unearned Income	Total Income
TAXABLE INCOMES	$103,180	$10,320	$113,500
Adjustments for tax preferences in excess of $30,000:			
1/2 of long term gain $62,500–30,000	(32,500)	32,500	
ADJUSTED TAXABLE INCOMES	$70,680	$42,820	$113,500

* * * *

Tax from Example 2 with no tax shelter	$82,255
Tax above with tax shelter	52,590
SAVINGS FROM $50,000 TAX SHELTER	$29,665

(1) Assumed for illustration to include no tax preference items.
(2) One-half of long term gain shown as deduction for adjusted gross income for illustration purposes.

COMMENTARY

An investor should study this chapter carefully before undertaking a program of tax shelters. For one thing, many tax shelters involve the items of tax preference enumerated by Mr. Upbin—items that create a tax even when every cent of income has been sheltered from regular income tax. This means that when the investor is evaluating a tax shelter, he should ask himself if there are tax preferences that may dilute the tax benefits of the investment.

Even more serious is the unsheltering of earned income from the maximum tax (IRC-1348) which Mr. Upbin illustrates in this chapter. Finally, Mr. Upbin thoroughly explores the maximum tax ceiling and shows why, in many cases, it will not eliminate the taxpayer's need for shelters. Since many writers in this book maintain that tax shelters become attractive only when the tax rate exceeds 50 percent, it is important for the investor to know just when and to what degree the 50 percent limitation under IRC-1348 does and does not operate. Mr. Upbin furnishes the answer to this question.

4

HOW TO MINIMIZE CORPORATE TAXABLE INCOME

Rudolph J. Englert

A corporation has entirely different objectives for its financial accounting and its tax accounting: with the former it tries to maximize its reported earnings, while with the latter it tries to minimize its taxable income. It is, of course, far from easy to achieve both of these goals together—but it can be done through tax shelter investments wisely made and skillfully handled.

This is one problem that does not afflict individual tax-shelter

MR. ENGLERT IS A PARTNER IN THE ACCOUNTING FIRM OF HASKINS & SELLS, NEW YORK.

investors, who usually have no need for accounting records that reflect the results of operations. But a corporation knows that when it attempts to minimize its income taxes, it must not penalize its reported financial earnings.

Let us define briefly the purpose of each type of accounting:

The purpose of tax accounting is to determine the amount of tax payable under the tax laws.

The purpose of financial accounting is to make a logical allocation of costs and revenues so that current and potential investors can appraise the company's performance.

It is obvious from these definitions that there will be major differences in the way costs and revenues are matched up and reported as between tax accounting statements and financial accounting statements. What are these differences? They fall into two main categories: *timing* differences and *permanent* differences.

TIMING DIFFERENCES

By timing differences we mean that income is reported in a different period for tax purposes than it is for financial purposes. Some timing differences can be unfavorable to the corporation, such as differences that accelerate income for tax purposes. An example: rental income is normally taxed when it is *collected,* but for reporting purposes it cannot be included in income until it is *earned.* Other unfavorable timing differences occur when tax deductions must be deferred. Deferred compensation illustrates this: it usually is not deductible by the corporation until it is paid, but for financial accounting purposes it should be accrued by charges against income over the active life of the employee holding the contract.

On the other side of the coin are those welcome *favorable* timing differences, which either defer the reporting of income or accelerate deductions for tax purposes. An installment sale aptly illustrates a transaction that defers recognition of income for tax purposes. If the company elects the installment method for recording sales for tax purposes, its income on the sales is taxed when the installments are collected, while for financial accounting purposes the entire gain on the sale is reported as income that year.

Equally helpful are timing differences that accelerate deductions for tax purposes. Consider depreciation, for example. Many companies now use accelerated depreciation for tax reporting purposes. This is one basis for a tax-sheltered investment: the income taxes are minimized with no unfavorable effect on reported earnings.

Such benefits, however, do not actually improve reported earnings. For example, even if in the current year the taxpayer deducts a $100 expense on his tax return but defers the charge a year for financial accounting purposes, his net favorable effect on reported earnings this year will be fifty dollars, assuming a 50 percent tax rate.

How Timing Differences Work

A slightly more complex example of this accounting principle is illustrated by the financial balance sheet (Exhibit 1) on page 43. Income before depreciation and taxes each year is assumed to be $1 million. During the first year, the company purchased machinery for $1,100,000, with an estimated life of ten years, after which it would have no salvage value. For financial reporting purposes, the company uses straight-line depreciation of $110,000 a year. But for tax purposes the company turns to the accelerated sum-of-the-years digits method, providing depreciation of 10/55 of the total cost for the first year, 9/55 the second year, 8/55 the third year, and so on.

A look at the timing differences in the tax accounting and the financial accounting reveals how tax benefits can be achieved without hurting reported earnings. For both tax and accounting purposes, income before depreciation and tax comes to $1 million. For financial reporting purposes, depreciation is $110,000, but for tax purposes it is $200,000, almost twice as much. Income before tax is thus $890,-000 for financial purposes, $800,000 for tax purposes.

Assuming a tax rate of 50 percent, the favorable effect on reported earnings is $45,000. This happy situation lasts only until the sixth year, however. The figures then are less favorable. Income before taxes and depreciation is still $1 million, and depreciation for financial reporting purposes remains at $110,000. But depreciation for tax purposes is now only $100,000. Thus, while income before tax for

Exhibit 1
ILLUSTRATION OF MANNER IN WHICH PROVISION FOR DEFERRED FEDERAL INCOME TAX IS COMPUTED

Financial Data—Corporation A

1. Income before depreciation and before tax for years 1–10: $1,000,000 per year.

2. Machinery acquired at beginning of year 1 at a cost of $1,100,000. Estimated useful life 10 years, estimated salvage is nil.

3. Depreciation method for financial reporting is straight-line, $110,000 per year. For tax purposes the sum-of-the-years digits depreciation is taken. This means that 10/55 of the total cost is depreciated the first year, 9/55 the second year, etc.

4. Tax rate assumed: 50%

Provision for deferred tax—Year 1 In year 1 the provision for deferred tax is $45,000 computed as follows:

Computation of Federal Income Tax—Year 1

	Financial Report		*Tax Return*
Net Income before depreciation and before tax	$1,000,000		$1,000,000
Depreciation $(1,100,000 \div 10)$	110,000	(1,100,000 $\times$ 10/55)	200,000
	890,000		800,000
Tax provision 50%	445,000	Tax Liability	$ 400,000
Net Income	$445,000		

Computation of Federal Income Tax—Year 6

	Financial Report		*Tax Return*
Net income before depreciation and before tax	$1,000,000		$1,000,000
Depreciation $(1,100,000 \div 10)$	110,000	(1,100,000 $\times$ 5/55)	100,000
	890,000		$ 900,000
Tax provision 50%	445,000	Tax Liability	$ 450,000
Net Income	$ 445,000		

An overall view of the impact of deferred tax accounting covering the ten year period may be illustrated as follows:

Year	Depreciation Per Books	Depreciation For Tax Return	Depreciation for Tax purposes higher (lower) than book depreciation	Deferred Federal Income Tax Decrease	Deferred Federal Income Tax Increase	Deferred Federal Income Tax— Credit Balance
1	$ 110,000	$ 200,000(10/55)	$90,000		$ 45,000	$ 45,000
2	110,000	180,000(9/55)	70,000		35,000	80,000
3	110,000	160,000(8/55)	50,000		25,000	105,000
4	110,000	140,000(7/55)	30,000		15,000	120,000
5	110,000	120,000(6/55)	10,000		5,000	125,000
6	110,000	100,000(5/55)	(10,000)	$ 5,000		120,000
7	110,000	80,000(4/55)	(30,000)	15,000		105,000
8	110,000	60,000(3/55)	(50,000)	25,000		80,000
9	110,000	40,000(2/55)	(70,000)	35,000		45,000
10	110,000	20,000(1/55)	(90,000)	45,000		—0—
	$1,100,000	$1,100,000	—0—	$125,000	$125,000	

financial reporting purposes continues to be $890,000, income for tax purposes is $900,000. The initial tax advantage of accelerated depreciation has become a disadvantage, because the tax liability now exceeds the amount which would have been payable had the company used straight-line depreciation for both tax and financial purposes.

This illustration, however, does not take into account any possible acquisitions of fixed assets after the first year. Normally, there is a constant cycle of replacements, providing new accelerated depreciation that again minimizes taxes without adversely affecting earnings. Theoretically, such continuous postponement of the so-called turn-around period can go on as long as the company keeps acquiring new fixed assets.

PERMANENT DIFFERENCES

These differences, unlike timing differences, are the result of statutory allowances that will not be offset by corresponding differences in subsequent reporting periods. Some of these differences enable a company to immediately reduce its taxes payable, without having to provide for deferred taxes in the financial earnings statement. The company thus has a higher net income for financial purposes. An example is municipal bond interest, which can be included in income for financial reporting purposes but is not taxable during that year or in future years. Since it is not a timing difference, no deferred taxes need to be provided. To evaluate such an investment, one would merely compare its yield with the after-tax income from an alternative investment whose income would be either partially or wholly subject to income tax.

Another example of a permanent difference is dividend income received from a domestic corporation. Statutory requirements provide that investing corporations may exclude 85 percent of the dividend income they receive from other domestic corporations from taxable income, but the entire amount can be included in income for financial reporting purposes. It should be kept in mind, however, that some types of permanent differences have an *unfavorable* effect on earnings. One example is life insurance premiums for company executives—these are charged against reported earnings but are not deductible for income tax purposes.

THREE TYPES OF TAX-SHELTER INVESTMENT

Going from the general to the specific, let us examine three kinds of tax-shelter investment and how they affect reported earnings:

1. **Real estate investment.** If a company builds an apartment house, a shopping center, or an office building, it can deduct for tax purposes its interest on the loans made to finance the construction, plus the real estate taxes paid during the construction period.

For financial accounting purposes, the firm can capitalize these costs and charge them to income over the estimated life of the building or buildings. Subsequent interest and real estate taxes incurred after the facility is completed should be charged against income.

Accelerated depreciation, discussed earlier, is a major benefit of real estate investment. This is illustrated in the financial statement and income summary (Exhibit 2) on pages 48–49. It should be noted that each year cash flow has substantially exceeded net income. These differences have been achieved by depreciation, amortization of deferred charges, and deferred federal income taxes. As shown by the notes to the financial statements, the company has used accelerated depreciation on certain of its buildings and equipment for tax purposes, while using straight-line depreciation for financial reporting purposes.

The note reads "that deferred federal income taxes have been provided by the Company and subsidiaries on statement income which differed from taxable income principally because of (a) deduction for tax purposes of real estate taxes, interest on indebtedness and other carrying charges during periods of construction while such costs have been capitalized for financial reporting purposes; and (b) the use of accelerated depreciation on certain buildings and equipment for tax purposes whereas straight-line depreciation has been used for financial reporting purposes—"

As a result of these timing differences, the company has provided deferred income taxes in the amount of $2,277,000, while paying current taxes of $121,000.

How have these timing differences affected the reported earnings? This is best shown by the comparative summary of income and cash flow. Net income per share decreased four cents in 1968 compared with 1967, but over the same period cash flow increased fifty cents per share.

2. Equipment leasing. Companies that lease equipment as a tax-shelter investment have two different accounting methods to choose from: the operating method and the financing method. With the operating method, the leased equipment appears in the lessor's balance sheet as property owned but being leased. On the income statement, equipment rentals are reflected as income as rents become due. The statement of income should also reflect as expenses the depreciation of leased equipment, maintenance, and other related costs, including the costs of any other service provided in the lease.

Under the financing method of accounting for leases, the property is treated for reporting purposes as though it had been sold. Instead of the property appearing on the balance sheet as an asset, the lease contracts receivable and residual values will appear. This financing type of lease is designed to compensate the lessor for the use of funds invested—the compensation is measured by the excess of aggregate rentals during the time of the lease over the cost of the leased property.

Income on the leased contract is recognized on a declining basis in much the same way as the interest portion of level payment obligations are accounted for by lending institutions.

How does one make the right choice between the operating method and the financing method when one is leasing equipment? Here are two basic guidelines:

•A company should use the operating method for non-payout leases—that is, leases under which the lessor does not recover his entire investment plus financing charges during the primary term of the lease.

Exhibit 2
EXCERPTS FROM THE 1968
ANNUAL REPORT OF
URIS BUILDINGS CORPORATION

URIS BUILDINGS CORPORATION AND SUBSIDIARIES
INCLUDING SHARE OF 50% OWNED CORPORATIONS
COMPARATIVE SUMMARIES OF INCOME AND CASH FLOW

	1968	1967	1966	1965	1964
			THOUSANDS OF DOLLARS		
Rentals	42,081	35,202	30,319	28,021	25,311
Hotel gross operating revenues	20,610	19,812	18,049	15,271	12,059
Construction	7	172	279	110	143
Interest	1,013	996	912	984	880
REVENUE FROM OPERATIONS	63,711	56,212	49,559	44,386	38,393
INCOME BEFORE PROVISIONS FOR DEPRECIATION AND AMORTIZATION	14,358	11,880	9,684	8,724	6,147
Provisions for depreciation and amortization of leasing, financing and hotel preopening costs	7,438	6,596	6,189	5,634	4,647
INCOME BEFORE PROVISION FOR FEDERAL INCOME TAXES	6,920	5,284	3,495	3,090	1,500

Provision for federal income taxes:					
Deferred	3,450	2,671	1,902	1,670	901
Current	121	(356)		(274)	312
INCOME FROM OPERATIONS, BEFORE EXTRAORDINARY CREDIT	3,349	2,969	1,593	1,694	4,729
Gain on sales of properties, less related income taxes	125	593	138	905	287
Extraordinary credit, reduction in income taxes from utilization of statement carry forward losses			192		
NET INCOME	3,474	3,562	1,923	2,599	5,016
PER SHARE OF COMMON STOCK:					
Income from operations, before extraordinary credit	$ .95	$ .85	$ .46	$ .49	$1.36
Gain on sales of properties	.03	.17	.04	.26	.08
Extraordinary credit			.05		
NET INCOME	$ .98	$1.02	$ .55	$ .75	$1.44
Pro forma net income per share*	.88	.91	.53	.69	1.24
Net income	3,474	3,562	1,923	2,599	5,016
Add, provision for depreciation, amortization of deferred charges and deferred federal income taxes	11,063	9,017	8,500	8,174	5,386
CASH FLOW	14,537	12,579	10,423	10,773	10,402
PER SHARE OF COMMON STOCK	$4.12	$3.62	$3.00	$3.10	$2.99
Pro forma cash flow per share*	3.51	3.07	2.57	2.65	2.56

*Assuming all warrents and stock options were exercised and the funds therefrom were used to reduce outstanding debts.

URIS BUILDINGS CORPORATION AND SUBSIDIARIES (CONSOLIDATED)
URIS BUILDINGS CORPORATION'S 50%-OWNED CORPORATIONS (COMBINED)
STATEMENTS OF INCOME
YEARS ENDED SEPTEMBER 30, 1968 AND 1967

	COMPANY AND SUBSIDIARIES		50%-OWNED CORPORATIONS	
	1968	1967	1968	1967
INCOME:				
Rentals	$36,559,561	$29,790,840	$11,042,255	$10,823,222
Hotels gross operating revenues			41,220,660	39,684,799
Construction	7,444	172,045		
Interest	939,898	947,712	145,883	95,299
	37,506,903	30,910,597	52,408,798	50,603,320
EXPENSES:				
Building operating	9,657,071	7,737,838	7,161,468	6,704,855
Cost of hotel services			18,060,829	18,610,595
Real estate taxes	8,289,340	6,529,874	5,493,686	5,335,319
Interest	8,457,732	7,675,514	7,841,854	7,916,809
General and administrative	1,385,916	1,130,479	3,272,323	2,978,667
Advertising and promotion			1,118,879	915,039
	27,790,059	23,073,705	42,949,039	42,461,284
OPERATING PROFIT BEFORE PROVISIONS FOR DEPRECIATION AND AMORTIZATION	9,716,844	7,836,892	9,459,759	8,142,036
Provisions for:				
Depreciation	4,030,680	3,441,916	4,328,482	4,285,171
Amortization of leasing, financing and hotel preopening costs (Note 2)	619,957	524,845	585,768	757,312
	4,650,637	3,966,761	4,914,250	5,042,483
OPERATING PROFIT	5,066,207	3,870,131	4,515,509	3,099,553

Share of net loss of 50%-owned limited partnerships, including provision for depreciation	418,663		136,017
INCOME BEFORE PROVISION FOR FEDERAL INCOME TAXES AND COMPANY'S SHARE OF 50%-OWNED CORPORATIONS' NET INCOME	4,647,544	4,545,509	3,099,553
Provision for federal income taxes (Note 3)			
Deferred	2,277,000	1,927,000	1,488,000
Current	121,000	(356,000)	
INCOME BEFORE COMPANY'S SHARE OF 50%-OWNED CORPORATIONS'			
INCOME AND EXTRAORDINARY CREDIT	2,249,544	2,163,114	1,611,553
Company's share of 50%-owned corporations' income before extraordinary credit	1,099,755	805,775	
INCOME BEFORE EXTRAORDINARY CREDIT	3,349,299	2,968,899	1,611,553
Extraordinary credit, reduction in taxes from utilization of 50%-owned corporations' statement carry forward losses	125,000	593,500	250,000
NET INCOME	$ 3,474,299	$ 3,562,389	$ 2,449,509
			$ 1,187,000
			$ 2,798,553
Per share of common stock:			
Income before extraordinary credit	$ .95	$ .85	
Extraordinary credit	.03	.17	
Net income	$ .98	$1.02	
Pro forma net income per share (assuming all warrants and stock options outstanding at end of fiscal year were exercised and the funds therefrom were used to reduce outstanding debt)	$ .88	$ .91	

The accompanying notes are an integral part of the financial statements.

URIS BUILDINGS CORPORATION AND SUBSIDIARIES (CONSOLIDATED)
URIS BUILDINGS CORPORATION'S 50%-OWNED CORPORATIONS (COMBINED)
BALANCE SHEETS
SEPTEMBER 30, 1968 AND 1967

| | COMPANY AND SUBSIDIARIES | | 50%-OWNED CORPORATIONS | |
	1968	1967	1968	1967
ASSETS:				
Land and buildings, at cost:				
Land	$ 43,279,666	$ 34,545,891	$ 17,787,352	$ 17,787,352
Buildings in operation	174,139,637	153,284,405	119,123,825	119,096,888
Buildings under construction	3,949,999	5,511,410		
Leasing and financing costs	12,377,626	12,049,567	6,188,998	6,187,852
	233,746,928	205,391,273	143,100,175	143,072,092
Less, Allowances for:				
Depreciation of buildings	21,498,562	17,467,882	13,896,422	11,051,017
Amortization of leasing and financing costs	3,054,176	2,434,219	2,023,704	1,608,087
	24,552,738	19,902,101	15,920,126	12,659,104
	209,194,190	185,489,172	127,180,049	130,412,988
Hotel furnishings and equipment, less allowance for depreciation, $6,540,472 and $5,049,600	19,382,688	18,350,914	8,440,515	9,634,579
Investments in and notes receivable from 50%-owned corporations (Note 4)				
Investments in and loans receivable from 50%-owned limited partnerships (Note 5)	693,760	1,116,173		
Cash and short-term cash investments	11,928,490	11,634,140	3,455,415	2,922,639
Accounts receivable	1,993,887	2,129,815	3,596,436	3,574,065
Hotel food, beverages and supplies, at cost, and operating equipment			1,409,022	1,452,914

Deferred charges and prepaid expenses	1,969,598		1,013,773	953,803
Claim for federal income tax refund		1,988,480		
Other assets	391,760	630,000		
		1,025,474		
	$245,554,373	$222,364,168	$145,095,210	$148,950,988

LIABILITIES:

Mortgages payable (Note 6) $171,278,771		$166,432,069	$ 90,423,025	$ 93,090,120
Construction loan (Note 7)	21,500,000	4,125,000		
6½% sinking fund debentures, due 1972 (Note 8)	5,633,900	7,489,000		
Notes payable to banks (Note 9)			4,843,500	8,693,500
Notes payable to stockholders (Notes 4 and 9)			30,525,823	32,480,763
Construction accounts payable	3,773,935	4,513,023		
Leasing commissions payable	2,366,863	2,993,764	328,128	416,994
Accounts payable and accrued liabilities	3,309,610	3,788,472	3,318,750	3,159,136
	207,863,079	189,341,328	129,439,226	137,840,513
Deferred federal income taxes (Note 3)	11,865,000	9,588,000	2,921,000	825,000
Commitments (Notes 1, 5 and 13)				

STOCKHOLDERS' EQUITY:

Common stock of Uris Buildings Corporation, par value 10¢ per share, authorized 6,000,000 shares, issued and outstanding 3,565,258 and 3,476,437 shares (Note 11)	13,977,725	12,942,785		
Capital stock of combined corporations, no par value, aggregate stated values of authorized, issued and outstanding shares			10,500,000	10,500,000
Retained earnings (deficit), as annexed (Notes 8 and 12)	11,848,569	10,492,055	2,234,984	(214,525)
	25,826,294	23,434,840	12,734,984	10,285,475
	$245,554,373	$222,364,168	$145,095,210	$148,950,988

The accompanying notes are an integral part of the financial statements.

URIS BUILDINGS CORPORATION AND SUBSIDIARIES (CONSOLIDATED)
URIS BUILDINGS CORPORATION'S 50%-OWNED CORPORATIONS (COMBINED)
STATEMENTS OF RETAINED EARNINGS (DEFICIT)
YEARS ENDED SEPTEMBER 30, 1968 AND 1967

	COMPANY AND SUBSIDIARIES		50%-OWNED CORPORATIONS	
	1968	1967	1968	1967
Retained earnings (deficit), beginning of year	$10,492,055	$ 9,011,196	($ 214,525)	($ 3,013,078)
Net income	3,474,299	3,562,389	2,449,509	2,798,553
	13,966,354	12,573,585	2,234,984	(214,525)
Cash dividends paid by Company, $.60 per share	2,177,785	2,081,530		
Retained earnings (deficit), end of year (Notes 8 and 12)	$11,848,569	$10,492,055	$ 2,234,984	($ 214,525)

STATEMENTS OF SOURCES AND APPLICATION OF FUNDS
YEARS ENDED SEPTEMBER 30, 1968 AND 1967

SOURCES OF FUNDS:

Income before Company's share of 50%-owned corporations' income and extraordinary credit	$ 2,249,544	$ 2,163,114	$ 2,199,509	$ 1,611,553
Provision for depreciation and amortization of deferred charges	5,094,896	4,499,370	4,914,250	5,042,483
Share of 50%-owned limited partnerships' provision for depreciation	330,426	107,438	(289,012)	(376,919)
Less, Additions to hotel furnishings and equipment				
Provision for deferred federal income taxes	2,277,000	1,927,000	2,346,000	1,488,000
CASH DERIVED FROM OPERATIONS (CASH FLOW)	9,951,866	8,696,922	9,170,747	7,765,117

Construction loans and mortgage financing	25,852,117	22,810,833		600,000
Mortgage refinancing		2,660,592		
Investment in 50%-owned corporations	152,481	244,004		
Exercise of stock options and warrants	1,034,940			
Federal income taxes	509,000	(905,703)		
	37,500,404	33,506,648	9,170,747	8,365,117
Cash and short-term cash investments, beginning of year	11,634,140	11,348,970	2,922,639	1,470,193
	$49,134,544	$44,855,618	$12,093,386	$9,835,310
APPLICATION OF FUNDS:				
Acquisition of land	$8,733,775	$5,953,943	$28,083	$141,412
Construction of buildings	19,621,880	18,977,730		
Investment in 50%-owned limited partnerships		495,266		
Mortgage amortization	3,630,415	3,639,067	2,667,095	2,518,684
Debenture sinking fund	1,855,100	1,172,100		
Net payment of loans from banks and stockholders			5,804,940	
Dividends	2,117,785	2,081,530		2,300,741
Net change in receivables, payables and accrued liabilities and other assets	1,247,099	901,842	137,853	1,951,834
	$37,206,054	$33,221,478	$8,637,971	$6,912,971
Cash and short-term cash investments, end of year	$11,928,490	$11,634,140	$3,455,415	$2,922,639

The accompanying notes are an integral part of the financial statements.

URIS BUILDINGS CORPORATION AND SUBSIDIARIES (CONSOLIDATED)
URIS BUILDINGS CORPORATION'S 50%-OWNED CORPORATIONS (COMBINED)
NOTES TO FINANCIAL STATEMENTS

1. The Company had six office buildings in operation throughout fiscal 1968 and a seventh office building was operated for a portion of the year. During fiscal 1967, five office buildings were in operation throughout the year and a sixth office building operated for a portion of that year. The Company's three 50%-owned corporations, together with their related wholly-owned subsidiaries, own and operate two hotels and one office building.

   In connection with its construction program, the Company is committed to the completion of two office buildings on which the remaining costs are expected to be approximately $103,000,000. In addition, the Company has started construction on the first phase of a suburban complex of office and research buildings and has announced plans to construct another office building. The remaining cost of the entire construction program stated above is expected to be $290,000,000 and it is anticipated that a substantial portion of this amount will be obtained through construction loans which will be replaced by long-term mortgages.

2. Deferred hotel preopening expenses were amortized by annual charges to income ($170,151 in 1968 and $367,296 in 1967) on a straight-line basis over a three-year period after commencement of operations until March 1968, when they were fully amortized.

3. The Company and subsidiaries will report a net operating loss on their consolidated federal income tax return for the fiscal year ended September 30, 1968. Deferred federal income taxes have been provided by the Company and subsidiaries on statement income which differed from taxable income principally because of (a) the deduction for tax purposes of real estate taxes, interest on indebtedness and other carrying charges during periods of construction while such costs have been capitalized for financial reporting purposes; and (b) the use of accelerated depreciation on certain buildings and equipment for tax purposes whereas straight-line depreciation has been used for financial reporting purposes. As a result of the construction program referred to in Note 1, it is anticipated that the Company and subsidiaries will incur over a period of several years substantial tax deductible expenses which will be capitalized for statement reporting purposes. Reduction of accumulated deferred federal income taxes will occur only whenever taxable income exceeds statement income.

   The three 50%-owned corporations file separate federal income tax returns. No income taxes are payable for fiscal 1968 as a result of utilizing net operating loss carry-overs. The corporations have available $2,797,000 to be applied against future taxable income, expiring as follows: 1969, $1,421,000, 1970 $473,000, 1971, $361,000, 1972, $270,000 and 1973, $272,000. Only $325,000 of such net operating loss carry-overs is available for utilization against future statements income. These corporations have provided deferred federal income taxes on statement income principally for the reasons (a) and (b) above.

The Company and subsidiaries' 1967 provision for federal income taxes was reduced (and net income increased) by an investment credit of $221,000. No provision has been made for the possible future utilization of investment credit carryovers by the Company and subsidiaries, $114,000, and by two of its 50%-owned corporations, $1,289,000.

4. The Company's investments in 50%-owned corporations ($7,055,076) are stated at cost, adjusted for its share of the changes in the underlying net assets. The Company has notes receivable totaling $12,327,612 from the three corporations. These notes, together with similar notes held by the other stockholders, are subordinated to all other notes payable by these corporations and total $28,807,323, including accrued interest at 5 1/2% to 6 1/2% per annum; $17,872,398 of such notes mature in fiscal 1971 and $10,498,000 in fiscal 1972.

5. The Company's investments in two 50%-owned limited partnerships are stated at cost, adjusted for its share of the changes in the underlying net assets. These partnerships have developed residential garden apartments. At September 30, 1968, the gross assets of the limited partnerships totaled $9,869,000 consisting principally of the cost of land and buildings after depreciation ($9,813,000). Liabilities consisting principally of mortgages on the partnerships' properties ($8,152,000) and loans payable to the Company ($385,000) amounted to $9,-750,000. The Company has agreed to make an additional investment of approximately $450,000 in one of the partnerships during the next three years.

6. Mortgages relating to buildings in operation, owned by the Company, totaling $155,614,868, bear interest at 4 3/4% to 6% and are secured by the operating properties. The mortgages are payable over remaining terms ranging from 13 to 24 years, in instalments applicable first to interest and then to reduction of mortgage principal. Payments required in reduction of mortgage principal in the succeeding five years are $3,830,000, $4,037,000, $4,259,000, $4,491,000 and $4,-736,000.

Additional mortgages totaling $15,663,903, presently bearing interest principally at 7 1/4% per annum, relate to certain land and buildings under construction or held for future development; it is anticipated that these mortgages will be replaced shortly by construction loans and, ultimately, long-term mortgages.

Mortgages payable by the 50%-owned corporations, bearing interest principally at 4 3/4% to 6% per annum, are secured by their land, operating buildings, equipment and tenant leases, and are payable over remaining terms ranging from 15 to 21 years, in constant annual amounts applicable first to interest and then to reduction of principal. Payments required in reduction of principal on these mortgages in the succeeding five years are $2,819,000 $2,979,000 $3,149,000, $3,329,000 and $3,524,000. Additional interest on the hotel mortgages is payable at 15% of annual net earnings (as defined in the mortgages) in excess of specified amounts.

7. A construction loan of $21,500,000 in connection with an office building is secured by a first mortgage on the property and presently bears interest at 7 1/4%. Operation of the building has started and the construction loan will shortly be paid from the proceeds of a short-term mortgage. It is anticipated that a long-term mortgage will be obtained before the maturity of the short-term mortgage.

8. The Company's debenture indenture requires sinking fund payments of $1,500,000 in the years 1969 through 1971, and $1,489,000 in 1972 payable in cash or by surrender of debentures. The Company has acquired $355,100 of debentures to

be used as part of the 1969 sinking fund payment. The indenture restricts the payment of cash dividends and acquisition of shares of the Company's stock. At September 30, 1968, under the indenture, $19,693,000 may be used for the payment of dividends and acquisition of shares of the Company's stock, and all retained earnings, $11,848,569, are available for such purposes.

9. Notes payable to a bank by a 50%-owned corporation in the amount of $1,718,500, for the purchase of hotel furnishings and equipment, presently bear interest at 6% and are guaranteed by Uris Buildings Corporation. Related notes payable to another stockholder in the amount of $1,718,500 have the same terms as the notes payable to bank. Aggregate annual payments required in reduction of all such notes, commencing in fiscal 1969, are $1,374,000, $1,374,000 and $689,000. The capital stock of another 50%-owned corporation is pledged as security for the balance of 5% notes payable to banks ($3,125,000). These notes are payable in equal annual instalments from December 1968 to December 1972.

10. In 1968, the stockholders approved the purchase for $15,000 by certain employees of the Company of a total of 5% of the capital stock of each of three subsidiaries which currently have buildings under construction. The Company has an option through November 1, 1973 to repurchase the stock at the then fair market value.

11. During fiscal 1968, the Company's common stock, including paid-in capital, increased by $1,034,940 resulting from exercise of warrants ($936,168) and stock options ($122,539), less the excess of cost of treasury shares over the related proceeds from the exercise of other stock options and warrants ($23,-767).

Under the Company's restricted stock option plan, there were options outstanding at September 30, 1968 to purchase 15,-193 shares of the Company's common stock at prices ranging from $9.63 to $17.99 (95% of the market value at the dates of grants). During fiscal 1968, options for 6,788 shares were exercised at prices ranging from $9.63 to $16.34 per share. Options for 13,133 shares were exercisable at September 30, 1968. All options under this plan expire from 1970 to 1972, and there are no shares reserved for future options.

In 1965, the stockholders approved a qualified stock option plan for employees under which 100,000 shares of the Company's common stock have been reserved. The first options under this plan were granted on October 15, 1968. On that date, options to purchase 30,000 shares at $44.50 (100% of the market value on October 15, 1968) were granted. Also outstanding at September 30, 1968 were options granted to directors for the purchase of 3,030 shares which expire in 1969 and 1970. The option prices on such shares range from $15.53 to $18.50 and are approximately 90% of the market prices at the dates of grant. During fiscal 1968, options for 6,620 shares were exercised at prices ranging from $15.53 to $18.50 per share.

An additional 764,692 shares of common stock are reserved for the exercise of warrants sold in connection with the debentures. The warrants are exercisable until May 1, 1975 at a price of $12.50 per 1.0609 shares (equivalent to $11.78 per share) in cash or by surrender of an equivalent principal amount of debentures.

12. None of the 50%-owned corporations may pay dividends while any of the notes payable of such corporation are outstanding.

13. The Company's subsidiaries have ground leases in connection with buildings in operation which provide for annual rentals (before consideration of any renewals and real estate taxes and other expenses payable by the subsidiaries) aggregating approximately $2,340,000. Of the aggregate annual rentals, $206,000 applies to leases expiring within 23 years, and $2,134,000 applies to leases expiring thereafter but prior to 2028.

    In connection with the acquisition and renegotiation of one of the leases, a subsidiary has issued promissory notes for $11,112,500 bearing interest at an effective rate of approximately 1 1/2% per annum. The notes, including interest, are payable approximately $250,000 annually over a period of approximately 72 years. To give recognition to the substance of the lease acquisition, the $250,000 annual payments under the lease purchase contract are being treated as additional lease rentals and are included in the annual rentals shown above. Payment of additional amounts, or acceleration of the payment of certain of the above amounts under this lease, may be required based upon operations of the buidling. In connection with a building under construction, a subsidiary has entered into a ground lease which expires in 2010 with renewal options for an additional 60 years. Such lease provides for aggregate annual rentals of $694,000 until September 30, 1971 and $1,181,000 thereafter (before consideration of any renewals and real estate taxes and other expenses payable by the subsidiary). Rentals incurred during the construction period are included in the cost of the building.

    One of the 50%-owned corporations has a ground lease in connection with the office building with a remaining initial term of approximately 25 years. The lease provides for an annual rental (before consideration of any renewal and real estate taxes and other expenses payable by that corporation) aggregating $1,133,000 with additional annual rent based on rental income.

    The two 50%-owned hotel corporations have management contracts with Hilton Hotels Corporation under which that company provides management services for a term of 20 years for 2% of adjusted net sales (as defined) plus $325,000 per year until certain indebtedness is retired or reduced below stipulated levels, and $375,000 thereafter.

14. Substantially all the Company's employees are covered by a pension plan. The Company's policy is to fund pension expense, which for the year ended September 30, 1968 was $100,000, including amortization of prior service cost over 10 years.

15. For purposes of comparison, certain items for fiscal 1967 have been reclassified to conform to the presentation accorded such items by the companies in fiscal 1968.

AUDITORS' REPORT

To The Board of Directors and Stockholders of
Uris Buildings Corporation:

We have examined the consolidated balance sheet of URIS BUILD-
INGS CORPORATION and SUBSIDIARIES and the combined balance
sheet of URIS BUILDINGS CORPORATION'S 50%-OWNED CORPORA-
TIONS as of September 30, 1968, and the related statements of
income and of retained earnings (deficit) and statements of sources
and application of funds for the year then ended. Our examination
was made in accordance with generally accepted auditing standards, and accordingly included such tests of the accounting records
and such other auditing procedures as we considered necessary in
the circumstances. We have previously examined and reported
upon the consolidated and combined financial statements for the
year ended September 30, 1967.

In our opinion, the aforementioned financial statements present
fairly the consolidated financial position of Uris Buildings Cporora-
tion and Subsidiaries and the combined financial position of Uris
Buildings Corporation's 509-Owned Corporations at September
30, 1968 and 1967, and the results of their operations and sources
and application of funds for the years then ended, in conformity
with generally accepted accounting principles applied on a consis-
tent basis.

LYBRAND, ROSS BROS. & MONTGOMERY

New York, November 18, 1968.

•If the term of the lease is approximately equivalent to the estimated life of the equipment, the financing method is usually the most appropriate method for financial accounting purposes, but the operating method should be considered for tax purposes. With this approach, a company could recognize greater leasing income for financial purposes than for tax purposes in the lease's early years.

3. Oil and gas investment. Accounting for oil and gas ventures is more complex than for either real estate or equipment leasing. This discussion will touch on just two of the major elements that create differences between accounting income and taxable income.

First is *intangible drilling costs.* Under this heading comes the cost of actually drilling the hole in the ground, including labor, supplies, and repairs, but not expenses directly related to the production of oil, such as storage tanks and casings.

For tax purposes, of course, a company will expense intangible drilling costs as they are incurred. For financial reporting purposes, however, many companies defer intangible costs and amortize them by charging to income when oil is produced. Three basic methods for deferring intangible costs are available:

BY WELL: the cost of drilling each successful well is amortized on the basis of its production.

BY FIELD: the cost of drilling an entire field of wells—both dry and producing—is deferred and subsequently amortized against income from the producing wells.

FULL COSTING: all intangible costs are deferred and subsequently amortized over the production from successful wells wherever they are located. This approach, of course, achieves the most favorable initial effect on reported earnings.

Depletion allowance is the second major element that creates differences between accounting income and taxable income. Depletion reflected on the financial statement is ordinarily based on cost, but depletion deducted for tax purposes is determined by statutory formula rather than the company's costs. Although the 1969 Tax Reform Act reduced this percentage from 27 ½ percent to 22 percent, the distinction between accounting income and taxable income is still necessary. The exception, of course, would be a situation in which cost depletion exceeded percentage depletion—in this case

Exhibit 3
ILLUSTRATION OF THE COMPUTATION OF A
TYPICAL PETROLEUM COMPANY'S TAX PROVISION

Pretax accounting income		$ 1,000,000
Adjustments for taxable income:		
Permanent differences:		
Excess of percentage depletion over cost depletion	$450,000	
Write-off of current year's intangible drilling costs	50,000	500,000
Timing differences (excess of tax depreciation over depreciation reflected in the financial statements, etc.)		100,000
Total		600,000
Taxable income		$ 400,000
Tax Provision (assuming a tax rate of 50%):		
Taxes currently payable (50% of $400,000)		$ 200,000
Taxes deferred (50% of $100,000)		50,000
Total		$ 250,000
Net Income (after tax provision)		$ 750,000

(For purposes of this illustration, no consideration has been given to the availability of tax credits, such as the investment credit, as a reduction of taxes currently payable. This can also cause the provision for taxes to be correspondingly less.)

cost depletion would be used for both accounting income and taxable income.

On this page is a simplified illustration (*Exhibit 3*) of how reported earnings are affected by the two factors of intangible costs and percentage depletion. Pre-tax accounting shows an income of $1 million from which is deducted $450,000—the excess of percentage depletion over cost depletion. This is a permanent difference that requires no provision for deferred taxes. The second deduction is $50,000, representing the intangible drilling costs during the year. It is being written off for tax purposes, but will be deferred and amortized for financial purposes.

Thus, taxable income has been cut in half, without any reduction in reported earnings. An additional deduction of $100,000, unrelated to the oil investment, makes the company's taxable income $400,000. Under the financial accounting, $200,000 has been deducted for current income taxes and $50,000 provided for deferred taxes. The over-all result is taxable income of $400,000 versus reported earnings of $750,000.

This has been only a sampling of how a company can achieve substantial tax-shelter benefits without adversely affecting its reported earnings. Every company, of course, must tailor its tax-shelter investments to meet its own particular tax problems. In so doing, it should be sure to take maximum advantage of the timing and permanent differences between taxable and accounting income to make the most of its reported earnings and the least of its taxes.

COMMENTARY

This excellent chapter is of particular interest to corporations which are (1) publicly held or (2) have been involved in an exchange or pooling of interests in which the number of shares of the acquiring company ultimately received by the corporation in the exchange depends on after-tax income. In the latter case, the acquired corporation is exceptionally anxious to reduce its tax but not its earnings.

NON-DEDUCTIBLE LIFE INSURANCE PREMIUMS

One point in the chapter deserves further comment. The author states that life insurance premiums on key-man insurance are charged against earnings but cannot be deducted for income tax purposes. There are several mitigating factors here. First, when the key man dies, the corporation realizes substantial tax-free income. Second, the policy's cash value is credited toward earnings. In many policies, after a few years, the cash value increase is greater than the premiums. Moreover, in mutual policies the insurance dividends can be added to income but are not taxable. They may also be used to buy paid-up additions to the policy—and the increased cash value is credited towards earnings.

THE PRO-RATING TECHNIQUE Even more important, the cash value or the death benefits in most policies ultimately exceed the aggregate premiums paid. This excess can be prorated over the entire life of the policy, which spreads the excess evenly. This means that the insurance will increase the per share earnings of the corporation even in the early years when the increase in cash value is far less than the premium.

This prorating technique can be illustrated with a footnote from the 1970 financial statement of Century Papers, Inc:

> *Note C - Deferred Charges.* During the year ended March 31, 1970, the Company changed its accounting for all new issues of officer life insurance policies, whereby the excess of total premiums over total cash value through age 65 is being amortized over the years remaining until the officer attains age 65. The effect of this change was to increase net earnings for the year by approximately $7,400 (0.01 per share).

Several large accounting firms utilize the prorating technique. One of them recently obtained an informal opinion from the SEC Regional Office in Houston approving prorating provided it did not increase per share earnings by more than 10 percent.

Prorating is not unanimously approved, however. An article in the November, 1970, issue of the *Journal of Accountancy* claimed that prorating was unsound because there was no assurance that the policy would be continued to the point where the cash value exceeded the accumulated premiums. This view ignores the fact that many other investments are valued at cost even when they may be lost if mortgaged principal and interest are not paid. And one method to offset even this questionable argument is to prepay premiums, a move which has the added advantage of earning a discount on the premiums. Although IRC-264 generally limits such prepayment to 20 percent of the expected total premium in each of the first four years of the policy. However, in most cases the gap between cash value and premiums paid can largely be eliminated by the payment of four premiums in advance.

Perhaps the most convincing arguments for prorating cash value over the first ten years of the insurance policy are contained in a study of the subject as it relates to insurance company accounting practices. The study may be found in the appendix.

5

AVOIDING THE ACCUMULATED EARNINGS TAX

Donald J. Malouf

As we go further into the 1970's, there is good reason to believe that vulnerable profit accumulation will move front and center on the tax litigation stage. The IRS, Congress, and the courts seem increasingly inclined to tighten up in this area. IRS agents, for example, who previously may have overlooked accumulations because of adjustments made in the balance sheet transferring earned

MR. MALOUF IS AN ATTORNEY IN THE FIRM OF ATWELL, MALOUF, MUSSELWHITE & BYNUM IN DALLAS, TEXAS.

surplus to capital, are now more alert to this maneuver and are questioning it on audit.

This means, obviously, that corporations trying to avoid the severe penalties of vulnerable accumulation must make doubly sure that the escape route they choose will not run straight into a brick wall of government resistance. This chapter will first take a look at the accumulated earnings tax itself, then discuss some ways to avoid it. (The reader should be warned, however, that what follows is an oversimplification of a very technical and complex subject. If he is left with enough information to question intelligently his tax consultant and other advisors, then the chapter will have accomplished its purpose.)

THE BIRTH OF A TAX

Congress brought forth the accumulated earnings tax in 1913, and revised it in 1916 and 1921. Since then the tax has remained relatively unchanged. Originally, it was imposed on a corporation's shareholders. This meant that if a corporation was "fraudulently availed" for the purpose of escaping the individual income tax by permitting the profits to accumulate at the corporate stage, the individual shareholder was taxed on that income. In 1916, however, the term "fraudulently" was dropped. Then, in 1921, Congress recognized the doubtful constitutionality of taxing shareholders on corporate profits and abandoned this approach in favor of levying a penalty tax on the offending corporation itself.

The tax is aimed at discouraging corporations from accumulating their earnings instead of paying them out as dividends to the individual stockholders. By accumulating its earnings, a corporation could later distribute them or capitalize on them in a way that would produce an aggregate lower tax. For example, the corporation could accumulate earnings over a number of years, then merge with a larger corporation in a tax-free transaction. The stockholders would thereby gain stock that they could later market, paying only a capital gains tax. The stockholders might also sell their corporation for cash and similarly enjoy the benefit of these accumulations at a capital gains rate. Or they could liquidate the corporation entirely at a capital gains rate. A gift of the stock to a charity might bring a full deduction for the fair market value, without a recognition of the gain for tax purposes. In the case of a single stockholder, he might hold the stock until his death. His beneficiaries would then acquire a new cost basis in that stock equal to the fair market value for federal estate tax purposes. The subsequent sale of the stock with this higher cost basis might well eliminate any tax at all.

It was to rob such devices of their appeal that the accumulated earnings tax was created. The tax is imposed on any corporation "formed or availed of" for the purpose of avoiding income taxes at the shareholder level by permitting earnings and profits to accumulate rather than be distributed. Personal holding companies, foreign personal holding companies, and exempt organizations are excluded, because they have their own restrictive rules. With these exceptions, all corporations are covered by the law: large, small, publicly held, closely held. However, since the penalty is imposed when the motive exists at the shareholder level, most cases involve closely held corporations. Publicly held corporations normally have strong pressures on them to pay dividends rather than accumulate earnings. For example, the dividends are often extremely important to the price of a stock, and shareholders naturally do not want the price of their stock weakened by low or nonexistent dividends.

In addition to closely held, non-public corporations, another type of corporation also becomes frequently involved in vulnerable accumulation cases. This type of company, increasingly popular in recent years, might be called quasi-public. It is dominated by a few stockholders, even though there may be a large number of public stockholders. For example, a company might have three or four thousand stockholders, but only two of those stockholders may control 90 percent of the stock. Taxpayers should not fall into the trap of thinking that public ownership of a small portion of their otherwise closely held stock protects their corporation against the accumulated earnings tax. The quasi-public corporation contains the common denominator of all accumulated earnings tax cases: concentration of ownership and control in a small group of stockholders.

It is the motives of this small group that the IRS will question in determining the intent to accumulate earnings.

HOW THE TAX WORKS

What is the tax itself? Being a penalty tax, it is imposed over and above the other corporate taxes. It has a dual rate structure: on the first $100,000 of *accumulated taxable income* there is an extra tax of $27\frac{1}{2}$ percent, while anything over that amount is taxed at $38\frac{1}{2}$ percent. Accumulated taxable income can be generally defined as the after-tax profit less dividends and what is known as the accumulated earnings tax credit. This credit is the amount the corporation retains to meet the "reasonable needs" of the business, but not less than $100,000. Thus, each corporation can accumulate $100,000 without having to justify that accumulation. This is not necessarily true, however, in the case of multiple corporations, a subject outside the scope of this chapter.

In view of these criteria, it is easy to see the role that tax shelters can play in avoiding this penalty tax. As a corporation reduces its taxable income with tax shelters for the purpose of reducing its federal corporate income tax, it also reduces its accumulated taxable income for the purpose of avoiding this penalty tax.

Two special types of corporations are dealt with somewhat more severely by the IRS than the ordinary corporation: holding companies and investment companies. A holding company—that is, one which does virtually nothing but hold properties and collect the income—has additional burdens to overcome in avoiding the accumulated earnings tax. So does an investment company, which the Treasury defines as any company whose activities consist substantially of buying and selling stocks, securities, real estate, or other investment property and derives its income from investment yield.

WHEN A CASE GOES TO COURT

The application of the accumulated earnings tax has a history of confusion, disagreement, and inconsistency. In one court, a taxpayer may have to overcome a presumption of guilt in order to win, while in another he may have to prove his case by the preponderance of the evidence. Confusion also exists over the criteria to be used in determining whether the penalty tax is warranted. Prior to 1969, some courts held that the intention of avoiding tax at the shareholder level had to be the *predominant* motive of the corporation. But the Supreme Court said that this intent only need be *one* of the motives for accumulated earnings.

One thing is clear, however. If a corporation can show that the accumulated earnings are for the reasonable needs of the business, it can reduce its accumulated taxable income by the amount retained for these reasonable needs.

But this immediately raises another question to which there is no simple answer: how do you define the reasonable needs of a business?

Until recently, there was a relatively narrow definition of reasonable needs. It has now been broadened to include not only the company's present business, but any business into which it might reasonably expand. This would cover, for example, a horizontal integration, a vertical integration, or a complete departure from the present business into an unrelated field. Bona fide expansion of the corporation's current business or replacement of plant are both acceptable as reasonable needs.

PERSUADING THE IRS

Whatever the reasonable need for which the earnings are being accumulated, the problem faced by the corporation is proving it to the IRS or a court. Let us assume, for example, that Able Corporation hopes to convince the IRS that it is accumulating earnings in order to build a new plant—an eminently reasonable need.

Able Corporation must anticipate that it may be challenged by IRS with, "Where's the evidence?" If Able has been sufficiently foresighted, it will have the evidence. At its annual directors' meeting, the minutes will show, the projected new plant was talked about at length. Plans for the new plant were shown on slides. Copies of accounting studies were distributed, comparing the costs of operating the old plant with those of the new one.

Such minutes carry much weight in vulnerable accumulation cases, because they document the corporation's claim at the time the earnings were being accumulated. Far less convincing to the IRS would be, for example, a set of architect's drawings hastily drawn up just before the confrontation with the IRS.

In another year, perhaps Able Corporation decides to accumulate its earnings in order to acquire another business enterprise. It could do this either by purchasing the business in its corporate form or purchasing the actual assets. At the directors' meeting, the minutes show this time that a list of possible acquisitions was distributed to the meeting. Accountants had made a study of the possibilities, which was also circulated. In addition, a time table for the acquisition was produced, to show that earnings were being accumulated now for a purchase that would be made three years from now.

The Tax Reform Act of 1969 has helped to settle (and, in some respects, unsettle) one area which has been the subject of considerable controversy. An addition to the Internal Revenue Code now provides that "reasonable needs of the business" include amounts needed (or reasonably anticipated to be needed) to accomplish a Section 303 redemption (i.e., a redemption of stock held by a decedent to pay death taxes, funeral expenses, and other administrative expenses) in the year of death and in later years.

WHAT WILL BE CHALLENGED

We have been examining evidence of *reasonable* needs for accumulation, but we should also touch upon what the IRS considers evidence of *unreasonable* accumulation. Making loans to shareholders and otherwise spending corporation funds for personal benefit to shareholders is frowned upon. So are loans having no reasonable relation to the corporation's business, such as loans to relatives or friends of shareholders.

Loans to brother-sister corporations fall into the challenged category. Such corporations are not subsidiaries or parents of the corporation, but are owned by the same individual shareholders. Similarly suspect are investment in properties or securities unrelated to the activities of the corporation. This is to be distinguished from actually diversifying into other businesses, which is acceptable as a "reasonable need." It is one thing to go into the automobile manufacturing business—it is another to merely buy 1,000 shares of General Motors stock.

At this point, the question logically arises as to how a corporation can establish that it is actually going into another business and not merely investing. According to treasury regulations, the corporation must acquire at least 80 percent of the voting stock. This will demonstrate that the acquired corporation is a mere instrumentality of the parent corporation, and that the earnings accumulated for the acquisition were intended to be used for going into another business. In addition, since it owned at least 80 percent of the stock, a corporation could elect to file a consolidated return with its new subsidiary, so that the unused benefits embodied in the tax-shelter subsidiary pass through to the parent organization.

If, however, a corporation purchases *less* than 80 percent of another corporation's stock, it will be challenged by the IRS to show that it exerts sufficient control to warrant the conclusion that it is actually participating in the business.

A DOUBLE-BARRELLED RISK

Buying another corporation is only one way to establish a "reasonable need" for accumulated earnings. Many tax-shelter investments do not operate most effectively within a corporate form, but rather through a syndicate such as a joint venture or limited partnership. Any corporation that invests accumulated earnings into a syndicate must face a double-barrelled risk, however. On the one hand, if the corporation only contributes its funds and takes a passive role in the operation of the venture, the IRS may decide it is merely making an investment and not involving itself in another business. This is particularly true, for example, if the corporation acquires a limited partnership interest or another type of non-operating interest. By law, a limited partner does not have the power to involve itself in the management of an operation. If it does, it loses its limited liability. Thus, in making a tax shelter investment, the corporation must be concerned not only with the form of the investment, but should make sure it is committed—and *per*mitted—to manage the investment.

On the other hand, what if the corporation—a printing firm, for example—does get involved in the management of a real estate operation or an oil and gas operation? It must then deal with serious management problems—problems it may not be qualified to act on wisely. If the risk of the enterprise is so great that the corporation's accumulated funds may well be lost, perhaps it would make more sense to go ahead and distribute these funds to the stockholders. They may have to pay their tax, but at least they will have something left over. Real estate ventures, for example, while often very successful, do have their risks. Investment in large rental projects such as office buildings, apartment houses, and shopping centers have become a popular corporate activity. Often a corporation has acquired a large tract of land for future plant expansion, but as community population grows, the corporation finds itself sitting on a choice location for a shopping center or housing development. In a time of tight money and rising costs, this may not be as fortuitous as it seems. Instead of enjoying the benefits of depreciation, a corporation may find that it must come up with more cash to cover the costs of the project. Another negative aspect is the effect on earnings: the same depreciation that reduces accumulated taxable income also must be taken on the financial accounting side, and will thus reduce earnings per share. While it has been possible in the past to use different depreciation methods for tax purposes and for financial accounting purposes, with the changes embodied in the 1969 Tax Reform Act a corporation may be forced to use straight line depreciation for both purposes.

INTERNAL PROBLEMS

A corporation trying to avoid the penalty tax for its accumulated earnings can face two internal risks. First, it may have problems with minority stockholders who disagree with the policy of the majority. In one corporation, for example, a minority stockholder who was a member of the board of directors showed up at a meeting with a written statement that was read into the minutes. This statement declared that the majority was accumulating the earnings within the corporation in order to save taxes at the shareholder level, that he had attempted to get the corporation to declare a dividend, and that the other directors should be held liable for any accumulated earnings taxes levied on the corporation. One might well imagine the joy of an IRS agent who discovers that kind of statement in the minutes of a board meeting.

A similar case occurred recently when stockholders brought legal action against the directors of a corporation that accumulated earnings and incurred a large accumulated earnings tax. The action was settled out of court—with the directors paying personally the $2½ million tax.

There is no doubt, then, that extreme caution is called for when a corporation seeks a viable tax-shelter investment with which to avoid an accumulated earnings tax. Before it makes the move, it should be able to affirmatively answer three basic questions:

1. Will the investment meet the IRS criteria for "reasonable needs"?

2. If the investment is into another business, does it actually involve the corporation in the management of that business?

3. Will the accumulated earnings be free from challenge by members of the corporate power structure?

DISCUSSION

Question: Please comment briefly on what I think is an exceptionally effective device for avoiding the accumulated earnings tax. It works this way: a company facing an accumulation problem makes a passive tax-shelter investment in the current year which gives either 100 percent deduction or close to it for the money invested. This deduction, to the extent that it wipes out the year's earnings, will eliminate the accumulated earnings tax and will render immaterial—for that year, at least—the question of whether the investment is a passive or active one. Moreover, if this investment is successful, the money will come back into the corporation as capital gain and will therefore be exempt under the definition of accumulated taxable income. Am I basically on the right track conceptually?

Mr. Malouf: Conceptually, yes. If you can find a way to expense an investment now or go into one of the tax-shelter investments that will create enough deductions now to eliminate the taxable income for this year, you have, by definition, eliminated the accumulated earnings problem.

Question: If you want to acquire a company, but you cannot purchase 80 percent of the stock, is it still possible to qualify the investment as a "reasonable need"?

Mr. Malouf: Yes, if there is a strong relationship between the two businesses. If you are buying control of a company with a business related to your own business, and you will actually have practical control of the subsidiary even though you have less than 80 percent of the stock, you would have a good case for establishing this as a "reasonable need" investment.

COMMENTARY

This Chapter deals expertly with an increasingly critical tax problem: the accumulated earnings tax. Although the tax—ranging from 27 ½ to 38 ½ percent of annual accumulated earnings—is at present applied rather narrowly, the President need do no more than give a mandate to the IRS to widen its application.

THE DONRUSS CASE

Any corporation vulnerable to this tax should be further alarmed by the Donruss case, in which the taxpayer's victory in the Federal District Court and Circuit Court of Appeals was overturned by the Supreme Court in one of its less brilliant decisions. In this case, the District Court judge had instructed the jury—in literal accordance with the exact wording of the Internal Revenue Code—that to impose the accumulated earnings tax requires not only that surplus must be accumulated beyond the reasonable business needs of a taxpaying corporation, but that the accumulation had to be for *the purpose of avoiding the surtax on dividends.* The jury found that although the Donruss Company had indeed accumulated surplus beyond its reasonable business needs, it did so out of business conservatism rather than for the purpose of avoiding taxes. The Supreme Court, however, maintained that tax avoidance only had to be *one* reason for surplus accumulation, not the *only* reason. Since it is extremely difficult to establish that tax motivation had nothing at all to do with a company's accumulation of earnings, this set a dangerous legal precedent.

TAX MOTIVATION FOR CORPORATIONS

There is possible disagreement with Mr. Malouf on only two points. First, he states that publicly controlled corporations have strong pressures on them to pay dividends rather than accumulate earnings, and that consequently no tax motivation could be found. However, this is not necessarily true of many publicly held companies that can be characterized as growth companies. The goal of such companies' managements may be accumulated earnings rather than dividend income. That this fact has penetrated the consciousness of the IRS is evident from the number of publicly held corporations being attached for the first time under Section 531. Most of these claims have been quietly settled out of court, since any attached company wants to avoid the kind of publicity that in the Trico case had led that company's minority stockholders to sue the controlling directors after exposure of the incurrence of a 531 liability. The case was settled for over $2,000,000.

REDEMPTION OF STOCK

The second reservation involves Mr. Malouf's statement that the 1969 Act permits redemption of stock with IRC-303 as a reasonable business need. Although this is a correct statement of the law, IRC-303 is a very narrow provision of the law which applies only in a limited number of cases and to a limited extent. The law itself is not necessarily restricted to its express provisions. In the case of the Emeloid Company, the court held that the borrowing of money to buy insurance on the life of stockholder management was motivated by a business purpose: to avoid the forced liquidation of stock to strangers in order to pay estate taxes at death. This court action seems to rule in favor of redemption whenever demonstrably necessary to avoid friction.

6

TAX SHELTER PITFALLS FOR THE INVESTOR

Howard M. Cohen

Before anyone starts to invest in tax shelters, he should be clear on two points: what he wants and what he does not want. In other words, he must understand precisely what objectives he wants to attain and be completely aware of the various pitfalls into which he might stumble in attempting to achieve them.

In specific details, of course, every investor has slightly different objectives, and the hazards he faces may also vary. But these elements are sufficiently similar to make this investor's-eye view of tax shelters useful to almost any potential investor.

MR. COHEN IS A PARTNER IN THE FIRM OF FINLEY, KUMBLE, UNDERBERG, PERSKY AND ROTH, ATTORNEYS AT LAW, GENERAL PRACTICE SPECIALIZING IN CORPORATE REAL ESTATE LITIGATION AND TAX SHELTERS.

Let us start with objectives. What do I want from my tax sheltered investments? My first objective, paradoxically enough, has nothing to do with taxes. I want, above all, a sound economic investment. Whatever my professional advisors may tell me, I know I am nevertheless putting cash into the deal—whether it is in the form of immediate investment or future tax payments without cash flow. Putting it bluntly, I want an investment, not a tax gimmick. Of course, I want to convert the investment into a shelter for my taxes. First, however, it must meet the criteria for a sound investment.

Another important objective is maximum leverage for the use of my money. Leverage is to tax shelters what margin is to stocks. With maximum leverage, I can create a capital asset with the use of as many tax dollars as possible.

TAX OBJECTIVES

What are my specific tax objectives? That depends, naturally, on a number of factors which may change from year to year. Such factors might include the size and nature of my income this year— and what they are likely to be in the next five or even ten years. Perhaps I have an unusual amount of ordinary income this year, so that I will be far more interested in this year's shelter than next year's. My objective then will probably be 100 percent deduction— or even 200 or 300 percent deduction—for every dollar that I put in, so that I can shelter the money I made this year.

On the other hand, let us assume that I am approaching retirement or my cash position is low. In either case, I may want to make an investment this year which would defer tax on my income for future years. This can be done, for example, by converting ordinary income this year into capital gains in a future year. An investment in cattle-feeding or oil might accomplish this.

As a corporation executive, I may want to sell some of my optioned stock before the end of the three-year period that would qualify the sale as a capital gain. This means, of course, that the stock sale will generate ordinary income, and my objective will be to shelter that income.

Still another objective might be future cash flow. Let us assume that I am on the rise in my corporation, and I am less worried about this year's tax than about whether I will be generating enough after-tax cash flow in future years to enable me to invest part of my then substantially increased income.

ECONOMIC PITFALLS

Once I have established my objectives for tax-shelter investment, I must start thinking about pitfalls and obstacles that could prevent my reaching those objectives.

In terms of the economics of the investment, what should I watch out for? First, I would take a long, hard look at the tax-shelter promoter's approach. The promoter and investment manager are, of course, entitled to fair compensation for their services and any risks to which they may be exposed. However, I would be wary of the promoter who unduly overloads the front end, thereby substantially reducing the chances of an adequate return with the slim funds that remain to be invested. I would be equally wary of the promoter who unduly overloads the back end. He will emphasize the wonderful tax benefits I will receive, but he may not draw attention to the fact that he retains for himself substantially all the equity in the property, the equipment, or the real estate. This approach will minimize or even eliminate the possibility of my achieving any economic gain other than a tax benefit.

Another pitfall may be the true amount and nature of the dollars I will be investing. Thus, in calculating the invested dollars, the taxes which may have to paid on future income without cash flow should be added to the after-tax dollars being invested initially. Moreover, in determining the amount of after-tax dollars being invested initially, the source of income from which they are derived is significant. For example, in my stock option situation, I know that if I hold the optioned stock for three years I will have a capital gain. Therefore, capital gains rates that are applicable at that time rather than ordinary income rates should be factored in when I am calculating my real investment and the potential return.

High interest rates are another pitfall I must avoid. I want to maximize my leverage, but not at the cost of borrowing at interest rates so high that they will make my investment economically unprofitable.

TAX PITFALLS

What pitfalls should I be alert for in the tax aspects of my investment?

I want to make sure that I participate not merely in a financing but in an actual investment. For example, a transaction in which I am reasonably assured of a return of all or a substantial part of my investment without further potential return or risk would run the danger of being deemed a financing. Thus, even if I think that the return of after-tax dollars plus a tax benefit constitute an adequate economic return, the absence of risk or potential may disqualify the arrangement as an investment and make it ineligible for the tax benefit.

I should also be wary of the deal in which the general partner of a limited partnership has no liability whatsoever, real or potential. Where liability is reasonably insurable, I will consider the joint venture preferable to the limited partnership.

I must also watch out for the tax penalties and risks. If an arrangement has no business purpose, I may lose my deductions completely. In the situation, for instance, in which the lender is, in effect, an equity holder rather than a true lender, I had better be prepared at the least for possible reallocation of deductions. I may not realize the deductions I anticipate getting in future years. Moreover, what I think will be capital gain may in fact turn out to be ordinary income.

I must also keep my eye open for statutory risks, such as recapture provisions. I want to avoid the real estate or cattle deal from which I am getting wonderful tax benefits today, only to have the recapture provisions turn what I had hoped would be future capital gain right back into ordinary income.

Future statutory changes, too, can vitally affect the whole

outlook. Therefore, I want to avoid, if possible, potential pitfalls as well as those that already exist. I want to be aware of all pending statutory changes so that I can anticipate how they will affect my tax-shelter investments. This lesson was well illustrated when the Tax Reform Act of 1969 caught my colleagues and myself by surprise with the 10 percent preference tax on option stock. We had not conceived of the possibility that we would have to pay the equivalent of an excise tax on gain from the exercise of an option granted prior to the Act. However, that is the exact effect of the new law.

Another way to avoid tax-shelter pitfalls is to consult accounting and tax counsel on possible interpretive challenges from the IRS and the courts. Remember that rulings and decisions resulting from these challenges may be retroactive, not merely prospective, in their effect.

Caution is my watchword when I study the documents relating to each prospective investment. I will carefully scrutinize all projections, such as income, expenses, financing costs, and debt service charges. I will question sharply all assumptions that are being made by the promoter—such as the tax bracket of the potential investor. It will make a substantial difference—both in terms of what it costs to go into the investment and what I may realize from it— if the promoter assumes a 70 percent tax bracket and I am only in a 50 percent bracket.

I will make a hardnosed, thorough investigation of the promoter. His ability, reputation, and integrity must be solid.

In addition, I will want competent experts to properly evaluate the risks and potential of any investment I am considering. If I am considering an oil investment, I will consult a geologist, or, at the very least, check on the reputation of the geologist involved in the investment. If I am considering a real estate deal, I will consult a real estate expert. It should go without saying that I will consult my accountant or my tax lawyer. I know that the risk of an investment cannot be completely eliminated. But as a prudent investor, I will seek out every possible source of expertise to uncover and minimize these risks.

GUIDELINES FOR CORPORATE EXECUTIVES

So far, we have examined tax-shelter investments from the point of view of the individual investor. Now let us point out some factors that should be considered by the corporate employee. His company's benefit programs may have been seriously affected by the Tax Reform Act of 1969. For example:

Stock Options

Under the old law, a corporate employee had a fairly good chance of realizing capital gains if he were willing to hold his options for three years, with his tax being limited to a capital gains tax. Under the new law, he must understand that, upon exercise of his option, he is subject to a possible 10 percent preference income tax on profits that he may never realize. Moreover, even if he holds the stock for three years, then sells it and realizes capital gain, up to one-half of that gain may be taxed as preference income. In addition, the amount of his earned income that will be protected by the 50 percent tax ceiling will be reduced by an amount equal to half of that capital gain.

There may be ways to minimize these disadvantages. As of this writing, the Treasury had not yet ruled on whether ordinary income realized from the sale of a stock option in less than three years after it is exercised would be considered nondeferred, earned income. One would think that, at the very least, stock sold in the same year that the option is exercised would so qualify. If so, any resulting income would be eligible for the maximum tax limitation. The 50 percent limit applicable as of 1972 is sufficiently close to the 40 percent effective rate applicable to capital gains in excess of $50,-000 that the advantage of waiting the full three-year period to achieve capital gains is substantially diluted. For one thing, if such stock is sold in less than the three-year required holding period for capital gains, unforeseeable market fluctuations in the stock will be avoided. Equally important, the funds derived from such sales may themselves be tax sheltered or otherwise invested in such a way that the resulting investments may be used as the basis for financing the exercise of additional future stock options.

The executive should also consider another interesting possibility in handling his stock options. If option stock is held for at least six months after the exercise of the option, the difference between the market price on the date of exercise and the market price on the date of sale is capital gain. However, if the stock goes down in value, it is not considered a capital loss but merely a reduction in the amount of the ordinary income which is realized.

The Tax Reform Act also reduced the attractiveness of restricted stock plans. Before the 1969 changes, restricted stock had very substantial advantages for both the corporation and its executives. When sufficient restrictions were placed on the sale of the stock, the executive could not realize gain on the stock until the restrictions were removed. He could then dispose of the stock, and his income from the sale was measured by the lesser of two differences: (1) the difference between the price at which he bought the stock and its market price at that time, or (2) the difference between the price at which he bought the stock and the market price at the time the restriction was removed.

However, the 1969 Act eliminated this important advantage. Now, although still deferred, the executive's tax is based on the difference between the original issue price and the price at the time the restriction is removed. This means that if the stock performs well, the executive's ordinary income from its sale will be greater under the new law than it would have been under the old.

For an executive willing to gamble, there is one way in which he might avoid this disadvantage. He can pay his tax at the outset on the difference between the issuance price and the market price at the time of purchase. If the stock goes up, everything he makes on it will then be capital gain. However, if it goes down, he will not receive any rebate.

Deferred Compensation Plans

Because the final version of the 1969 Act did not include proposed changes to eliminate individual deferred compensation contracts, such contracts are still permissible. Their object, of course, is to defer the tax on an executive's income to a future date when his tax rate will presumably be lower.

The 1969 Act did, however, strike a serious blow against a major advantage of qualified deferred compensation and profit-sharing plans. A company may still make deferred payments to its executives, on which they would pay no tax until the money is actually distributed—usually on retirement or earlier termination of employment. Under the old law, only a capital gain tax applied to both the company's base contributions and any increments to these contributions that accumulated before distribution. Under the new law, any company contributions made after January 1, 1970, are treated as ordinary income at the date of distribution, although increments to these funds remain as capital gains. The new law does permit averaging in certain cases, which for some executives can substantially ameliorate the tax burden of such a lump sum payment.

Pension Plans

Although not normally considered a tax shelter, pension plans actually did serve that purpose under the old law. In addition to the benefit of tax deferral, an executive about to retire had the option of choosing either a lump sum payment or an annuity. If he chose the lump sum, the entire amount was capital gain.

Under the new law, contributions made by employers after January 1, 1970, are treated as ordinary income, even if the money is paid in a lump sum at retirement. As in qualified profit sharing plans, any increments will still be capital gains. And here, too, the law has ameliorated the effect of this change. Under certain circumstances it permits a seven-year averaging, and remuneration received in the year of retirement does not have to be factored in.

Other Plans

Paid insurance, vacations, medical and dental plans, tuition plans, guaranteed loans—all of these can be considered tax shelters provided by a company for its employees. Indeed, a company can even make a tax-shelter investment on behalf of an employee. All such plans are subject to IRS challenge, but this risk can be minimized by making the plan as objective, broad, and unselective as possible.

Ordinary Income

Surprisingly, ordinary income could be an executive's most effective tax shelter. If the tax limits on earned income remain unchanged, the executive who is presently in a bracket over 50 percent may well find that straight salary increases are his best shelter.

DISCUSSION

Question: You stated that when liability is reasonably insurable, you preferred a joint venture to a limited partnership. Please expand on that.

Mr. Cohen: I based my opinion on the Treasury's implication that it may challenge a limited partnership oil deal in which neither the corporate general partner nor the limited partners have any significant potential liability. The situation could be further aggravated if the general partner is a corporation without financial substance. As a result, a number of oil operators have formed joint ventures instead of limited partnerships. Their reasoning is that while for all other purposes they can set the joint venture up as a limited partnership, it does have at least potential liability for negligence, explosion, and third-party liability—all of which may be covered by insurance. As long as the risk is there, the fact that you are covered by insurance still protects you tax-wise.

Question: It is my understanding, however, that recently the IRS ruled that when a corporate general partner has $250,000 net worth or 10 percent of the limited partners' contribution—whichever is higher —they would not tax that. Also, in applying the net worth standard, the IRS is satisfied with actual fair market value of the corporate general partner's assets and does not restrict him to a book net worth. In other words, he might have a book net worth of only $1,000, but discovered reserves of several million dollars in actual value. The Treasury evidently will accept that.

Another point: when the SEC is accepting or denying prospectuses for limited partnerships, it does not turn them down on the liability issue. Instead, it asks the promoter to list the possible non-compliance with Treasury guidelines as an additional investment risk. This seems to mean that the Treasury is only trying to make sure that the general partner is not a mere instrumentality of the limited partners. Thus, even if the general partner has net worth of only a nickel, the limited partnership should be able to successfully resist an IRS challenge. This could be done by demonstrating that the partnership was operated as a bona fide business enterprise and that the general partner was not a mere instrumentality being used by the limited partners to limit their liability while at the same time they actually made the business decisions. Would you agree with this assumption?

Mr. Cohen: No. I would question that assumption. Referring to the specific question raised, it is my understanding that the IRS has indicated that irrespective of compliance with its financial guidelines, potential liability of the general partner will be considered a factor in determining the bona-fides of the limited partnership.

Question: If a top executive has a restricted stock option, can the corporation give the stock to him at a time when its value is low, so his tax bite will be smaller?

Mr. Cohen: I assume the question concerns a nonqualified option to purchase restricted stock. A company can accomplish this in two ways: it can try to time the option in terms of the market conditions, or it can boost the purchase price. Naturally, the second approach would be less attractive to the executive, since he would need more funds to buy the stock.

Question: Let me expand on my question with a hypothetical example. Assume that an executive in a corporation has an option for 5,000 shares of stock over a five-year period, and can purchase 1,000 each year. Let us also assume that the stock is priced at ten cents a share in the first year but by the fifth year has gone up to ten dollars. My question is, instead of getting his 1,000 shares each year, could he get the whole 5,000 shares in the first year when the price is only ten cents?

Mr. Cohen: In the case of qualified stock options, the purchase price must be 100 percent of the market price, and the options must be exercised within five years. I have already covered above the various tax consequences of the exercise and sale of qualified option stock. If you are referring to unqualified options, then the option may be at any price that the company desires, irrespective of market price. If there are no restrictions on the transfer of the stock, the difference between option and market price at the time the option is exercised will be ordinary income at that time to the optionee. If the option is actively traded and has a readily ascertainable market value, then the tax may be imposed upon receipt of such action. If there are restrictions on transfer, the difference between option price and market price at the time the restrictions are removed will, generally, be ordinary income to the optionee. The optionee has the alternative, however, of restricting the ordinary income to the difference between option price and market price at the date of exercise of the option if he pays a tax on that amount for the year in which he exercises the option. Any subsequent increments will be capital gain if the stock is held more than six months.

COMMENTARY

In this refreshingly realistic appraisal of tax shelters from the investor's viewpoint, there are few points on which it is possible to have a difference of opinion.

Near the beginning of the chapter, Mr. Cohen writes about deductions of 100, 200, or 300 percent of the dollar investment. Most investors would be wise to aim no higher than 200 percent—to go for 300 percent deductions can be extremely dangerous.

THE PROMOTER'S INVESTMENT

Later, Mr. Cohen warns against the promoter who unduly overloads the front end or the back end of a tax shelter. His warning is quite justified, but it should go even further. No limitation on the promoter's return can be guaranteed to work in the taxpayer's interest unless the promoter invests his own money, dollar for dollar, to the extent of 20 or 25 percent of the total investment. This conclusion is based on a series of this commentator's bitter experiences with promoters who seemed to have a duly limited reward for their efforts, but made no substantial investment of their own in the program.

SALE OF STOCK OPTIONS

Mr. Cohen seems unduly concerned as to whether ordinary income on the sale of stock options will be considered deferred income and therefore not earned income. In excepting *defered income* from the definition of *earned income,* Section 1348 excluded deferred income only if it is not received in the year following the year in which rights become non-forfeitable. This language does not seem to apply to the ordinary exercised stock option.

DISTRIBUTION OF DEFERRED COMPENSATION

Mr. Cohen separates his discussion of the taxability of distributions of deferred compensation into two sections, one on non-qualified plans, the other on pension plans. This may suggest that he is referring to different plans, but he is not. Distributions under non-qualified deferred compensation plans are always treated as ordinary income and should not only be spread, but also should be set up to recurringly qualify for the tax ceiling under IRC-1348.

In pension plans and profit-sharing plans, the seven-year averaging provisions on lump sum distributions can substantially reduce the tax and even bring it below the capital gains tax. A long-term payout would make lower brackets available. Moreover, a relatively new annuity contract is available whereby the lump sum payment can be used to buy a variable annuity whose investments are managed *by the employee himself* or placed in a mutual fund designated by him. This arrangement spreads out the payment while permitting liquidation and diversification of the pension or profit-sharing credit. It also defers and reduces the income tax on distribution and preserves estate tax immunity.

JOINT VENTURE VERSUS LIMITED PARTNERSHIP

Coming to another point, it is easy to understand Mr. Cohen's preference for a joint venture over a limited partnership when investing in various types of tax shelters. However, limited partnerships or general partnerships provide many advantages under IRC-704 in allowing varying allocations of losses and gains. The question and answer discussion indicated how the benefits of partnership setups can be retained within the guidelines laid down by the Internal Revenue Service.

QUALIFIED STOCK OPTIONS

Non-restricted, non-qualified stock options may now appear more attractive than qualified options, particularly in two circumstances:

1. When the corporation is in a higher tax bracket than the employee;

2. Where the direct and indirect taxes on capital gains can add up to more than the ordinary income tax on earned income, which benefits by the ceiling under IRC-1348.

7

GUIDELINES FOR SELECTING A TAX SHELTER

Jules M. Baron

Consider the term *tax shelter.* It is full of promise, conjuring up visions of major tax savings to ease the tax burdens that weigh down both the individual and the corporation alike.

Indeed, tax shelters *can* provide such relief, but only if the investor, after thorough study and evaluation, chooses his tax shelter wisely. Unfortunately, many investors are so dazzled by the perfectly valid *concept* of tax shelters that they are blinded to an important

MR. BARON IS EXECUTIVE VICE PRESIDENT OF THE AIMS GROUP, INCORPORATED.

fact of life: there are good and bad tax shelter investments. And the time to find out whether a particular tax shelter investment will be good or bad for the investor is *before* he commits his resources to it. In this chapter, I will point out some of the pitfalls that await the uninitiated tax shelter investor and suggest some questions that he should ask in order to avoid such pitfalls.

Perhaps the investor's first move should be to drop the term *tax-shelter investment* and replace it with the term *tax-incentive investment.* Not only is this term more apt and constructive, but it could also be used more effectively with the Internal Revenue Service in the event of the ever-possible audit.

Why do I stress the terminology? Primarily because the term *tax-incentive* investment puts the entire subject in more balanced perspective by emphasizing the importance of an investment that is sound economically as well as tax-wise. Too frequently over-emphasis is placed on the tax savings and not nearly enough on the other economic aspects of the deal. Indeed, it should be a warning signal to an investor when a promoter or a prospectus stresses the tax-savings aspect of a deal and skims over its business advantages. Regardless of tax deduction considerations, the most significant factor in a tax-incentive deal is whether it is a sound investment. The investor should commit his resources only after he is convinced that there is underlying economic potential in the deal. As a matter of fact, this is essential if the investment is to qualify for favorable tax treatment. There must be economic viability *apart* from the relief provided by tax losses.

UNRAVELING THE COMPLEXITIES

The investor should next recognize the fact that the tax-shelter field is treacherously complex. Even tax experts have difficulty unraveling the complexities, particularly in the current decade while the tax changes of 1969 are still being sorted out.

These factors emphasize the need for a thorough understanding of tax and legal considerations, most of which must be developed with the assistance of such experts as an attorney and an accountant.

And when they are consulted, it should be done early enough to give them sufficient lead time. One cannot expect instantaneous answers to the complex questions raised by tax-incentive investments.

Time is essential in evaluating the conomic as well as the tax aspects of a tax-incentive investment. It may be necessary to make a geophysical study, obtain certain documents, develop engineering reports—all of which can be time consuming.

Another point that the investor should keep firmly in mind: many tax-incentive investments fall into the low-liquidity category. Seldom can he merely pick up a phone and promptly sell a leased computer, a shopping center, or an interest in an oil deal. At this time there is simply no organized market mechanism for transferring such ownerships—still another reason why the investor must consider the practical as well as the tax consequences of committing his resources for extended periods.

For the individual executive, this inflexibility requires that he think ahead to the possible changes that could affect his tax rates. Can he be sure there will be no significant decrease in his salary? Have bonuses been important and can he count on them in the future? Has he anticipated the possibility of a merger that could change his status? What about his health—could it force an early retirement? Does he intend to stay with his present company? All these questions must be considered *before* the executive commits himself and his resources. If he has an employment contract, he should go over it carefully with his lawyer. A most important consideration should be the possibility of early retirement, a contingency which could dramatically reduce the attractiveness of a tax-incentive investment.

EVALUATING AN OPPORTUNITY

It is, of course, difficult to make accurate projections in evaluating a tax-incentive opportunity. Two basic elements should be considered: first, the stream of losses from intangible drilling expense, accelerated depreciation, and construction costs. These usually comprise immediate tax benefits that provide the return *of* capital. Second, capital gains achieved on disposition of the property, provide the return *on* capital. Some deals offer rapid recovery of capital and a small annuity or residual thereafter. In others, the asset's residual value represents a major factor in determining return.

Here are three rough rules of thumb that can be used in measuring these investments:

1. Few tax-incentive deals will prove attractive to the investor with a tax bracket very much under 60 percent.

2. Cash outlay should come back within four years.

3. Within another four years, the net cash retrieved should should have almost doubled.

These are only general rules. When an executive considers a tax-incentive investment, he must understand how a particular deal affects the balance of his total investment program. He must maintain the most advantageous balance among such investments as securities, real estate and insurance.

To achieve this balance, the executive must thoroughly evaluate and understand his over-all financial picture. Only then can be choose the kind of tax-incentive investment that is most appropriate for his portfolio. Evaluation starts with examination—perhaps by the executive's attorney—of the employment contract, stock options, pension plans, income tax returns and divorce or separation agreements. These documents can frequently throw light on the way in which a specific tax-incentive investment will affect the executive's financial position.

Next, before commitment, the executive should determine whether his present portfolio meets basic balance requirements among essential physical assets, working capital and necessary reserves. Existing investments must be considered. Does he have an effective diversified portfolio of marketable growth securities? The executive should regard tax-incentive investments as the icing on the cake, to be considered *only* after his total portfolio objectives have been firmly established.

MONITORING THE INVESTMENT

The task of monitoring the investment should also be attended to ahead of time. In many cases, this can be a complex, time-consuming job. The executive must ask himself whether he can budget the time necessary to measure actual performance against projections, or to adjust the deal when it is affected by changing economic conditions or shifts in the tax rules. Added to this is the problem of providing whatever degree of management a particular property may require. If, for example, the investor is obligated to do structural repairs under the terms of a net lease, he can safely bet that roof repairs will be necessary within six years. Does he know how to get bids for the job?

Often, the executive will decide to delegate these responsibilities to an individual or organization. Although it may be painful, such delegation is necessary to reduce day-to-day involvement and to obtain expert professional assistance. He should just make certain to take the costs of legal, accounting, and managerial services into account when he is projecting his return.

REAL ESTATE INVESTMENT

Now let us consider two types of tax-incentive investments in terms of some questions the potential investor should ask before making his commitment.

First, real estate. There seems little doubt that real estate will continue to be attractive as an inflationary hedge with high leverage advantages. Once that is accepted, however, the investor faces the difficult question of deciding what kind of real estate investment makes sense for him.

When considering an apartment house, for example, the quality of the operating management is invariably a key factor—whether it be luxury, middle income or low rental housing.

As to shopping centers, the investor is faced with a wide

variety of types. One may be a neighborhood shopping center, another a community center that draws customers from a three to five mile radius, or a regional center that draws from as far as twenty miles away. Depreciation advantages tend to be greater with a regional center—but so do the risks. He must keep in mind that highway and traffic patterns can change, seriously affecting a shopping center's drawing power.

Office buildings require equally careful consideration. What about the quality of the operating management? Are there specific risks, even though a net lease is involved? Which structural repairs, for example, will remain the owner's responsibility? What constitutes an adequate reserve for repairs? Is there a complete, reliable evaluation of heating, elevator, and air conditioning equipment—or should an engineer be hired to examine these facilities?

OIL INVESTMENT

Oil continues to represent a most attractive form of tax-incentive investment. But what kind of an oil investment makes sense for the specific individual? Is a specific lease or group of leases more advantageous than a public program? What about overhead costs which so closely affect the potential for profit?

It is most important for the potential investor in oil to read the fine print in a prospectus—and understand it. For example, what kind of diversification is provided for in order to spread the risk? Is it diversification over a broad spectrum of leases, or diversification of drilling operators? How meaningful is the claim of diversification when the prospectus permits the manager of a fund to sell the fund all of the oil leases to be drilled? Is there almost a contradiction of avowed intention to diversify when the fund permits the acquisition of leases in this manner?

These, of course, are merely random examples of the questions an investor must ask before he commits himself to a tax-incentive deal. They are presented to point up the necessity for thorough evaluation, no matter how attractive the opportunity may seem at first glance. The investor must get the facts—and he must understand what they mean to him specifically. Only then will he be able to invest wisely and end up with the deal that is right for him.

COMMENTARY

This chapter deals comprehensively with the important business aspects of tax shelter investments. My major reservation is Mr. Baron's generalization that tax-incentive deals are not attractive to investors under the 60 percent tax bracket. Much depends on the specific tax-shelter needs and overall goals of the investor. Another factor is whether the return from a tax-sheltered investment is itself taxable as income or as capital gain. Assume that the return is taxable as capital gain at the old 25 percent rate, because only limited capital gain is taken in any one year and there are no other items of tax preference. If the return equals or exceeds the investment and is received fairly quickly, then an investment deducted at 50 percent rates may compare attractively with a tax on return of 25 percent.

This point becomes even more valid if the return is tax-free, as with life insurance. A recent calculation on minimum deposit insurance demonstrates that a thirty-five-year-old man can carry insurance over a twenty-year period at an after-tax cost of seventy-eight cents a thousand when he is in only the 40 percent tax bracket. Considering the leverage from even twenty years of premium payments at this annual after-tax cost for tax-free insurance, one fact seems obvious. If the investor needs insurance he will find it attractive even in the 40 percent bracket when the minimum deposit method makes the cost of the insurance ultimately tax deductible while the proceeds are tax free.

Another factor is that the investor seldom knows

what his tax bracket will be in the future—five years from now he may be averaging income from the 70 percent level. If so, he may find it extremely valuable to have a deduction that cuts the brackets for the preceding averaged in four years to the 30 percent level.

Indeed, if the investment's income is sheltered, the investment may be an attractive one with no deductions at all. For example, many qualified pension or profit-sharing plans permit voluntary contributions by the employee. Such contributions are not deductible by the employee, *but the income earned on the contributions is accumulated in the trust, free of tax, until ultimate distribution.* This tax holiday, permitting the rollover of gains and their tax-free escalation until distribution date, can be a tremendous boon—particularly if the proceeds are distributed over many years in relatively low brackets. It is also possible for the tax-payer to invest in a variable annuity; he controls the investment and the income is not taxed to him until the annuity payoff begins.

THE INVESTOR'S GOAL

Another questionable generalization is that a tax-shelter investment must be paid out within four years. This may be a valid requirement when the investor's goal is immediate or relatively quick improvement of his tax position. But some investors have longer-range goals, and for them such tax shelter programs as pension trusts or minimum deposit insurance—which usually take far longer than four years to pay off—may be more appropriate than quick-paying shelters.

8

TWO WAYS TO ESCAPE HIGH CAPITAL GAINS TAXES

Gustave Simons

Traditionally, most tax shelter investments have aimed at converting ordinary income into capital gains. In almost all cases this was a perfectly sound goal—but then came the Tax Reform Act of 1969. Under the Act, there now exists a potential *65 percent* on capital gains. Rarely would a capital gains tax rise above 45 percent, but it can happen—and the wise investor should take steps to make sure it will not.

MR. SIMONS IS A SENIOR PARTNER OF GUSTAVE SIMONS AND ASSOCIATES AND PRESIDENT, AMERICAN MANAGEMENT COUNSEL.

How could the capital gains tax mount up to 65 percent? It works this way:

Depending on the size of the capital gain and the amount of tax preferences, the Federal Capital Gains Tax will be 35 percent in 1972. Half of the capital gain is treated as a tax preference item and taxed at 10 percent, bringing the total tax so far to 40 percent. Then the investor should figure on a state tax of around 5 percent, bringing his tax up to 45 percent.

In addition, tax preference items in one year can in future years remove some of the taxpayer's income from the shelter of the 50 percent maximum tax on ordinary income. Assume, for example, that a taxpayer has $300,000 worth of tax preference items in the current year. Five years from now, even if he has had no more tax preference items, his tax will be adversely affected. Under the 1969 tax law changes, the amount of his average tax preference over the past five years in excess of $30,000 a year is knocked out from the taxable income sheltered by the 50 percent maximum. In this case, the basic $30,000 a year allowance would add up to $150,000. This leaves an excess of $150,000, averaging out to $30,000 a year. For each of the next five years, then, $30,000 of the taxpayer's income will not be sheltered by the 50 percent maximum tax on earned income. This brings his total capital gains tax to 65 percent. Thus, having avoided the pitfalls of excess deduction account, accelerated depreciation recapture, and all the other rules that can turn a capital gain into ordinary income, the taxpayer still carries an enormous burden.

How can he avoid it? Here are two examples of innovative conversion procedures that can avoid a high capital gains tax—one from the viewpoint of the individual taxpayer and the other from the viewpoint of the taxpaying corporation.

USING A PRIVATE ANNUITY

In the first case, we have a 46-year-old man with a family business. Wishing to diversify, he makes a tax-free exchange of his securities for those of another company. Now he wants to get rid of a million dollars' worth of these securities.

He is still receiving a large salary from the corporation, which means that if he sells the securities he will be hit for the previously mentioned 65 percent tax on most of his capital gain—and he will be hit for five years.

The alternative—a private annuity

What does he do? He sells his securities in exchange for a private annuity. Such a sale can be made to a member of the family or to a private trust. Under the terms of this particular private annuity (by definition, a private annuity is one that is not granted by a financial organization), a male taxpayer, age 45, receives $76,209.10 a year in quarterly installments. Of this amount $46,084.20 would be referred to as the excluded portion and the balance of approximately $30,000 a year as the included portion.

Until a Revenue Ruling in 1969, the excluded portion was totally tax-free until the annuitant had recovered his basis. It was then taxed as a capital gain, but was subjected to no capital gains tax after it had added up to the value of the asset exchanged for the private annuity.

However, in the 1969 Revenue Ruling, the Internal Revenue Service took a different position: the excluded portion would be subject to taxation immediately on the same proportionate basis as that of an installment sale (the excluded portion would be taxable in proportion to the fair market value of the assets over the basis). Then, after the fair market value of the property was recovered, the continuing excluded portion would be taxed as ordinary income. This ruling is being challenged at this writing.

How does one determine the excluded portion in a private annuity? Simply take the fair market value of the asset and divide it by the annuitant's life expectancy. This is similar to all annuities, which are based on the concept that the annuity payor will dissipate the capital and interest at an assumed rate on the declining balance and will just break even on the day the actuary tells the annuitant he is going to die.

Deducting the excluded portion from the annuity leaves the

included portion, which is always taxed as ordinary income. This amount usually hovers around 2 percent of the total value of the asset, although in one case the interest assumption was 4 percent.

Avoiding the preference tax

Returning to our example, the annuitant is receiving $46,084.20 a year of capital gain on $1,000,000 of assets with a zero basis only. Assuming that he has no other capital gains, he does not as yet exceed the 25 percent federal limitation on the capital gains tax, because the increased percentage starts only after $50,000 a year of capital gain is realized annually by a joint return taxpayer. Since the exluded portion is only $46,084.20, the married taxpayer would receive the benefits of the old rates in the absence of other capital gains. Assuming further that he has no other tax preference items, he will not have any tax preference tax, because half of his capital gain is only $23,042, below the $30,000 exemption. Thus, none of his earned income will be removed from the shelter of the 25 percent maximum, assuming no other capital gains or items of tax preference.

The beauty of the private annuity derives from the fact that the annuitant really pays no capital gains tax on his original capital gain from the sale of his securities. He pays a capital gains tax only on the part of the new income generated by his capital gain. This million dollars of capital gain remains intact—assuming that it earns the required annuity, e.g., 7.62 percent at age 45.

What if the annuitant dies soon after the agreement is signed? In that case, the annuity ceases to exist. There is no capital gains tax, no ordinary income, no tax preference, no gift tax (this assumes, of course, that the annuitant was in good health at the time of the transaction—the IRS would certainly question an agreement with an annuitant who had a terminal illness). Nor would there be an estate tax, although there could be a tax when the grantor of the annuity disposes of the property.

Rules for Foreign Trusts

If the annuity grantor is a foreign trust created by a nonresident alien (such as a relative in Canada), and the alien reserved certain rights specified in Sections 671–678 of the Internal Revenue Code, then a 1969 ruling permits the trust to distribute all the "excess" to U.S. beneficiaries without any tax to them. The "excess" is the amount retained by the trust over the amount of the annuity payments, and is determined by two factors:

1. How long the annuitant lives and the aggregate paid to him, and

2. The amount earned over the annuity.

To qualify for the tax-free distribution, the trust must have enough "kick-off assets" to avoid a claim of sham. Most of the income derives from reinvesting the proceeds of the cash sale, but these investments must be determined by an advisory committee of which at least one member is a non-resident alien.

If these tests are not met, the final distribution of the "excess" to the U.S. beneficiaries is taxable as earned income or as capital gains dependant on the original status of the increment. However, the deferment of tax on the original gain and on excess receipts by the trust provides a long period of tax-free rollover of gains. In fact, if the eventual distribution is spread over many people and many years, the tax, if any, is usually offset by increments during the tax holiday. Thus, this procedure not only shelters the original gain from tax, but also shelters the eventual distribution partially or sometimes completely.

The arrangement can also be made with a U.S. individual or trust company, but the annuity grantor must seek tax-sheltered investments, because the annuity grantor receives no deduction for payments and is taxable on the accounting gains realized.

LIFE INSURANCE AS A TAX SHELTER VEHICLE

The second case history involves a conversion procedure which takes ordinary income and converts it into a gain which from a business standpoint is capital gain but from a tax standpoint is tax-free. The vehicle that accomplishes this is a salary continuance program funded by life insurance.

The schedules at the end of the chapter (see pgs. 112–114) show the way this plan works in the case of a 47-year-old top executive with a wife of the same age. His company is renewing his employment agreement and wants to give him worthwhile pension and death benefits. Because the existing group pension and insurance plan won't meet his requirements, the company decides to design a salary continuance program for him individually.

The company's goal is to provide the executive with $30,000 a year from ages 65 to 75, and to accomplish this it insures his life for $350,000. Note from Column 1 of the schedule that the company does not borrow the premium of $12,132 in the first year—this is to meet the stipulation of Section 264 of the Code that the company may borrow premiums only in three out of the first seven years of the policy. (Although instead of paying all of the premium in four out of seven years, the company may, by combining convertible term with ordinary life, pay half of the premium and borrow half of the premium in six out of seven years.)

So far, as can be seen from Column 5, there is a cumulative expense of $12,132. This is also the amount of debits in Column 7—it is, however, a book debit rather than a cash expenditure. Column 9 shows the net death benefit if the executive obliges by dying in the first year at $337,000. In actuality, the corporation would receive $350,000, but it would reimburse itself first for the first year's premium.

The next key figure is in Column 10—$253,000. This is based on a provision in the plan that if the executive dies at any time before age 75, his beneficiary will receive the amount of the salary continuance until he would have been 75.

What the Fund Earns

The assumption is made that this unsegregated fund will earn 3 percent net of taxes on the declining balance from the first year, when the widow as well as the insured executive was 47, to the 28th year, when the widow is 75 and the insured would have been 75 had he lived. The amount produced, according to these assumptions, is $13,500 annually. Assuming a 55 percent tax rate (which would be the combined federal and state tax rate in New York), this permits the company to pay to the widow or other beneficiary the yearly sum of $30,000 and to take a deduction of that amount which would give them an after-tax "cost" of the $13,500 aforementioned.

There is, of course, the chance that a tax-law change in the next 28 years may disallow the deduction of salary continuance. A company concerned with this possibility could stipulate in the contract that the beneficiary will get the before-tax salary continuance that will have an after-tax cost of $13,500 a year. Even if the deduction of salary continuance is totally disallowed, the widow would receive $13,500 a year for 28 years—still a worthwhile benefit.

Moving over to the last column, we see that the company would have a profit of $84,553 if the executive died in the first year, This profit takes on great importance later on.

In the second year of the plan, the policy has sufficient cash value for the company to borrow the premium. In that year, then, the company pays no premium out of pocket, no interest, and has no net outlay. The cumulative outlay is still $12,132, but the loan of the same amount creates a book debit of two years' premiums: $24,264.

The death benefit grows

In this case, the insurer is a mutual company and the dividends have been used to buy paid-up additions. (Exhaustive computer tests have established that with most contracts and most insurance companies this is the optimum use for dividends.) This increases the gross death benefit in Column 8 by $2,100. The net death benefit will now be $352,100 minus the $12,132 loan against it, or $339,968. However, the figure $327,836 appears as the net death benefit in Column 9, Line 2 because the company should get back the $12,132 premium it paid out in the first year.

Since the widow is now one year older, there is one less yearly payment to her the company must make, bringing the figure in

Column 10 down to $247,509—and leaving the company with a profit of $80,327.

The company continues to alternate between paying the premium and borrowing it until the eighth year, when it borrows out all the cash value it has not used up till now. This, however, is subject to a limitation, because the insurance company will lend only 95 percent of the policy's cash value. The loan comes to $29,835. The company pays the premium and the interest on the loan, then deducts the interest of $1,819.80 in Column 3, minus an assumed tax of 55 percent. Thus, the company gets back approximately $29,000, giving it an aggregate cost up till now of about $22,000, or about $2,000 a year. After 28 years, this cumulative cost in Column 5 has risen to only $48,836.70, or less than $2,000 a year to carry a tremendous program of tax-free insurance. This optimum leverage is provided by three factors:

1. The interest on the premium loan is deductible.

2. The salary continuance is deductible.

3. The profit on the insurance is tax-free.

To see the gains to be made from this particular plan, let us move on to the 19th year, when the executive—if he lives—will be 65. At this point the company sets aside about $116,000 in order to pay him his salary continuance of $30,000 a year for ten years. If he dies at the age of 75, the company has recovered all of its costs, has paid him $300,000 over 10 years as salary continuance—and ends up with a profit of $27,000.

Does it really work? Here is but one striking example: A West Coast company started a similar plan 13 years ago to cover 69 of its executives. At this point, the company has recovered all of its insurance, salary continuance, and interest costs and is actually showing a profit of $200,000. And from this point on, since the insureds will begin dying more rapidly, the company's profits will increase.

It is true, of course, that executives who live to an unusually ripe old age can put a crimp in the plan's profits. However, if there is one executive who dies at 65, the profits from his insurance will carry the cost of another executive who lives to be 90. In actual practice, this writer has never observed a plan with a large group of executives that did not become self-funding after a few years.

If the executive leaves . . .

What happens if the executive decides to leave the company—does he lose out? For the answer to that question, look at the A and B schedules at the end of the chapter. Assuming that the executive leaves the company in the ninth year of the plan, the company sells him the policy for its loan value or cash value, and he carries it on. His net death benefit will continue to go down as shown in Column 9, but remember that his wife's life expectancy is shortening every year.

The next schedule shows what would happen if the executive died in the 11th year of the program. His widow would be guaranteed a monthly income by the insurer of $1,561 for 10 years and for as many subsequent years as she might survive. Now, if the executive lived to 75, she would have an income of actually $16 a month more, even though the total net death benefit has gone down. And even if he lives to this age, his average after-tax cost per $1,000 per year is only $0.56. Compare this with the cost of term insurance, beginning at age 54, which is $13.20 per thousand per year. At 60, it is $19.56, and one cannot get it age 76 in any company this writer has heard about. This program, then, gives him insurance—depending on when he dies—at one-fortieth to one-sixtieth of the cost of term insurance.

Not orthodox, but effective

The two conversion procedures described in this article are unconventional, to be sure. But they have been proven to work in situations where they can be applied. The first—a private annuity—permits the taxpayer to liquidate a capital asset with a tax only on new income. The second—a salary continuance program funded by life insurance —gives a company a tax-free profit while providing a tremendous fringe benefit for its executives. Either of these procedures would certainly seem a more effective shelter than one on which the capital gains could be taxed at 65 percent.

SCHEDULE: SALARY CONTINUANCE PROGRAM FUNDED BY LIFE INSURANCE

JULY 28, 1970   Male Age 47

Year	Age	You Borrow	You Pay or Withdraw	Loan Interest @ 5%	Net Outlay	Cumulative Outlay	Total Loan	Total Debits	Gross Death Benefit	Net Death Benefit	Present Value @ 3% of $1,125 Mo. to Age 75	Surplus Death Benefit
1	47	00	12,132	0	12,132.00	12,132.00	0	12,132.00	350,000	337,868	253,315	84,553
2	48	12,132	0	0	0	12,132.00	12,132	24,264.00	352,100	327,836	247,509	80,327
3	49	0	12,132	606.60	12,404.00	24,536.97	12,132	36,668.97	354,550	317,881	241,367	76,514
4	50	12,132	0	606.60	272.97	24,809.94	24,264	49,073.94	357,700	308,626	235,076	73,550
5	51	0	12,132	1,213.20	12,697.94	37,487.88	24,264	61,751.88	361,550	299,798	228,636	71,162
6	52	12,132	0	1,213.20	545.94	38,033.82	36,396	74,429.82	366,100	291,670	221,994	69,676
7	53	0	12,132	1,819.80	12,950.91	50,984.73	36,396	87,380.73	371,000	283,619	215,636	67,983
8	54	41,967	- 29,835	1,819.80	-29,016.09	21,968.64	78,363	100,331.64	376,600	276,268	208,103	68,185
9	55	12,665	- 533	3,918.15	1,230.17	23,198.81	91,028	114,226.81	382,900	268,673	200,853	67,820
10	56	13,220	- 1,088	4,551.40	960.13	24,158.94	104,248	128,406.94	389,550	261,143	193,374	67,769
11	57	12,914	- 782	5,212.40	1,563.58	25,722.52	117,162	142,884.52	396,900	254,015	185,679	68,336
12	58	13,556	- 1,424	5,858.10	1,212.15	26,934.67	130,668	157,602.67	404,950	247,347	177,741	69,606
13	59	14,118	- 1,986	6,533.40	954.03	27,888.70	144,786	172,674.70	413,350	240,675	169,574	71,101
14	60	14,191	- 2,059	7,239.30	1,198.69	29,087.39	158,977	188,064.39	422,450	234,386	161,163	73,223
15	61	14,847	- 2,715	7,948.85	861.98	29,949.37	173,824	203,773.37	431,900	228,127	152,496	75,631
16	62	15,268	- 3,136	8,691.20	775.04	30,724.41	189,092	219,816.41	442,050	222,234	143,573	78,661
17	63	15,730	- 3,598	9,454.60	656.57	31,380.98	204,822	236,202.98	452,550	216,347	134,379	81,968
18	64	16,167	- 4,035	10,241.10	573.50	31,954.48	220,989	252,943.48	463,050	210,107	124,916	85,191
19	65	16,019	- 3,887	11,049.45	1,085.25	33,039.73	237,008	270,047.73	473,900	203,852	116,821	87,031
20	66	16,137	- 4,005	11,850.40	1,327.68	34,367.41	253,145	287,512.41	485,100	197,588	116,821	80,767
21	67	16,572	- 4,440	12,657.25	1,255.76	35,623.17	269,717	305,340.17	496,650	191,310	116,821	74,489
22	68	16,898	- 4,766	13,485.85	1,302.63	36,925.80	286,615	323,540.80	508,200	184,659	116,821	67,838
23	69	16,957	- 4,825	14,330.75	1,623.84	38,549.64	303,572	342,121.64	520,100	177,978	116,821	61,157
24	70	17,290	- 5,158	15,178.60	1,672.37	40,222.01	320,862	361,084.01	532,350	171,266	116,821	54,445
25	71	17,290	- 5,158	16,043.10	2,061.40	42,283.41	338,152	380,435.41	544,950	164,515	116,821	47,694
26	72	17,623	- 5,491	16,907.60	2,117.42	44,400.83	355,775	400,175.83	557,900	157,724	116,821	40,903
27	73	17,955	- 5,823	17,788.75	2,181.94	46,582.77	373,730	420,312.77	571,200	150,887	116,821	34,066
28	74	18,287	- 6,155	18,686.50 19,600.85	2,253.93	48,836.70	392,017	440,853.70	584,850	143,996	116,821	27,175

Dividends are not guaranteed

8

(A) $30,000 ANNUAL DEFERRED COMPENSATION/SALARY CONTINUATION PLAN

August 5, 1970 $350,000 LIFE INSURANCE @ AGE 47—ANNUAL PREMIUM $12,132.00

		You Borrow	You Pay or Withdraw	Loan Interest @ 5%	Net Outlay	Cumu-lative Outlay	Total Loan	Total Debits	Gross Death Benefit	Net Death Benefit	Present Value @ 3% of $1,125 Mo. to Age 75
Year	Age										
1	47	0	12,132	0	12,132.00	12,132.00	0	12,132.00	350,000	337,868	253,315
2	48	12,132	0	0	0	12,132.00	12,132	24,264.00	352,100	327,836	247,509
3	49	0	12,132	606.60	12,404.97	24,536.97	12,132	36,668.97	354,550	317,881	241,367
4	50	12,132	0	606.60	272.97	24,809.94	24,264	49,073.94	357,700	308,626	235,076
5	51	0	12,132	1,213.20	12,677.94	37,487.88	24,264	61,751.88	361,550	299,798	228,636
6	52	12,132	0	1,213.20	545.94	38,033.82	36,396	74,429.82	366,100	291,670	221,994
7	53	0	12,132	1,819.80	12,950.91	50,984.73	36,396	87,380.73	371,000	283,619	215,636
8	54	41,967	-29,835	1,819.80	29,016.09	21,968.64	78,363	100,331.64	376,600	276,268	208,103
9	55	12,665	- 533	3,918.15	1,230.17	1,230.17		91,028	382,900		291,872
10	56	13,220	- 1,088	4,551.40	960.13	2,190.30		104,248	389,550		285,302
11	57	12,914	- 782	5,212.40	1,563.58	3,753.88		117,162	396,900		279,738
12	58	13,556	- 1,424	5,858.10	1,212.15	4,966.03		130,668	404,950		274,282
13	59	14,118	- 1,986	6,533.40	954.03	5,920.06		144,786	413,350		268,564
14	60	14,191	- 2,059	7,239.30	1,198.69	7,118.75		158,977	422,450		263,473
15	61	14,847	- 2,715	7,948.85	861.98	7,980.73		173,824	431,900		258,076
16	62	15,268	- 3,136	8,691.20	775.04	8,755.77		189,092	442,050		252,958
17	63	15,730	- 3,598	9,454.60	656.57	9,412.34		204,822	452,550		247,728
18	64	16,167	- 4,035	10,241.10	573.50	9,985.84		220,989	463,050		242,061
19	65	16,019	- 3,887	11,049.45	1,085.25	11,071.09		237,008	473,900		236,892
20	66	16,137	- 4,005	11,850.40	1,327.68	12,398.77		253,145	485,100		231,955
21	67	16,572	- 4,440	12,657.25	1,255.76	13,654.53		269,717	496,650		226,933
22	68	16,898	- 4,766	13,485.85	1,302.63	14,957.16		286,615	508,200		221,585
23	69	16,957	- 4,825	14,330.75	1,623.84	16,581.00		303,572	520,100		216,528
24	70	17,290	- 5,158	15,178.60	1,672.37	18,253.37		320,862	532,350		211,488
25	71	17,290	- 5,158	16,043.10	2,061.40	20,314.77		338,152	544,950		206,798
26	72	17,623	- 5,491	16,907.60	2,117.42	22,432.19		355,775	557,900		202,125
27	73	17,955	- 5,823	17,788.75	2,181.94	24,614.13		373,730	571,200		197,470
28	74	18,287	- 6,155	18,686.50	2,253.93	26,868.06		392,017	584,850		192,833

CORPORATE OWNERSHIP

INDIVIDUAL OWNERSHIP

Dividends are not guaranteed

(B)   Schedule of Benefits with Executive Deceased in Eleventh Year of Program

AGE	SURPLUS DEATH BENEFIT	MONTHLY INCOME 10 YEAR CERTAIN*	AVERAGE COST PER $1,000 (NET)
47	84553		
48	80327		
49	76514		
50	73550		
51	71102		
52	69676		
53	67983		
54	68165		
55			
56			
57		1561.52	
58			
59			
60			
61			
62			
63		1569.10	.42
64			
65			
65			
66			
67			
68		1572.65	.40
69			
70			
71			
72			
73		1579.94	.43
74			
		1577.37	.56

NOTES

Figures shown for years 1–8 represent corporate payments. Figures shown for years 9–28 represent insured's payments.

Net Death Benefit - Years 1–8 represents Gross Death Benefit less Total Debits.

Net Death Benefit - Years 9–28 represent Gross Death Benefit less loan.

Monthly Income - 10 Years Certain assumes Wife same age as Husband.

Average Cost per $1,000 of insurance represents average annual cost divided by average insurance protection from year 9.

* Includes excess interest which is not guaranteed.

SECTION II:

THE EXPERTS LOOK AT SOME SPECIFIC TAX SHELTERS

9

OIL: A BASIC GUIDE FOR INVESTORS

David A. Gracer

There seems little doubt that the oil industry will continue to be the huge and profitable business that it has been in the past. Indeed, experts predict that during the 1970's as much oil will be consumed as in the previous 110 years—since Colonel E. L. Drake drilled the first oil well in 1859.

In light of this strong demand for oil, it seems fair to assume that investors in this field will enjoy ample opportunities to make

MR. GRACER, A NEW YORK CITY INVESTMENT ADVISOR WHO SPECIALIZES IN OIL/GAS, IS NATIONALLY RECOGNIZED AS AN EXPERT ON STRUCTURING PUBLIC DRILLING FUNDS AND PRIVATE PLACEMENTS.

substantial profits. One fact that has inhibited the growth of oil drilling operations has been a sharp rise in drilling costs without a corresponding rise in the price of oil. Now, however, our reserves are down to a perilously low point. It is obvious that there must be higher oil prices as an incentive to greater drilling activity. These higher prices will make oil investment a more attractive and lucrative field to high-tax-bracket investors.

To an oil investor, however, the most important incentive is often the opportunity for tax savings. Here, too, the future for oil investment appears bright. The 1969 Tax Reform Act, which severely hurt a number of other traditional tax shelters, left oil investment virtually unscathed. In comparison with most other tax shelters, oil has become even more attractive than it was before the 1969 changes.

Despite the opportunities in oil investment, many investors fail to achieve the gains they hope for when they put their money into an oil drilling venture. Some, indeed, have lost not only their investment but all their personal assets as well. Only after it was too late did they realize that their mistakes could easily have been avoided had they selected their investment more wisely.

Thus, the first reality that a potential investor in oil must recognize is that there is a negative side as well as a positive side to oil investment. Then he must take steps to accentuate the positive and minimize the negative aspects if he wants the best possible chance for realizing his expectations. This chapter will try to give him some useful guidelines.

WHO SHOULD INVEST IN OIL

Initially the prospective investor might ask himself whether he should be investing in oil at all. Does he have a large annual income in a very high tax bracket? Has he had a windfall profit from exercising a stock option, from receiving a profit-sharing distribution, or from selling securities or real estate? Does he control a corporation in top tax brackets, or one that needs some way to avoid accumulation of excess surplus?

HOW OIL INVESTMENT SHELTERS INCOME

If the prospective investor can answer *yes* to any of the foregoing questions, he should certainly consider oil investment as a tax shelter device. Next, he should learn *how* oil investment can shelter his income. The main basis for tax savings is the deductibility of *intangible drilling and development expenses,* which include most of the expenses of drilling, such as labor and materials with no salvage value. This provision of the Internal Revenue Code was left untouched by the 1969 Tax Reform Act. There are still no limits on the amount of intangibles a taxpayer can deduct against salaries, fees, profits, rents or any other income he might have. And he can normally list these intangible expenses as a deduction in the first year of investment. Assuming an 80 percent write-off in the first year on a cash investment of $10,000, a taxpayer in the 50 percent bracket would have a tax savings of $4,000, making his net after-tax cost only $6,000. The 60 percent taxpayer (the maximum bracket in 1971) would fare even better, with a net cost of $5,200.

In terms of return on investment, the 50 percent taxpayer would make a 66 percent profit with a return of his before-tax investment of $10,000. Moreover, 22 percent of his gross income from successful wells is tax-free, courtesy of the depletion allowance. (Although the 1969 Tax Reform Act reduced the depletion allowance from 27½ to 22 percent, this has not appreciably reduced the attractiveness of oil investments as tax shelters. The primary tax shelter is the deductibility of intangible expenses.)

Finally, still another plus for oil investment is the fact that the sale of oil interests is treated as a long-term capital gain.

HOW DRILLING FUNDS ARE ORGANIZED

Once the taxpayer understands how an oil investment can shelter his income, he should learn something about the way in which an oil drilling program is actually set up. For most taxpayers, participation in a drilling fund will serve as the most advantageous form of investment. A drilling fund is set up so that it is not taxed as a corporation—otherwise the individual investors would not receive the intangible expense deductions. Therefore, drilling funds are usually organized as a general partnership, a limited partnership, a joint venture or some other arrangement in which the combined contributions of many individual investors can finance the drilling of several wells. Each investor has an interest in all the wells drilled.

In some ways, the drilling fund can be compared to the mutual fund. In both, a management group brings together interested investors who combine their capital to obtain the benefits of professional management, diversification, risk reduction and convenience. Among the basic differences in the two types of organizations is that a mutual fund investment can be cashed in at any time, whereas drilling fund investments are more difficult to dispose of immediately.

The Management's Profit

How does the management of a drilling fund get its compensation? There are four basic ways.

1. Money is taken "off the top"—that is, management immediately takes a portion of the investor's capital contribution. This is not particularly favorable to the investors, but it is acceptable in some cases if the investors get other important concessions in return.

2. Management can also make money "off the middle" by taking an overriding royalty on the income from drilling. This amounts to a share of the oil income, but not a share of drilling or production expenses. A variation of this is the carried working interest, in which the management has a share of the oil income and the production expenses, but not the drilling expenses.

3. Management can make money "off the bottom" by arranging for a share of the profit after the investors have gotten their money back. This approach is known as a reversionary working interest, and operates best for the investor on an overall program basis rather than on an individual well basis.

4. Management makes money through reimbursement of part of its overhead expenses, including the salaries of the general partner's officers. In addition to these reimbursements, the general partner may want a substantial share of the profits. Investors will usually find that this arrangement is too costly.

The Investor's Profit

The investor naturally wants a reasonable chance of getting his profit from a drilling fund. Normally, the operating oil company receives production income monthly and deducts operating and other expenses. The direct owners then receive their share. However, some oil funds do not distribute income in the early years; instead they use it to drill additional wells. This arrangement sometimes has definite advantages for the investor. First, his additional investment may bring him a greater return. Second, he can take additional intangible expense deductions without adding new money. On the other hand, he exposes himself to greater risk and defers the use of his cash.

Suppose the investor wants to sell his interest in an oil drilling fund? He may have difficulty finding a purchaser, since the purchaser would not receive the benefit of intangible drilling deductions. For this reason, a purchaser would probably want to pay less than the investor's cost for the interest. Moreover, the drilling fund normally restricts the transfer of participation units in order to avoid taxation of the program as a corporation. Because of such difficulties placed in the way of selling an interest in a drilling fund, the investor should always have other assets upon which to rely should he unexpectedly need cash.

Personal Liability

Must the investor in a drilling fund concern himself about personal liability? In most cases, the answer is *no.* It is true that costly accidents can occur during drilling. A well may blow up, poison a stream, or cause some other calamity. But the personal liability that might be incurred from such accidents is an insurable risk, and liability insurance is normally carried by oil companies in sufficient amounts. (Naturally, there is always a possibility that the damages will exceed the insurance, but such catastrophes are rare.) Some drilling funds may further protect investors through fixed-price drilling contracts. In some funds, the investor is a limited partner and would be liable only for the amount of his investment and any undistributed profits. However, limited partners should inquire whether the company plans to drill in certain states and Canadian provinces that do not recognize this limitation of liability.

WILDCAT VERSUS DEVELOPMENT DRILLING

When considering an oil program, the investor can choose between two types of drilling or a combination of the two. One is exploratory—also known as wildcat—drilling, in which the company attempts to discover completely new oil or gas fields. The other is development drilling, in which the company develops the reserves of already existing fields. Some drilling funds do both exploratory and development drilling.

Exploratory drilling is a high-risk gamble for the investor, as is shown by the fact that nine out of every ten wildcat wells drilled are dry. On the other hand, there can be tremendous profits if a big new field is discovered. To decide whether or not he should put his money into wildcat drilling, the investor should ask himself some important questions. Does he have sufficient assets to sustain the losses that he is likely to incur from much of his investment in exploratory drilling? And is he emotionally prepared for the disappointment that he will probably have to face? If he can answer *yes* to both questions, he may wish to consider exploratory drilling.

If he cannot, he would be wiser to go into development drilling or a combination of development and exploratory. Since development drilling is performed in fields where oil and/or gas has already been discovered, it is far less risky than wildcat drilling. And with smaller risk, of course, goes smaller potential return. Development drilling is often the answer for investors who have high annual income but low net worth. Although they will have less potential return on their investment, they can gain substantial tax savings to shelter their income—without as much risk of great losses.

EVALUATING A PROGRAM

As with any type of investment, the investor in oil should go into a deal with his eyes wide open. Here are some suggestions to help him avoid pitfalls and problems:

He should consult his tax advisor to determine whether or not he needs the tax shelter of an oil investment. He should also determine with that advisor how much he should invest in order to get the deductions he wants.

When considering a specific drilling fund, he should thoroughly evaluate its management, its past programs and its operations. He should always invest in a company with a reputation for good management and proven success. He can often establish a drilling fund's reputation by consulting his own bank. If his bank is not familiar with the specific fund, it can make inquiries through a correspondent bank in the fund's home city.

If possible, he should meet the fund's management personally. They are the people who will decide where and how to drill with his money. His impression of them should play an important role in whether he wants to entrust his investment to them.

Evaluating an oil company's past programs is not as easy as it might seem. From the prospectus, the investor will learn how many wells were producers and how many were dry holes. He will also find the cash returns to date on earlier investments. Though useful, this information is not sufficient for him to accurately measure past performance. For example, a company may have a high batting average in locating producing wells, but the wells may be low-yielding ones. On the surface, the program seems successful, but it may actually have been an investment failure. High cash payout for a year or two can also be deceptive, since the wells may have little or no remaining reserves.

On the other hand, the program with many dry holes and small initial payout might indicate a more successful performance— if a few highly profitable, long-life wells were drilled.

Consulting An Engineer

All of these factors make it important for the investor to obtain a sound, authoritative opinion on the extent of reserves in the company's producing wells. He will not find this information in the company's prospectus, because prospectuses are supposed to contain facts, not opinions. His best bet is to consult the company's independent petroleum engineer, whose reputation should be checked out to determine how much credence to place in his appraisal. Generally, if he is consulted by banks as well as oil companies, one can rely on his appraisal, since banks prefer conservative appraisers to optimistic ones. It should be kept in mind, however, that even a conservative engineer's opinion on reserves is based on the assumption that the wells will be properly operated and maintained. A well may have $1 million worth of potential, but it can be worth much less if improperly operated.

Evaluating Previous Profits

The investor must also make a sound evaluation of the return earned by previous programs. Return on oil wells is not calculated like an investment earning compound interest. In an oil investment, money gradually becomes available for additional investments within the producing life of the wells, whereas money deposited at compound interest does not become available for additional investment until the end of the term.

An evaluation of the return on oil investments should be expressed in terms of annual rate of return, not total return. Oil people tend not to use the term "return on investment." Instead, they refer to "payouts," meaning how much the well may be expected eventually to pay the investors. But whether this is a high or low return would depend on how long it would take.

GETTING THE BEST TAX DEAL

The prospective investor should always keep in mind that the major objective is to shelter his income. He should strive for 100 percent deduction of his investment during the first year, unless the economic opportunities of the investment are attractive enough to compensate for taking a smaller percentage of deduction.

How can the investor get 100 percent deduction in the first year, when part of the cost of drilling a well is not deductible immediately, but depreciable over a number of years? One answer is an arrangement wherein the oil company's investment in the deal covers all non-deductible costs. In exchange for this tax benefit, the investor, of course, must give up part of the return on the deal. This also means that the investor is putting his money into the more risky drilling costs—although they are deductible—while the company is investing in the less risky operating costs after they have had a chance to "look at the bottom of the well." In exploratory drilling, wherein normally 80 to 90 percent of the wells drilled are dry, the company definitely benefits, because it does not have to spend money on these dry holes. In development drilling, the company must put up completion costs on nearly every well, which means that it is less likely to go into this kind of arrangement.

Another way to obtain 100 percent deduction is to lease the equipment that creates tangible costs. Or, if the oil company has a good line of credit, it can borrow to buy the equipment.

THE OPERATOR'S INVESTMENT IS CRUCIAL

The investor should choose a deal in which the oil company makes at least some investment of its own money. A company may be reluctant to put money into the program because it is contributing the know-how without which the program could never succeed. Nevertheless, an investor can sleep better at night if he knows that the oil company is risking some of its own money in a venture. For example, the company might pay the costs of registering the offering, which can run from \$40,000 to as high as \$100,000. The company should also be willing to pay all sales expenses, which can also be substantial, what with traveling, hotels, commissions, meals and entertainment. And if the company is profitable, why should it not invest its funds just as the limited partners are doing? To do so will certainly increase the investor's confidence that the company is justified in claiming that its program is the best.

VERIFYING THE TAX BENEFITS

The investor should also make sure that the program will actually produce the desirable tax benefits the sponsoring company claims for it. If the IRS ends up disagreeing with the company's claim, he is the one who will pay. Some oil companies are foresighted enough to get an IRS ruling on the program they are offering, in which case the investor can request a copy for his files when he makes his investment.

If an IRS ruling is not available, the investor should, at the very least, obtain a letter from the company's attorneys stating their opinion on the tax consequences. He should ask his own lawyer to interpret the opinion for him.

The preceding guidelines have covered only the most important factors that the investor must weigh in selecting the oil investment program that is best for him. There are many others he should consider as well. Whether he relies on an expert advisor or becomes knowledgeable himself is up to the investor himself. Whatever his approach, he should make sure that every aspect of the oil investment program has been thoroughly checked out before he commits his funds. Only then should he expect to obtain the substantial tax benefits—and possible income—that a good oil investment can provide.

COMMENTARY

Since oil is undoubtedly the most controversial tax shelter of all, it is not surprising that, despite the excellent points made by this article, there are some debatable ones as well.

DRILLING TO AVOID EXCESS SURPLUS

Mr. Gracer suggests that drilling for oil is an effective way for a corporation to avoid the accumulation of excess surplus. True, the deduction for drilling does reduce income subject to this label and to the IRC-531 tax if it is imposed. But it is a two-edged sword, because in most situations drilling for oil would be treated as an unrelated investment and thus invite unreasonable accumulation treatment.

This means that if a corporation does drill for oil, it should be sure it has drilled away its surplus accumulation in excess of the $100,000 exemption and the clearly demonstrable reserves calculated in accordance with the cycle formula developed in the Bardhal Oil case. The corporation must expect an examination of prior open years. Therefore, its position must be very sound. Moreover, it must count on continuing to drill for oil in subsequent years unless a radical change in its business situation occurs. Indeed, if this device is anticipated early enough, the company charter should include drilling for oil as one of its regular purposes, and then carry out a certain amount of drilling every year.

THE DEPLETION ALLOWANCE

Mr. Gracer is correct in his view that reducing the depletion allowance to 22 percent does not appreciably damage oil as a tax shelter, since the primary basis of the shelter—deductibility of intangible expenses—was left untouched. It is important to keep in mind, however, that the depletion allowance is now a tax preference item that may subject the investor to the minimum tax under IRC-57 and may even spill over and infect his earned income subject to the IRC-1348 ceiling.

WILDCAT DRILLING VERSUS OFFSET DRILLING

Although, as Mr. Gracer states, offset or development drilling is less risky than wildcat drilling, it is still possible to get stuck with dry holes. In one case, offset drilling produced seven dry holes in a row because of a bad fault structure, despite the high reputation and past record of the operator. In another case, eleven out of twelve offset wells turned out to be producers, but because there was a minimum risk, the return was mediocre in proportion to the money invested, even after allowing for drilling deduction and other tax benefits.

It might be wise, then, for the investor not to put all his money into offset drilling, but to put at least a share of it into widely diversified wildcat drilling operations.

CHECKING ON THE PROMOTER

Despite all the checking an investor can do on the promoter of an oil program, such checking cannot provide the security that comes from being certain the promoter has his own money in the operation in the form of some share of the drilling investment on a par with other investors. As for bank references, it is unwise for the investor to depend too heavily upon them, particularly if they are from the promoter's own bank. The same goes for any geologist whom the investor consults—he should be an independent geologist, not working for the promoter. Since time is required to obtain an independent opinion on prospective drilling, the investor should not wait until late in the year to make his investment decision.

SALES EXPENSES

Mr. Gracer is correct in saying that the promoter should be willing to pay all sales expenses. He might have gone further and pointed out that unwary investors might actually be indirectly paying these expenses if the promoter charges more than the standard drilling expenses. This is one way in which a promoter can make money whether the well produces or not.

10

OIL: THE ECONOMIC ASPECTS

Barnett Serio

By its very nature, investment in oil exploration is highly speculative—no one yet has invented a divining rod that will unerringly detect potential gushers. Moreover, in recent years drilling-program operators have found it increasingly difficult to locate sufficient oil reserves to make an investment profitable. This difficulty has been ignored by many investors, who delude themselves with the nebulous hope that tax benefits will make it all come out right in the end. Often, they are wrong.

However, there are some specific ways in which an investor can reduce the risks. By investing his money cautiously and wisely,

MR. SERIO IS PRESIDENT OF SERIO EXPLORATION COMPANY.

he can boost his chances for making a profit as well as sheltering his income.

He can begin by observing a few basic principles:

He should not invest in oil at all unless he himself meets certain tests of suitability. That is, he should be in at least a 50 percent income bracket or have enough net worth or cash flow to stand the loss—cushioned though it may be by tax benefits—from an unsuccessful investment.

He should invest in a program that is diversified both in the number of wells and in the areas of search, thus spreading the risk.

He should invest for a period of several years rather than just one, which means he must have the resources to pay his share of the cost of additional development drilling if there is an oil find.

Assuming that none of these requirements eliminate him from oil investment, he is ready to consider specific programs offered to him. He can further reduce his risks by careful investigation and analysis of three major elements of any program he is considering:

1. The operator's past record of success in finding profitable quantities of oil.

2. The amount of economic pressure on the operator to expend wisely the funds entrusted to him by investors.

3. The tax advantages offered by the program.

Let us look at each of these factors in more detail.

THE OPERATOR'S PAST RECORD OF SUCCESS

The operator's proven ability to find oil in profitable quantities should be a prospective investor's major concern. In evaluating this ability, the investor will be wise to rely more on the operator's record of success or failure in recent years than on his lifetime "batting average." Generally, the record of the past three to five years will reveal highly significant statistics from which the operator's oil-finding talents can be judged.

Keep in mind that the operator's record should be evaluated in terms of how well he does for his investors, not for himself. The mere fact that he consistently finds productive oil wells does not mean that he is making money for his investors. A well may produce oil, but not enough to compensate the investor for the loss of use of his money during the producing period. The well must return several times its cost—within a reasonable period of time—to be profitable to the investor. In addition, the productive wells must bear the cost of the dry holes in the program.

THE AMOUNT OF ECONOMIC PRESSURE ON THE OPERATOR

The investor should look for an oil program which makes it difficult for the operator to profit from the drilling of wells unless the investor profits, too. Since even most of the larger and more popular drilling programs have not found oil for investors at profitable levels recently, it is important to ensure that maximum economic pressure be put on the operator to spend wisely the invested funds entrusted to him—and to accept no more funds than he can spend in this manner. To determine whether a given program meets this criterion, the investor might ask these probing questions:

1. Can the operator make money simply by spending money?

2. Can the operator continue to profit—or at least break even —by spending excess funds on sub-standard drilling prospects?

3. Will the operator lose money—or at least reduce his profits on prior discoveries—if he spends his remaining funds unselectively?

It is, unfortunately, far easier to ask these questions than to obtain meaningful answers to them. Frequently, it is difficult to discover from available information—usually the prospectus—just how much pressure there is on an operator to come up with profits for the investor. One prospectus, while it satisfies SEC disclosure standards, may not reveal all the information disclosed in another prospectus—thus making them difficult to compare.

For example: Company A does not maintain its own staff of operators, but its prospectus describes the basis on which it intends to contract with outside operators. Company B, on the other hand, also a non-operator, may simply state in its prospectus that arrangements will be made with outside operators, without specifying the percentage of the profit that goes to these operators. Some companies may attach an actual operating agreement form to their prospectus, while other companies simply state that their agreements will be on terms customary in the industry.

THE LANGUAGE CONFUSION

Confusion over terminology adds to the difficulty of analyzing and comparing different oil drilling programs. The term *net profit* is used in so many varied and wonderful forms that it can be easily misinterpreted by the unwary investor. Some investors fail to distinguish between a *net profit* interest, in which the operator receives nothing until payout, and a *net operating profit* interest, in which the operator shares immediately in the production.

Still another problem is that prospectuses often fail to reveal how many stages of promotion an oil program has gone through before it is presented to the investor. The more promotion stages in developing an oil prospect, the less percentage of profit is left to the investor, even though the final promoter may be taking only a small overwrite as compared with the operator who develops the prospect himself. A prospect may be originally conceived by an independent geologist, then acquired by a major oil company which conducts further evaluation and acquires additional leases, then farmed out to an independent operator who promotes it to the investor. The cost to the investor in this case may actually be more than if he pays for the single promotion being handled by an independent operator without preliminary stages.

In view of these factors, the investor should watch out for programs in which the operator's primary function is simply to raise money and allocate it among various outside operators or in which the operator has a staff but not the capacity to originate drilling prospects.

Despite the difficulty of obtaining adequate information about an oil drilling program, the potential investor should persevere until he can determine whether or not the program has the features that will exert the greatest economic pressure on the operator to come through with profitable wells.

A program in which the operator shares the well costs exerts greater economic pressure on him than one in which he receives a cost-free interest. The investor should not be misled by so-called *subordinate interest* programs in which the operator shares income after payout. Such programs exert less economic pressure on the operator than do cost-sharing programs, because they usually permit investor payout before operator profit only on a property-by-property basis rather than on the program as a whole. And even a program which requires investor payout on the whole program before operator participation ignores the fact that the investor has lost the use of his money during this period, while the operator, with none of his cash tied up, can afford to wait.

Therefore, as a general rule the operator should bear more than 25 percent of the program costs if he is to receive as much as 50 percent of the revenue—or at least there should be some specified ratio between the sharing of costs and the sharing of receipts. When an investor evaluates such a formula, the real test is how much money he will recover within that period in relationship to his total investment. Unless he can expect to recover his total investment in an oil program within five to seven years, he would probably be better off putting his money into some other form of investment.

THE TAX ADVANTAGES OFFERED BY THE PROGRAM

In comparing the tax features of competing oil investment programs, the investor should seek answers to the following important questions:

1. What percentage of the investor's expenditures are deductible in the year of expenditure?

With some program formulas only about 70 percent of the expenditures charged to the investor may be written off. The reason for this is the fact that the typical drilling program requires the capitalization of lease costs and equipment related to productive wells. Depending on depth, area, and the ratio of completed wells to dry holes, these costs will amount to approximately 30 to 50 percent of the cost of each productive well and between 20 to 35 percent of total program costs.

However, there is another program formula: the *functional allocation* formula. Under this formula, all capital costs are borne by the program operator, so that investor expenditures are 100 percent tax deductible. The leverage offered by federal income tax deductibilities can create a spectacular difference between the after-tax consequences of the 70 percent formula and the functional allocation formula. Indeed, the hard-dollar cost to the investor in a 70 percent formula will be almost twice as much—for the same interest and reserves—as the cost in a 100 percent deductible program.

2. Has program deductibility been derived from techniques that are costly to the investor?

Certain financial devices can be useful in creating program deductibility—but they sometimes increase the investor's cost to the point where even the tax savings are offset. One example is "turn-key drilling," wherein the operator pays a drilling contractor a flat sum to drill a well to the casing point. Another is equipment leasing, in which such items as tanks, pumps and flow lines are leased on a monthly basis with the investor recapturing the charge-off feature rather than taking depreciation on the equipment as if it were a capital item. If these devices are being used in a program the investor is considering, he should make sure they will actually benefit him.

3. What are the after-drilling tax consequences of the program?

Most programs are alike in offering both the depletion allowance and the opportunity to make charitable contributions or assignments to a family trust or other entity in a lower federal income tax bracket. However, some programs offer the investor a further advantage: the opportunity to sell his interest or exchange it for common stock to take advantage of capital gains or—in some stock exchange deals— of a tax-free exchange.

Even following the guidelines laid down in this chapter will not, of course, guarantee profits for the oil-program investor. It will, however, reduce his risks to a reasonable level and assure him of at least a fighting chance to come out ahead when the results are in.

COMMENTARY

DEPENDING ON A BATTING AVERAGE

Although the promoter's lifetime batting average can serve as one useful guideline in evaluating his program, the investor should not depend on it too heavily. Such a record is not always a reliable guide to future performance; in addition, it can sometimes be manipulated to appear better than it actually is.

THE PROMOTER'S INVESTMENT

It is true that the investor may feel more secure if he can persuade the promoter to invest some of his own money in drilling costs. However, the investor should make certain that the agreement is worked out in such a way that the promoter's investment is indeed tied up in the program. In one case, an investor negotiated with an operator who finally agreed to put up his own money for 25 percent of the drilling and completion expenses. As soon as the operator signed the agreement buying the interest, however, he sold it to another investor, thus freeing himself of any incentive for making the program successful. Moral: the investor should always obtain the promoter's stipulation that he will not sell his interest in a program until it is actually successful.

EXCHANGING AN OIL INTEREST FOR COMMON STOCK

At the end of his chapter, Mr. Serio suggests that the investor can exchange his interest in an oil program for common stock in order to achieve capital gains or a tax-free exchange. Although this is feasible, some caution is necessary. First, not every exchange of an interest for stock is tax free. Second, the investor who makes such an exchange too frequently may find himself in trouble with the IRS. Finally, while some exchanges have worked out well for the investor, others have resulted in a dilution of interests and loss of direct ownership. For example, the investor would lose the benefit of the direct individual depletion deduction and then find himself having to pay a painfully high capital gains tax.

Another example can be cited in the case of an investor who had exchanged his interest in an oil program for 50 percent of the stock of a highly successful oil company. After corporate and individual taxes, he netted only $4,800 a year on the corporation's $500,000 oil income.

This investor had the additional problem of a $2 million non-business bad debt, which could be offset only against capital gains. He therefore in later years exchanged his 50 percent interest in the oil company for an undivided 50 percent interest in the oil-in-place, which he received as a corporation partner. The oil-in-place, appraised at $2,012,000, was treated as a capital gain, since he had completely liquidated his interest. But the gain was offset by his $2 million outside capital loss. He paid a $3,000 tax on $12,000 excess gain and took cost depletion by dividing the estimated number of barrels in reserve into $2,012,000. Thus, a major portion of his revenue was free of tax as recovery for the stepped-up basis on a cost depletion writeoff. In this particular case, cost depletion was more beneficial than percentage depletion because of the stepped-up basis offset by the investor's otherwise useless bad-debt capital loss. The conclusion then, is that an investor might profit from going into a corporation, but he might profit even more from getting out of it.

11

OIL: THE TAX ASPECTS

Edward J. Fitzsimmons

When a decision has been made to invest in oil and gas, the investor must carefully select the best method of organization. There are four types which he can use:

1. A corporation
2. A Subchapter S Corporation
3. A joint venture
4. A limited partnership

MR. FITZSIMMONS IS ASSISTANT TREASURER AND DIRECTOR OF TAXES, CARRIER CORPORATION.

THE CORPORATION

In many cases, the corporate form of organization is the least advantageous, but it has certain significant benefits.

The first benefit concerns the high risk of loss in an oil and gas operation—for example, the costs of a blowout or other major disaster. Because of this risk, some investors feel that the limited liability protection afforded by a corporation is important. Another feature which some investors desire is the ability to dispose of their investment as easily and quickly as possible. Obviously, a stock certificate is more readily transferable than an interest in a joint venture.

In addition, the corporation has the privilege of making certain elections, such as methods of accounting and depreciation, choice of a taxable year, and expense versus capital treatment of intangible drilling costs.

For the investor, however, the corporate form has a number of disadvantages which often outweigh the advantages. The investor should consider the potential double tax incurred by operating in the corporate form. To the extent that a corporation has income, the tax must be paid. When the after-tax income is distributed to the stockholder, additional taxes may be incurred. It should be noted, too, that in computing its earnings and profits (from which dividends are paid) a corporation is allowed to deduct only cost depletion rather than the percentage depletion which is used to determine taxable income. Thus, the corporation has earnings and profits, for tax purposes, which may be higher than the sum total of the amounts of its taxable income. If the corporation pays out as a dividend amounts in excess of its taxable income, the stockholder is, in effect, paying a tax on the excess percentage depletion claimed as a deduction by the corporation.

Investors should also be aware that upon the liquidation or sale of stock of the corporation, the Internal Revenue Service may contend that the gain is ordinary income, rather than capital gain, because the corporation may be "collapsible."

SUBCHAPTER S CORPORATION

As noted, a double tax can be levied on income earned by corporations. To alleviate the pressure of the double tax on smaller corporations, Congress permits certain corporations to flow their income through to the stockholders, thus bypassing the corporate income tax. This form of corporate organization is known as the Subchapter S Corporation. In order to qualify, certain tests must be met. Among the tests are:

_1._ There can be no more than 10 stockholders, all of whom must be either individuals or estates.

_2._ There must be only one class of stock.

_3._ No more than 20 percent of the corporation's income may be from such items as dividends, interest and royalties.

_4._ Affirmative election to be considered a Subchapter S Corporation must be made.

Should these restrictions be violated, the corporation's special tax status will be terminated with possible adverse tax consequences to the stockholders.

Stockholders in Subchapter S Corporations must treat as income their pro rata share of the income of the corporation. Similarly, they are entitled to deduct a pro rata share of the losses of the corporation to the extent that the total losses do not exceed their investment (stock and debt) in the corporation. Because the investors in a Subchapter S Corporation lose the benefit of percentage depletion, this form of organization is not often adopted.

THE JOINT VENTURE

Until recent years, this form of organization was probably the most widely used in oil investment. Since it is not unusual to have joint ownership of oil and gas properties, it is customary to have properties jointly operated as well.

To be certain of obtaining the tax benefits of a joint venture, the participants must avoid having the joint venture treated as an association taxable as a corporation. Such a classification can be made if the joint venture has the features of a corporation. IRS regulations list these features as:

1. Associates.

2. An objective to carry on a business and divide the gains therefrom.

3. Continuity of life.

4. Centralization of management.

5. Liability for corporate debts limited to corporate property.

6. Free transferability of interests.

In order to forestall such classification, which would give rise to the corporate problems previously discussed, it is customary to delete the objective to carry on the business for a joint profit. This may be accomplished by agreeing that each participant has the right to take the oil or gas and dispose of it. The parties normally would enter into an agreement to share the expenses of development and operation of the property. One party is designated the operator and is responsible for the payment of the expenses incurred in drilling for and producing the oil.

In a joint venture, each person's share of the income and expenses is reported in his own tax return. Thus, he has the right to make his own election to deduct or capitalize intangible drilling costs; the right to determine the method of depreciation to be used in recovering his investment in tangible assets; and the option to expense or capitalize delay rentals which are payments for the privilege of deferring drilling.

Making an Election

In order to be treated as a joint venture, all members of the group must make an election in the first income tax return (a partnership return) filed by the venture. These formalities can be handled by a competent tax man who is familiar with Income Tax Regulation 1.761.

While the joint venture has advantages which make it attractive to the investor taxpayer, it does have its drawbacks. One of these concerns management decisions. Before the operator can take action, he must give notice to and secure consents from all the members. This can cause problems, especially when the title to the lease is held by many different parties living in different locations. Another drawback is the problem of joint and several liabilities. In a joint venture, it is possible that each participant would have unlimited liability for the commissions or omissions of the operator. On the other hand, it is sometimes easier to sell individual interests or to enter into farmout arrangements and other transactions.

LIMITED PARTNERSHIP

Recently, increasing numbers of investors in oil have been turning to the limited partnership form of organization. One reason is the fact that this vehicle has the advantage of limiting the liability of the investor-limited partner. In addition, the individual partner reports in his own tax return his share of the income or loss of the limited partnership. A further advantage which may be present is the ability to allocate certain deductions in amounts which may differ from the investor's percentage ownership of the limited partnership. Limited partnership agreements have provided that items such as intangible drilling costs shall be allocated to the limited partners. It is the view of some tax practitioners that this is permitted by Section 704 of the Internal Revenue Code, which states that the partners' share of any item of income or deductions shall be determined by the partnership agreement unless the principal purpose of the provision in the agreement is the avoidance of tax. The IRS has been concerned about the allocation of deductions to limited partners and recently issued a revenue ruling which narrowly interprets this section. Investors would be well advised to discuss this feature with their tax advisors before entering a limited partnership.

The limited partnership also faces the problems of avoiding classification as an association taxable as a corporation. If the general partner is a corporation and if the limited partners own in the aggregate directly or indirectly 20 percent or more of the stock of the corporate general partner, whose net worth does not meet certain tests, the IRS is inclined to treat the limited partnership as a corporation. This area is in a state of flux and is another matter which must be discussed with tax advisors.

Although each investor must examine his own needs in determing the form of organization best suited to him, limited partnerships and joint ventures, in most situations, will usually present the more significant tax saving possibilities.

COMMENTARY

What Mr. Fitzimmons says about the use of a limited partnership is correct, but the reader should supplement this by referring back to the IRS guidelines discussed in the question-and-answer section following the chapter by Mr. Cohen.

12

OIL: THE FEDERAL LEASE PROGRAM

Laurie C. Jones

Mention the word *oil* to an investor and his eyes will light up with images of bonanza riches and black gold flowing from the ground. Actually, his chances of striking it rich in oil are about as good as his chances of striking a mother lode with a pick and shovel. There is, however, a way in which the investor in high tax brackets can employ his tax dollars to create an opportunity for substantial capital gains by investing in a relatively unknown sector of the petroleum industry: the Federal Oil and Gas Leasing Program.

Through this program, the investor can take advantage of the government's beneficial tax incentives for developing oil resources

MISS JONES IS VICE PRESIDENT, OIL AND GAS, STEWART CAPITAL CORPORATION, A FIRM SPECIALIZING IN TAX SHELTERED INVESTMENTS.

and the favorable land rights provisions created to aid this essential facet of our economy. He can, in fact, realize a sizable return on an investment in oil leases even if not one drop of oil is produced from the land he leases.

The government makes this possible by leasing the mineral rights to its vast land holdings on an equal basis to all citizens through a lottery, at a fixed rate of 50 cents per acre per year. Any citizen has as good a chance to win a valuable property as the largest oil company, because an individual or a company can only file once for a given parcel of land. Whoever wins the rights to the land is then in a position to sell his lease to an interested oil developer at its real value, ordinarily with a cash bonus per acre and an interest in any future oil production. The cash bonus can be as much as 100 to 200 times the 50 cents an acre which the lottery winner pays.

For a high-bracket taxpayer, the costs of participating in the Federal Oil and Gas Leasing Program can be substantially reduced, because until a lease is actually won all expenses incurred—including the Bureau of Land Management fees and filing services fees—are fully deductible. When a lease is won, the filing fee and any service charges for the lease must be capitalized, but the full annual rental fee can be deducted. Thus, the money saved from tax deductions underwrites a considerable portion of the investment.

Consider the example of an investor who files on 20 leases in a given month. Each lease filing costs $25 ($10 filing fee plus $15 service fee), giving him $500 of deductible expenses. If he wins one lease in this month, he can still write off the fees on the other 19 lease filings as well as the full rental on the won lease, which could be as high as $1,280. His only capitalized expense would be the $25 for filing on the won lease.

HOW THE PROGRAM BEGAN

This form of investment got started in 1920, when the government began leasing at 50 cents per acre the mineral rights to public-domain land which had never been homesteaded because of its unsuitability for farming or ranching. When the leasing program began, leases were awarded on a first come, first served basis—the investor who got his application in first won the lease.

As leasing of U.S. owned lands gained in popularity, this system began to create major problems. Every month there was a mad scramble at each land office to find out what leases had expired and become available. In order to get their application in first, some investors camped outside the land office all night, and by the time the doors opened in the morning there might be 50 to 75 men and women rushing in to get their hands on the record books. Women were knocked down, men fought, record books were torn, and the Bureau of Land Management wondered what could be done to end the chaos. In 1960, they came up with the answer: a lottery system.

With this system, the government now awards leases on parcels of public-domain land—ranging from a minimum of 40 acres to a maximum of 2,560—in Wyoming, Colorado, Utah, New Mexico, Alaska and other oil-producing states.

HOW THE LOTTERY SYSTEM WORKS

On the third Monday of every month each land office posts a list of available parcels of land on which investors may file applications. The list gives the location of each parcel, the number of acres, and the amount of annual rental (based on 50 cents per acre). For a fee of $24 to $48 a year, most land offices will mail out their monthly listings.

Once the investor decides to apply for a lease to a particular parcel, he fills out a Simultaneous Oil and Gas Drawing Entry Card, available from any Bureau of Land Management Office. Two checks must accompany the application card:

1. A check for $10 to cover the cost of filing. This may be a personal check, money order, or cashier's check.

2. A check to cover the amount of the first year's rental (for example, the investor filing an application for a 200-acre parcel would attach a check for $100). This check—which must be a cashier's check, certified check, bank draft or money order—is returned to the investor if he fails to win the lease.

To be eligible for the drawing, an application must be received by the fourth Monday of the month or one week after the list of parcels is posted. A few days later, the drawing is held—the stub portions of all applications for a specific parcel are mixed up in a bin and one is drawn. That application wins the lease.

THE BENEFITS FOR THE LEASE WINNER

What, then, are the advantages to the winner of a lease? First, there are the tax benefits previously mentioned, which apply to the initial expenses. Then, there is the possibility of capital gains treatment on the money received for the sale of the lease. If, for example, a lease winner holds his lease for more than six months and then sells it for a cash bonus plus a production payment, the cash bonus may be taxable at capital gains rates. This would mean a maximum tax of 25 percent, providing that capital gains do not exceed $50,000 in the tax year.

Still a third benefit is possible if the seller retains an interest in any production that might result from drilling. This interest can be in either of two forms: a production payment or an overriding royalty. A production payment is a fixed price per acre taken out of a specified percentage of production, while an overriding royalty usually entitles the owner to a percentage of the income for the entire producing life of any gas or oil wells drilled on the land. Thus, if oil or gas is discovered on the lease, he receives a continuing, tax-protected return on his investment, since the money received, although treated as ordinary income, is subject to the 22 percent oil depletion allowance. Even if the drilling is unsuccessful, the investor has received some cash for his lease—and he has not borne any of the expenses of the unsuccessful drilling.

Here is an illustration of how the after-tax cost of a public-domain lease is considerably less than the investor's actual outlay—based on the IRS ruling that the oil lease is totally deductible as an expense.

Assuming that the investor has won a 2,000-acre parcel of land, his first year's rent is $1,000. For an investor in the 50 percent tax bracket, the after-tax cost of the investment would only be $500. Thus, even if the lease turns out to be unsalable and he abandons it, he has reduced his loss substantially. If he decides to retain the lease, he can write off his rental payments for succeeding years. If he sells the lease, his return may be taxed at capital gains rates (if he waits six months from the effective date on the lease). This means that if he sells the lease for the $1,000 he paid for it, he makes a profit of $250 after taxes, a substantial 25 percent gain.

The mathematics of this is very simple:

When the lease is won,

there is a CASH OUTLAY OF: $1,000.00

In the 50 percent tax bracket

there is a TAX CREDIT of: 500.00

This leaves a cost

AFTER TAXES of: $500.00

If the lease is sold for the

original 50 cents/acre the gross is: $1,000.00

Assuming capital gains

treatment - resultant tax 250.00*

Net gain after tax $750.00

Less original cash investment 500.00

Results in net profit $250.00

HOW TO EVALUATE LEASING SERVICES

These, then, are the opportunities for a successful tax-protected investment offered by the Federal Oil and Gas Lease Program. The problem faced by the investor is how he can capitalize on these opportunities. How does he find out what parcels are available? How does he know which leases have immediate or nearly immediate salability to operating oil companies? How does he get all his filing done economically and on time? If he wins a lease, how does he go about selling it at the best possible price?

For most high-bracket investors, the answer is: through a

---

*Based on 1971 capital gains tax assuming individual has less than $50,000 capital gains.

service. Successful investment in federal oil and gas leases is a time-consuming process—it demands great expertise to analyze available leases in terms of their potential marketability. Most high-bracket investors will not want to immerse themselves in such complexities. Yet even selecting a service requires great care. There are many seemingly inexpensive services which cater to the small, relatively unsophisticated investor who is willing to gamble a $10 filing fee every month. These services may handle all the required paper work of filing the forms with the right offices and they might even offer some "tips" on which of the available properties is the best bet, but there are a number of dubious practices these otherwise legitimate services might try on an inexperienced investor.

One of these is to state an exaggerated value for a specific lease, thus giving the impression that the winner of that lease will be able to sell it for far more than he will actually be offered. Such inflated valuations are based on the dubious assumption that oil will be discovered on the land. With this assumption, the value of the land can be estimated to include the overriding royalty that the investor would receive if he retained an interest in the lease when he disposed of it. More conservative lease services do not include this purely speculative possibility when they evaluate a lease; instead, they base their value estimate only on the likely selling price of the lease. They prefer to be cautious about establishing a value, because once a lease is won they would rather have the client be able to sell it for more than their estimate, not less. A striking example of how these two different approaches can affect the estimated value set on a lease is shown by the recent case in which one lease service valued a particular parcel at $32,000, while another, more conservative service pegged the same land at $5,800. Eventually, the investor who won the lease sold it for $11,600.

Another questionable practice is for the lease service to use its own address when filing an application on behalf of a client. This means that if a client wins a lease, any offers to buy it will come to the service rather than the client. For his own protection, the investor should make sure that if he wins a lease, buying offers will come directly to him so he is sure of the exact amount of the offer.

What a Good Service Should Offer

In addition to seeking a lease service that follows ethical practices, the high-bracket investor should look for one that specializes in clients of his type. To attract this sort of clientele, the service must develop a methodical, planned approach to oil and gas leases that will increase the client's chances of winning worthwhile leases.

Some services of this kind offer an investment program on a yearly basis. The cost of investing in such a program might be around $7,500 a year, which would include filing fees, advisory fees to the lease service, bank charges for issuing the cashier's checks used to file for the leases and approximate interest on the cashier's checks. In addition, the client would place on deposit the sum of $1,280 to cover a cashier's check for the rental on the largest possible parcel of land that he could win: 2,560 acres at 50 cents an acre. All of these expenses are entirely deductible except when a lease is won—then just the $10 filing fee plus the advisory service fee must be capitalized. This would amount to about $25 (assuming a $15 advisory service fee per lease).

An investor in such a program cannot, of course, get any guarantee that he will win a worthwhile lease—or any lease at all, for that matter. He can, however, make sure that the lease service maximizes his chances of winning a valuable parcel. A good service retains experienced landmen in the areas of oil leases. These men keep current maps on all federal leases in which the service may someday have an interest. Each month, the landmen obtain from the various Bureau of Land Management offices the complete lists of leases available. From these lists they determine which are the best leases from both the standpoint of availability (how much competition is there?) and its desirability. The estimate of a lease's desirability is based on its salability, not on speculation as to its possible oil and gas reserves.

The better services perform the actual filing of applications for their clients—approximately 250 to 300 filings during the year. If a client wins a lease, any sale is handled by an independent broker, the service deriving no income from the sale of leases.

In some cases, a client may win no lease at all during the year, although the law of averages usually yields something with continued application. And, as some of the following examples show, even winning one lease can put the investor ahead of the game.

—Client A invested $7,605 and filed applications on 243 parcels during the year. He won one lease, which although originally valued by the service at only $12,000, was subsequently sold for $65,000. Assuming a 50 percent tax bracket (as we will in all the examples) and capital gains treatment on the sale price, the client's after-tax gain is $45,097.00. This is an actual example in which the sale occurred prior to a change in the law applicable to capital gains rates.

—Client B invested $67,565 over a period of seven years. Out of 2,428 filings, he won 10 leases. So far, he has received $76,961 for his leases and still holds parcels valued at $3,500. With a 50 percent tax bracket, this leaves a net gain of $42,000 after taxes.

—Client C invested $9,865 and made 347 filings. He won one lease which he sold for $8,690. Assuming a 50 percent tax bracket, his gain after taxes was $1,585.00.

—Clients D and E—who are husband and wife—each invested $8,770 and filed 352 times. Client D won three leases and has sold two for a total of $16,844. He still holds a lease valued at $4,799. Assuming a 50 percent tax bracket and including his unsold acreage, his net gain after taxes is $11,847. Client E also won three leases and has received $2,100 while still holding acreage valued at $7,798. Assuming a 50 percent tax bracket her net gain after taxes is $3,031.

As these examples illustrate, there is potential for profit in the Federal Oil and Gas Leasing Program. While the lottery for leases is basically a gamble, the investor has good odds because his tax dollars underwrite the investment and even a single won lease can mean a profit. With careful planning and the aid of a reputable service, the smart investor can turn his tax dollars into tax-sheltered dollars.

COMMENTARY

This chapter is a fair, balanced description of the federal oil lease program. There is nothing wrong with the investor doing some gambling—so long as he recognizes that it *is* gambling.

13

REAL ESTATE: THE ULTRA-SENSITIVE INVESTMENT

Peter C. Faherty

When an investor thinks about real estate, what may come to his mind first is tax benefits. True, real estate investment *can* provide healthy tax benefits. To achieve them, however, the investor should consider real estate first as a sound economic investment, then as a tax shelter. Why? Because without one, he will not get the other. Indeed, the tail is wagging the dog when the investor looks upon real estate purely as a tax shelter.

MR. FAHERTY IS VICE PRESIDENT OF EASTDIL REALTY INC.

ESSENTIAL INGREDIENTS

This means that the potential real estate investor should begin by asking a basic question: what are the essential ingredients of a successful real estate investment?

There are many, of course, but this chapter will focus on two of the most important:

• Leverage. A successful real estate investment must be highly leveraged, because real estate without debt performs minimally when compared with any stock or any company with a dynamic growth pattern.

• Appreciation. The investment must have the potential for capital appreciation, so that the principal can grow through intelligent management and normal inflation.

With these two components present—proper leverage and the potential for appreciation—the investor will have not only a sound economic investment, but an effective tax shelter as well.

THE NEED FOR PROFESSIONAL GUIDANCE

To the uninitiated investor, this may sound simple. But the simplicity is deceptive. In actuality, selecting a sound real estate investment is complex and hazardous. For this reason, the neophyte investor should not try to select and manage a real estate investment on his own. He needs professional guidance of two kinds: first, from his own investment counselor, who knows his capacity to hold debt, his earnings potential, and all the other factors that asset managers consider in determining a recommended portfolio mix for a client.

Second, he needs a professional experienced in dealing with the problems of real estate. This professional must be able to recognize potential problems in the investment. So many investors are concerned with the short-range benefits of a real estate investment that they completely neglect the possibility of what can happen in the long run. For example, in the initial stages of a real estate investment, the investor receives substantial tax benefits because his depreciation is high and the proportion of his mortgage payments allotted to principal is low. Eventually, however, as depreciation decreases and payments on principal increase, the two lines cross, and the investor finds himself paying a larger portion of his tax dollar on that part of the debt which is principal, and because his deduction allowance is reduced, he ends up paying that principal out of earned income. For specific illustration, consider a case in which the investor's property brings in $100,000 annual income and has debt service and expenses of $99,000—leaving a real estate cash flow of $1,000. Assume that eventually principal payments exceed depreciation deductions by $5,000. If the investor is in the 50 percent tax bracket, he will have a tax of $2,500. Thus, he will be paying $1,500 more than he earns from the property—a situation scarcely calculated to make him happy.

Besides being able to recognize the potential problems inherent in a real estate investment, the professional must also use his skill and experience to structure the joint venture, whether it be a general partnership, limited partnership, or some other form. Then he must set up operating and control procedures to make certain that the investment will perform as it should. He does this usually by establishing objectives for the investment on a yearly basis, and monitoring the performance of the investment so that problems can be spotted as early as possible. This is vital, because in real estate corrective measures take time. If taxes go up, the investor cannot immediately raise his rents. That is why it is important to anticipate problems and act on them early. The investor should keep in mind that good management can make a basically mediocre investment perform well, while poor management can turn a potentially good investment into a disaster.

Although the investor should seek expert professional guidance, he should nevertheless have at least a rudimentary knowledge of the problems and pitfalls involved in real estate investment. Here are three major ones:

SENSITIVITY OF THE INVESTMENT

Because of its high leverage, a real estate investment is extremely sensitive even to small decreases in income or increases in operating expenses, and it is usually impossible to compensate for these changes immediately.

Let us consider an apartment house as an example of this problem (Figure 1). In this case, the investor has assumed that his apartment house has a potential income of $100,000. Because of a vacancy factor of 5 percent, however, it produces only $95,000 income. His operating expenses are $38,000—based on a 40 percent income-expense ratio—and his debt service is $47,500. This leaves him a cash flow of $9,500.

Figure 1

	SITUATION A	SITUATION B
Potential income	$100,000	$100,000
Vacancy factor	5,000	10,000
	95,000	90,000
Operating expenses	38,000	36,000
	57,000	54,000
Debt service	47,500	47,500
Net cash flow	9,500	6,500

Now suppose that for some reason the vacancy factor rises to 10 percent, providing a gross income of only $90,000. Expenses drop to $36,000, but the debt service remains at $47,500. The result: net cash flow dwindles to $6,500. Thus, with only a 5 percent drop in gross income there has been a loss of almost 33 percent in net cash flow.

Real estate is equally sensitive to increases in expenses. Figure 2 shows what can happen in such a circumstance. The same investor has been hit by a $5,000 increase in real estate taxes, raising his operating expenses from $38,000 to $43,000. His income-expense ratio has risen only 5 percent, but his net cash flow has been cut by more than half. To earn the same cash flow he had before the tax increase, he would need to boost his gross income to $100,000—and there is probably no way he can do it immediately.

THE NEED FOR CASH FLOW

A certain amount of net cash flow is necessary both to carry the leverage and maintain the resale value of the property—and net cash flow is a most difficult factor to estimate with any accuracy.

Because of this problem, the investor would be wise to err on the conservative side when he estimates the potential income of a real estate property. Otherwise, here is what can happen. Let us say that he estimates a potential income of $100,000 and is 10 percent too high. This means that even if the property earns its true potential income of $90,910, the investor is already almost $10,000 below his calculations. On top of this, he could have other problems. He might suffer losses when tenants do not pay their bills. Moreover, even with "full occupancy," there can be a substantial vacancy rate. Assume that the investor's project is an apartment building with 100 units and that eight tenants move out every month. Even if he leases all eight, they will each be vacant for approximately two weeks. This actually amounts to four vacant apartments over the year, for a vacancy rate of 4 percent. This could knock another $3,640 off the gross income, reducing it to $87,270. And yet, if occupancy was calculated on a monthly basis, the record would show that the project was 100 percent occupied.

The investor who falls into this trap will be hurt in two ways. First, the property may not be able to carry the leverage that has been placed upon it. Many investors assume that as long as they have 90 percent leverage, they are guaranteed a profitable investment on an after-tax basis. But this will not be the case if they are forced to pay the debt service out of their own pockets or from some other source. In a sound investment, the leverage debt must be paid out of the income generated by the project.

Nor should the investor count on the fact that the operator or general partner in the deal is supposed to carry all deficits. The operator cannot carry the deficits forever. Eventually he would call on the investor for additional capital or drop out of the deal, leaving the investor holding the bag.

Moreover, the resale value of the investor's property will be calculated on its cash flow—and if the investor overestimates his cash flow, he will find it difficult to eventually refinance the property or to sell it without taking a loss.

COORDINATING LEVERAGE AND APPRECIATION

The two most important elements in a sound real estate investment—leverage and appreciation—are so closely intertwined that if they are improperly coordinated the investor will ultimately suffer.

In order to get more leverage, an investor may pay more for a property than it is actually worth, forgetting that the property must appreciate in value to carry the additional leverage. Here is an example. An investor is offered a property for $1,000,000. Since the property has a 75 percent mortgage, equity of $250,000 is necessary for the purchase. The investor, however, does not think that the property is worth that price at this time. He therefore agrees to buy it for the $1,000,000 figure provided the seller will give him an additional $150,000 purchase-money mortgage payable in ten years. By then, the investor estimates, the property will actually be worth $1,000,-000.

This means that the cash flow must increase substantially during the next ten years. At present, the cash flow is $21,000. Calculating 12 percent of equity as a fair return, this is more than adequate, since the investor has put in only $100,000 of cash equity. But what happens in ten years? The investor must pay off the $150,-000 purchase-money mortgage, and he now has $250,000 equity in the project. To maintain his 12 percent return on equity, his cash flow must have increased to $30,000—over 35 percent. If it has remained at $21,000, his return will be only 8.4 percent.

A variation on this transaction might be the situation in which the seller would come down to $925,000 if the investor puts in $175,000 equity. But the investor does not want to put in that much cash. Therefore he pays the $1,000,000 price in order to get the additional leverage of a $150,000 purchase-money mortgage. If he had put in the $175,000 equity instead, the property's cash flow would not have to increase in order to maintain a 12 percent return. But he has paid a higher price in exchange for more leverage—and the property must pay for that additional leverage eventually.

These then, are some of the problems of which an investor in real estate must be aware. The tax-shelter benefits are there—but only the investor who makes sure he is getting into a sound, properly structured economic investment will be able to realize them.

COMMENTARY

It can be fairly said that it is almost as difficult to find a good deal in real estate investment as it is in oil investment. However, the investor does have the advantage of being able to evaluate a structure and a neighborhood more accurately than he can evaluate the possibilities of oil ten thousand feet beneath the surface.

On the other hand, the 1969 Tax Reform Act hit real estate harder than it did oil. The investor should keep in mind these points:

1. The possible disallowance of excess investment interest over $25,000 a year (IRC-163[d]).

2. The potentially heavy tax on capital gains.

3. The toughened recapture provision on accelerated depreciation (IRC-1250).

4. The minimum tax on accelerated depreciation.

14

TAX SHELTERS THROUGH LIMITED PARTNERSHIPS

Sheldon Schwartz

The quest for tax sheltered income has brought the limited partnership into the limelight as a favored investment vehicle. The business and tax features which accompany the limited partnership are well suited to real estate shelters. Its successful use nevertheless depends upon a thorough understanding of its characteristics and the technical requirements for achieving a tax saving result.

MR. SCHWARTZ PRACTICES AS A TAX ATTORNEY WITH THE FIRM OF ROSEN AND READE, IN NEW YORK CITY, AND LECTURES ON THE TAX ASPECTS OF REAL ESTATE TRANSACTIONS AT THE NYU REAL ESTATE INSTITUTE.

ADVANTAGES OF THE LIMITED PARTNERSHIP

A limited partnership is defined by statute as a partnership consisting of at least one general and one limited partner. It has traditionally offered two quite basic business advantages that have not simultaneously been available to any other form of business operation—*limited liability* and *single level taxation*.

Limited Liability

Once having made the initial investment in a partnership, limited partners need not fear that the creditors of the business will look to the partners' personal assets for the satisfaction of business obligations. The general partner or partners, on the other hand, do not have the benefit of limited liability. They are the managers of the business of the partnership and are subject to unlimited liability for partnership obligations. A condition to the limitation on the limited partners' liability is that they maintain only a passive position, as mere investors, without taking part in the management of the business. (The degree of managerial participation which will cause the loss of the protection of the statute has been the subject of recent consideration.[1])

Single Level Taxation

The second advantage of limited partnership operations is the manner in which the participants are taxed. Notwithstanding the limited liability of the partners, the business enterprise may be treated as an ordinary partnership for income tax purposes. There is no tax at the entity level, unlike the incorporated business which pays a corporate income tax. The only tax falls upon the partners, who are required to report their proportional distributive shares of partnership income or loss. The limited partners thereby achieve the best of all possible

---

[1]"The Limited Partnership with a Limited General Partner." *Southwestern Law Journal,* Volume 24, No. 2, May 1970, pp. 285–304.

business worlds—the limited liability of corporate investors and the single level of taxation enjoyed by partners.

Significance of Pass Through of Losses

Of particular interest to the real estate industry is the pass through of partnership losses. The Internal Revenue Code, in taxing partners directly, allows the deduction by the partners of partnership losses as well as gains. This feature is directly responsible for the ascending popularity of the limited partnership vehicle in real estate operations.

Those who are closely associated with the industry are familiar with the "shelter-of-income" concept which has become so important to many operations. Generally, when the depreciation deductions generated by improved real estate exceed the operating profits of the business, we have a "net operating loss" for income tax purposes which acts as a shelter for the taxpayer's income from other sources. These losses are available to the partners of partnership-owned real estate in the same manner as if the realty were owned directly by the partners. In the case of high bracket taxpayers such losses can produce tax savings of up to seventy cents for each dollar of deductible loss.

FHA Popularity

The Tax Reform Act of 1969 sharply curtailed the use of the accelerated depreciation methods which produced the largest deductions (and therefore the largest losses) for the real estate industry. In addition, the 1969 Act strengthened the recapture provisions applicable to accelerated depreciation methods, thereby converting a larger portion of the gain at the time of sale to ordinary income.

The fast write-offs and former more liberal recapture provisions are, however, still available for a type of real estate investment which lends itself quite well to the limited partnership form of operation. This is residential rental real estate constructed under the provisions of the National Housing Act, or state statutes which similarly provide for public assistance to those sponsors who build low and moderate income housing.

The 1969 Act specifically exempts such new residential real estate from the restrictions on accelerated depreciation. It further provides that the pre-1969 depreciation recapture rules shall continue to apply to these investments. Thus, publicly assisted housing can be sold without the conversion of any part of the gain to ordinary income, at any time after it is held by the seller for a period of 10 years.[2] This is true regardless of the method or amount of depreciation taken.

Because it qualifies for accelerated depreciation and the old, more liberal, recapture rules, the publicly assisted housing project, or so called "FHA job," has become a very attractive investment for high bracket taxpayers who are seeking the tax losses to shelter income from other sources.

Moreover, it should be noted that operations motivated purely by "tax shelter," of the type mentioned above, have been quite obviously sanctioned by Congress, as evidenced by the 1969 Act provisions referred to. Publicly assisted housing is restricted by law to a limited cash return of no more than 6 percent in most cases. The only possible economic motivation for such investments is the anticipated large "net operating loss" brought about by the accelerated depreciation, and which need not be given back to the government through recapture. The real estate tax shelter is, therefore, one of the few remaining tax saving devices which cannot be defeated because it was motivated principally by tax avoidance desires.

The limited partnership vehicle is ideally suited to bring these tax advantages to the investor. It provides the following:

a. Permits high bracket (non-real estate oriented) investors to participate in a project without any managerial responsibility, with limited liability for partnership obligations, and with a degree of anonymity which may be most desirable;

b. Allows the pass through of net operating losses generated from large depreciation deductions, and liberal recapture, both of which specifically are sanctioned by Congressional act; and

c. Permits the builder-sponsor to erect the project without

---

[2]Rehabilitated dwelling units are an important exception to this rule. I.R.C. §1250 (a) (1) (c) (iv).

any investment, by "selling" the anticipated tax losses to the limited partners in exchange for a cash investment in the partnership which is sufficient to furnish the funds necessary to make up the difference between the government insured financing and the full construction costs.

OBTAINING PARTNERSHIP TAX TREATMENT

Since investors rely so heavily upon the expected partnership tax treatment, it is essential that a limited partnership not be so structured as to convert it into an "association" for tax purposes. An association is a non-incorporated organization that more nearly resembles a corporation than a partnership. If an organization is found to be an association it will be treated as a corporation for federal income tax purposes.

The fact that a particular organization is treated as a corporation or partnership under the state law is not determinative. The essential criteria for determining corporate status, as set forth in the Treasury regulations, are as follows:

☐ Centralized management
☐ Continuity of life
☐ Free transferability of interests
☐ Limited liability for investors

Whether a particular organization will be taxed as a partnership or an association must be determined by taking into account the presence or absence of each of the above corporate characteristics. An organization will be taxed as an association if the corporate characteristics are such that it more nearly resembles a corporation than a partnership. This apparently means that partnership tax treatment will be available if it can be demonstrated that two of the four corporate characteristics are absent.[3]

---

[3]Treas. Regs. §301.7701–3 (b) Example (2).

Centralized Management

It would appear that most limited partnerships do in fact have the corporate characteristic of centralized management. This is especially so in view of the fact that the limited partners will own, percentage-wise, the greatest interest in the partnership, so that their interests as investors are represented by a central board of managers in the form of the general partners.

Continuity of Life

The opinion of the IRS, as expressed in private rulings, is that a limited partnership formed under a statute which is substantially the same as the Uniform Limited Partnership Act, automatically lacks continuity of life since the Uniform Act permits the general partner or partners to dissolve the partnership at any time without the consent of the limited partners. The vast majority of states have adopted the Uniform Limited Partnership Act in substantially unchanged form, and so an absence of continuity of life is achieved by the simple act of forming the limited partnership under local statute. Care should be taken, in drafting the articles of limited partnership, not to modify or abrogate the general partner's right to dissolve as contained in the statute.

Free Transferability of Interests

Free transferability of investors' interests can be avoided by inserting a prohibition on the transfer of a limited partner's interest in the articles of limited partnership. It is often felt that such an absolute bar to transfer is unsuitable since the sale of his interest may become necessary to a partner at some future date. Most articles of limited partnership do therefore contain a modified form of transferability wherein the permission of the general partner or partners is required to effectuate a change in ownership. Such a modification is deemed by the Treasury regulations to be a lack of free transferability of interests.[4]

---

[4]Treas.Regs. §301.7701–2(e) (1).

Limited Liability

Along with continuity of life, limited liability is generally an easy criterion to negate, and usually provides one of the two required "absent characteristics."

Though it may seem anomalous to say that limited liability does not exist in limited partnership, the Treasury regulations are clear in pointing out that if any partner (even a general partner) has unlimited liability, then the limited liability does not exist for purposes of determining the tax treatment of the entity—this notwithstanding the fact that all of the limited partners enjoy limited liability.[5]

In determining whether or not unlimited liability exists for the general partner or partners, we must go beyond the technical legal liability which is always present under the state law. We must look to the assets of the general partner in order to see if he is in fact subject to exposure. If he is insolvent and selected as a general partner only because of his judgment proof nature, the IRS will not recognize him as having unlimited liability. Though a corporation may serve as a general partner in a limited partnership, it may not be a mere dummy corporation. It must have substantial assets exclusive of its interest in the partnership, although the assets do not have to equal a substantial portion of the liabilities of the partnership.

USE OF A SOLE CORPORATE GENERAL PARTNER

The use of a corporation as the sole general partner of a limited partnership is becoming a popular technique. There are some obvious advantages to this device.

---

[5]Treas.Regs. §301.7701–2(d) (1).

Continuity of Management

A corporate general partner is not subject to the infirmities of ill health, death, insanity or other human frailties. It provides continuity of management which will survive the active managerial years of the individual sponsor of the venture. Moreover, there appears to be no clear restriction against one or more limited partners serving on the board of directors of the sole general partner corporation, thereby giving them an indirect voice in the management of the patnership.

Limited Liability

Insofar as the builder-sponsor of the project is concerned, a sole corporate general partner may act as a shield which gives him the same limited liability enjoyed by his limited partners. Such a shield can be most desirable in the operation of a low income housing project, should there be building department violations, tenant relations problems or other difficulties that are more easily overcome by corporate management.

The IRS, as well as the builder-sponsor, recognizes that the sole corporate general partner offers complete limited liability to all individuals concerned, almost to the same extent as direct corporate ownership of the realty, and so certain additional requirements have been engrafted upon the criteria set forth above for testing partnership versus corporate tax attributes.

Safe Harbor Rules

The IRS has adopted the so called "safe harbor rules," which must be complied with before an advance ruling will issue to the effect that an entity will be taxed as a partnership rather than as association. The additional requirements embodied in the "safe harbor rules" are applicable only to those situations involving a corporation which is acting as sole general partner of a limited partnership. The added requirements are:

☐ *Capital requirements:* If the capital contributed to the partnership by the partners is less than $2,500,000, the sole corporate general partner must maintain at all times a net worth at least equal to 15 percent of the total partnership capital, but not more than $250,000. If the contributed capital is $2,500,000 or more, the sole corporate general partner must maintain at all times a net worth at least equal to 10 percent of the total partnership capital. There appears to be no reason why the corporate general partner cannot lend its assets to the partnership since this would not reduce the net worth of the corporate general partner.

☐ *Ownership requirements:* The limited partners may not own, individually or in the aggregate, more than 20 percent of the stock of the corporate general partner. In determining such ownership, stock owned by members of a partner's family may be attributed to the partner if certain degrees of relationship exist.

The foregoing "safe harbor rules" do not appear in any revenue ruling published for the general guidance of the taxpayer, nor are they found in, or directly supported by, the official Treasury regulations. They exist only as an internal guideline which must be adhered to by the rulings division in issuing private rulings on partnership tax status. It is difficult to assess the weight that would be given the rules by the tax court in a litigated controversy. They are, in effect, the opinion of the IRS—merely an adversarial position. Notwithstanding the lack of authoritative support, most taxpayers who are setting up limited partnerships with sole corporate general partners will attempt to comply with the "safe harbor rules," either because they intend to apply for an advance ruling, or because they wish to avoid any possible controversy on audit. The validity of the rules nevertheless is an open question.

MAXIMIZING THE PASS THROUGH OF LOSSES

Having established that a limited partnership will receive partnership treatment for federal income tax purposes, we must turn our attention to those features of the partnership which maximize the tax benefits to be derived from the venture. The primary tax benefit of a partnership real estate venture is the pass through of a depreciation deduction in the form of a partnership net operating loss. The objective is to put the loss where it belongs—with the high bracket investors who save up to 70¢ on each dollar of deductible losses.

Giving the Limiteds all the Losses—The Economic Rationale

The Internal Revenue Code allows any item of gain or loss to be allocated among the partners in accordance with a partnership agreement. The only restriction to such freedom of allocation is that the allocation must have some economic substance and that it not be motivated principally by tax avoidance desires.[6] It is possible to allocate the gains and losses of a limited partnership entirely to the limited partners since they have, typically, contributed all of the cash invested in the partnership. There is an economic rationale for allowing this result. The rationale is that they are being permitted to recoup their initial cash investment through the receipt of partnership profits and losses before the noncontributing general partners may share. The entire net operating loss of the partnership thereby can be placed where it belongs, namely, with the high bracket passive investors who went into the deal in order to share in the usually predictable tax losses.

A typical limited partnership agreement would provide that the general partner (builder or his corporation) shall be equal partners with the limited partners as a class; however, all gains and losses of the partnership shall be allocated to the limited partners until they have recouped their initial investment through cash distributions. The agreement will further provide that the cash flow from the realty will be distributed currently to the limited partners. This provision adds to the economic substance of the allocation since the limited partners are thus receiving any cash generated by the business during the time that all profits and losses are allocated to them.

If the partnership owns a publicly assisted housing project, the cash return may be restricted to as low as six per cent of the investment and so the limited partners will receive all losses for many years before they recoup their cash investment from distributions. If

---

[6]I.R.C. §704(b) (2).

a sale or refinancing of the property should occur prior to the recoupment by the limiteds of their investment, they would receive so much of the proceeds as would, together with all prior cash distributions, equal the initial investment, and the remaining proceeds would be shared equally among the general and limited partners. The general partners thus retain a full 50 percent of the "residual" interest in the realty, profiting equally with the limited partners should there be substantial equity appreciation. When the limiteds have recouped their investments all partnership profits and losses are thereafter shared equally.

OBTAINING "BASIS" FOR THE MORTGAGE

Most of us know that the depreciation deductions generated by a building are based upon the full cost of the building to the owner, including therein the amount of any purchase money mortgage.[7] An equity investment of $100,000 with a $900,000 purchase money mortgage produces $1 million of depreciable basis. The owner therefore has purchased a million dollars of depreciation with $100,000 cash outlay—the concept commonly known as "leverage."

The successful use of a limited partnership vehicle in realty ownership requires that the leverage be made available to the limited partners. If the partnership constructs or purchases a building with 10 percent cash, it may depreciate the full cost of the building even though 90 percent of the funds are borrowed. The important factor, however, is to make certain that the net operating loss generated by the leveraged depreciation deduction can be passed through in full to the limited partners.

The general rule is that partners can deduct partnership losses only to the extent of their "cost basis" for their partnership interests. When the aggregate of his losses equals the cost basis of his partnership interest, a partner cannot pass through any additional losses. The cost basis of a partner's interest in a partnership is his cash contribution plus his pro rata share of the partnership liabilities.

---

[7]Crane v. Commissioner, 331 U.S. 1.

Liabilities (including mortgage liability) are added to basis because the partner is potentially liable to the creditors of the partnership and may be called upon for additional contributions to satisfy such liabilities. In the case of a real estate partnership the additional basis for the partners' pro rata share of the mortgage liability is essential if he is to be able to pass through the losses generated by the leveraged depreciation deductions.

The difficulty with the limited partnership vehicle (as opposed to a general partnership) is that the limited partners are not personally responsible for the partnership liabilities. They cannot be required to satisfy the liabilities with additional contributions and so the rationale for adding their pro rata share of the mortgage liability to their cash contributions is absent. A special technique supported by the Treasury regulations must be utilized in order to overcome this difficulty.

How to Comply with the Regulations

The Treasury regulations specifically state that a limited partner does not get additional basis for the liabilities of the partnership, except in one particular instance. If no partner, general or limited, is personally liable on the partnership mortgage (or for any other liability of the partnership), then the partners, both general and limited, can add the mortgage liability (or any other liability) pro rata to the basis for their partnership interests, in accordance with the manner in which they share partnership profits.[8] The limited partnership must bring itself within this single exception, lest it lose the primary tax benefit of the limited partnership form.

Under this rule, if the partnership agreement allocates all profits and losses to the limited partners, presumably they will be entitled to add the entire amount of the mortgage liability to their cash contributions, and thus will have sufficient "basis" so that all losses of the partnership from the leveraged depreciation deductions may be passed through to them.

Avoiding personal liability on the partnership mortgage

---

[8]Treas.Regs. §1.752–1(e).

means paying a great deal of attention to construction loan and permanent mortgage commitments. The tax posture of the transaction must be considered at its inception. All commitments must provide for exculpatory clauses in the mortgages which relegate the lender to foreclosure as his only remedy on default in the payment of the mortgage obligation.

The exculpatory clause in the mortgage eliminates the personal liability of the partnership, or any of the partners. Thus each partner can increase the basis for his partnership interest by his pro rata share of the mortgage. The same result can be achieved by having the mortgage executed by a nominee of the partnership. The nominee would sign the mortgage, and convey title to the realty to the partnership "subject to" the mortgage obligation, but with no partner, nor the partnership, personally liable on the mortgage. It is essential that one of these techniques be employed, if the limited partners are to get "basis" for the mortgage obligation, and thereby obtain the benefits of all of the operating losses to be generated by the partnership.

CONCLUSION

The limited partnership is uniquely suited to bring all of the tax saving features of real estate operations to the passive investor. The intended benefits do not, however, come about automatically. The organizational details require careful consideration. Much attention must be given to the Treasury regulations and guidelines that determine tax status, especially if there is to be a sole corporate general partner. The losses must be channeled to the investors. Financing provisions will be crucial. It is only when all of the key factors are brought into alignment that the optimum tax saving result is achieved.

THIS CHAPTER IS BASED ON AN ARTICLE, "HOW TO FIND TAX SHELTER AS A LIMITED PARTNER," BY SHELDON SCHWARTZ, AND IS REPRINTED BY PERMISSION FROM REAL ESTATE REVIEW, SUMMER 1971 EDITION.

COMMENTARY

This is an excellent analysis of the advantages of limited partnerships. The author does particularly well on how the limited partner can increase his depreciation basis through non-recourse loans and on the "Safe Harbor Rules." I would, however, express some doubt about the guideline precluding the ownership by limited partners of more than 20 percent of the stock of the corporation—that is, the general partner. I would also like to suggest that the use of family trusts as limited partners should always be considered.

15

REAL ESTATE: OFFICE BUILDINGS, SHOPPING CENTERS AND APARTMENT HOUSES

Jenard M. Gross

Both as an income producer and a tax shelter, real estate is an increasingly attractive form of investment. Consider these facts: In the next thirty years, the U. S. population will probably

MR. GROSS, PRESIDENT OF GROSS BUILDERS, IS ONE OF THE SOUTHWEST'S MOST PROMINENT INVESTMENT BUILDERS.

grow by over 100 million. This will create a tremendous demand for housing—it is estimated that by 1990, at least 68 million more residential units must be built merely to maintain our housing at its present inadequate level. To meet even this goal will require a sharp boost in housing starts over the current rate of 1,300,000 a year. And in addition to dwellings, our growing population will need places to work, to shop, to eat, and to go for entertainment.

Moreover, since construction costs will continue to rise rapidly, real estate acquired now for the long term can provide a substantial inflationary hedge. As construction costs go up, so do rents. For example, at this writing, the General Motors building in New York is renting smaller offices for as much as $19 a square foot. Although this is an extreme case, it forcefully illustrates the fact that rents will continue to rise—to the benefit of the investor.

All of these facts are important to the individual or corporation looking at real estate investment as a tax shelter. Unfortunately, too many such investors say blithely that they do not care if they get any income as long as they get depreciation. This is a serious mistake. When a real estate investment does not make sense as an income producer, it does not make sense as a tax shelter. The investor who goes into real estate purely for tax-avoidance purposes will probably regret it in the end. To give just one example, let us assume he has put his money into a real estate development which must maintain 98 percent occupancy in order to break even. Because this level cannot possibly be maintained consistently, there will be times when he has to come up with more cash to keep the project afloat. This is scarcely what he had in mind when he invested his money originally.

ECONOMIC SOUNDNESS

Investors who ignore the economic soundness of a real estate investment can also get into trouble by overextending themselves. Real estate deals are almost always high leverage transactions—the investor can ordinarily borrow from 75 to 85 percent of the total costs of a real estate development as a first mortgage. The problem is that some investors go farther and take second and third mortgages, eventually ending up with an overload of financial debt they cannot carry.

Keeping these hazards in mind, the potential real estate investor should first make sure a venture is basically sound and properly financed so that it will produce cash income on its own. Only then should he proceed to consider its possible benefits as a tax shelter.

What benefits should he seek? There should be two major benefits for the individual investor: he should be able to shelter both his real estate and other income for a number of years and then be able to convert his real-estate income into a long-term capital gain by selling his property. For the corporation—if it is sufficiently adroit —the benefit can be a permanent avoidance of tax payments on its real estate income.

Comparing the Rates of Return

But before an investor—whether individual or corporate—goes after these benefits, he should learn something about the varying rates of return and tax-shelter characteristics of different types of real estate investment. Let us compare three popular types: office buildings, shopping centers, and apartment houses.

Office buildings are the most expensive to construct. They have the greatest longevity but the lowest return on investment: 8 or 9 percent. Since they require a forty-five to fifty-year depreciable life, office buildings do not provide as much tax shelter at the outset as do shorter-lived shopping centers or apartment houses. On the other hand, they are superior in terms of long-range income stability.

While shopping centers do not match office buildings in this respect, they do offer stable income, as well as minimum maintenance and operating costs. The shopping center's stability derives from its long-term leases with national tenants. However, this stability is weakened by the local tenants, who pay higher rents but have shorter leases. A shopping center can be expected to last thirty years and give a 10 to 12 percent return on investment.

Because it has individual tenants with short leases, the apartment house is the least stable of these three types of investment, but it offers the highest return on equity—13 to 16 percent—and the biggest depreciation. The building can usually be written off in thirty to thirty-three years, while the equipment, such as carpeting and appliances, can be written off in from five to ten years.

AVAILABLE DEPRECIATION METHODS

What depreciation methods can be used on these properties? Before the 1969 tax-law changes, first users of all three types were allowed double declining balance accelerated depreciation. Under the new laws, however, only the first user owners of new residential projects can use this method. Owners of new shopping centers and office buildings are restricted to 150 percent accelerated depreciation, and investors in used real estate must use only straight line depreciation.

These changes, obviously, make residential projects even more attractive as a tax shelter. Not only can owners of new apartment houses use double declining balance accelerated depreciation, but they have a further advantage: they can depreciate by components. Thus, the building shell, electric wiring, plumbing, carpeting, and air conditioning equipment can be depreciated individually over different lives. For example, consider depreciation on carpeting. Allowing a four-year depreciation life and using the double declining balance method, the owners would get 50 percent the first year and 50 percent the second year. Then they could convert to straight line depreciation in the third year, to gain more depreciation than they would get by continuing the accelerated method.

TWO CASE HISTORIES

To show how a real estate investment can be effectively used as a tax shelter, let us look at two actual cases. Both examples deal with apartment projects, which have the highest income and highest tax loss (and, it should be added, the highest risk).

In one case, improvements costing $1,046,000 were made in

an existing apartment house. At the end of thirty months, there was $304,000 in depreciation—almost 30 percent of the total depreciable value. This tremendous write-off in the early years resulted in a net tax loss. Thus, investment in these improvements provided an excellent tax shelter.

The second case involves a new apartment house which cost approximately $3,500,000—with $400,000 of this being cash equity and the remainder a mortgage. During the first year, the project had $110,000 worth of deductible items, including real estate taxes, sales taxes, and construction interests. In addition, there was depreciation of $260,000. On the credit side was cash flow of $100,000 and principal reduction of the mortgage of $36,000. The result was a net tax loss of $234,000.

In the second year, the tax loss was $148,000. Although at this writing, there are no further figures on this building, they can be projected with a fair degree of certainty. At the end of the seventh year, $13,000 of the cash flow would be taxable, and that would increase to $77,000 by the tenth year. By the twelfth year, all the cash flow would be taxable, and after the twelfth year part of the principal reduction on the mortgage would be taxable as well. This, of course, is about as long as the owners should wait before selling the project and converting it to a capital gain.

Figuring the Gain

Let us assume that the owners sell after ten years. What have they gained during this period? First, they have received $1,000,000 in income which was covered by the depreciation of deductible items. Second, they have reduced principal indebtedness by $544,000. Third, they have shown a tax loss of $349,000.

Assuming they sell the project for its actual cost—$3,500,000 —the owners have a capital gain of $1,778,000 on which they owe approximately $445,000 in income tax. Also, at the time of sale, they get back their $400,000 equity and the amount of the principal reduction of the mortgage, $544,000, which more than pays the tax on the capital gain. Any profit made on the sale would, of course, be in addition to this.

An individual investor in such a project would achieve substantial tax savings. If, for example, he were in a 50 percent tax bracket and had $234,000 of tax loss in the first year, he could in effect avoid the payment of $117,000 worth of tax which ultimately would be converted to a long-term rate.

For a corporation, the possibilities are even more interesting. By steadily investing in real estate ventures it can sell off its projects at the appropriate time and shelter the capital gains with its tax losses on other properties.

FINDING A GOOD DEAL

How does a neophyte real estate investor go about finding a sound venture into which to put his money? First, he should be aware of the various investment channels available to him. He can place his money with:

1. Building developers—there are many who are generally short of capital and are looking for added investment funds for their ventures.

2. Investment houses—several in New York have departments specializing in real estate deals.

3. Mutual funds and syndicates.

4. Real estate and mortgage investment trusts—they provide some tax shelter through tax-free income, but they do not provide pass-through depreciation to the beneficiaries in excess of the trust's income.

In almost all cases, an investor going into real estate for its tax-shelter benefits should contribute his money and leave the management of the project to the participants equipped to handle it. This means his key decision is picking his partners—they must be competent and experienced in successfully developing and handling real estate properties.

Despite the appeal of real estate as an investment for both income and tax shelter, the potential investor should be cautioned that real estate has one major drawback: it is a non-liquid asset. When an investor buys real estate, his money is locked in and cannot be retrieved as easily as money invested in stocks and bonds. And, inevitably, he will want his money most when the market is depressed and he cannot get a decent price for his property. Despite the bright long-range prospects for real estate, an investor must expect short-term fluctuations in demand due to cycles of underbuilding and overbuilding. These possibilities should be carefully considered by the investor before he ties up his funds in a real estate venture.

No type of investment is a sure thing—and this includes real estate. But, if an investor uses good sense in deciding where to commit his money, he will find that real estate can be an excellent source of income, tax shelter, and capital enhancement.

DISCUSSION

Question: When an individual goes into the kind of real estate investment described here, how can he determine whether or not he will get a good return?

Mr. Gross: Without experience in the field, it would be unwise for an individual to attempt to evaluate a prospective real estate investment. He must depend largely on the help and advice of a person knowledgeable and experienced in the real estate business. That is why it is so important that the potential investor investigate any individuals with whom he is planning to join forces to make certain of their capability and reliability.

Question: How does one evaluate the other individuals with whom he is going to invest in terms of whether he will be able to get his money out by selling the property?

Mr. Gross: Examine their financial strength, their length of experience in the business, and their past performance. Particularly, examine their staying power—that is, their ability to wait it out if the market is not right for selling the property. Naturally, the potential investor should have this kind of staying power, too.

COMMENTARY

As Mr. Gross pointed out in the previous chapter, the investor should keep in mind the following: the provisions of the 1969 Act concerning depreciation recapture; heavier burdens on capital gains; minimum tax on accelerated depreciation; infection of tax-ceiling protected earned income by tax preferences resulting from capital gains and accelerated depreciation; partial non-deductibility of excess investment interest in highly leveraged accounts; and Internal Revenue Service guidelines on limited partnerships.

16

REAL ESTATE: OPPORTUNITIES IN PUBLIC HOUSING

E. Burton Kerr

In recent years, the government has created incentives to encourage investment in the construction and rehabilitation of low- and middle-income housing. These incentives provide some attractive opportunities for the investor, both in economic and tax-shelter benefits.

What are the economic benefits? In 1968, the Housing and Urban Redevelopment Act created what are known as "Section 236

MR. KERR IS A PARTNER IN THE LAW FIRM OF COHEN, SHAPIRO, POLISHER, SHIEKMAN AND COHEN.

programs" to provide economic incentive through a mortgage interest subsidy or supplemental rental income payments. The act promotes forty-year FHA-insured mortgages, covering 90 percent of the estimated land and building costs of a project at an effective mortgage interest rate of 1 percent, with the individual investor contributing the 10 percent balance. The U.S. Department of Housing, and Urban Development makes constant monthly amortization payments, directly to the mortgagees, of the difference between the current prevailing rate of $8\frac{1}{2}$ percent, and the effective one percent rate being charged under the Section 236 programs. The monthly payments made by HUD include the difference between the principal portion and the interest, plus the mortgage insurance premiums.

As might be expected with these benefits, the FHA does stipulate some major restrictions on the owners or sponsors of the projects. First, rent charges are limited. As the tenants are from low- and middle-income families, and the government is assisting on the mortgage interest rates, rents are kept 25 percent to 40 percent lower than the prevailing rents of similar properties.

A second major restriction is on the cash flow distribution from the project to the owners. As of this writing, the rule of thumb is a 6 percent return on the 10 percent actually invested by the sponsors. Moreover, the owners or sponsors of the property cannot refinance the project within twenty years of the basic commitment without first obtaining FHA approval.

What about the tax benefits of public housing? There are basically three major benefits:

ACCELERATED DEPRECIATION ON REHABILITATION EXPENDITURES

Public housing, in general, is entitled to the same depreciation methods available for any type of residential real estate. *New* real estate is entitled to the double declining-balance method and the sum-of-the-year-digits method of accelerated depreciation. If *used* property is acquired, the taxpayer is entitled to use a 125 percent declining-balance depreciation method if the property has a remaining useful life of at least twenty years. However, if the property's useful life is less than twenty years, the taxpayer is permitted only a straight-line depreciation method.

The 1969 Tax Reform Act added a new section, 167 (k), to the Internal Revenue Code which provides a special depreciation method for expenditures on the rehabilitation of certain low-income public housing. The purpose of the new section is to encourage the improvement, remodeling, and restoration of existing slums and substandard housing.

Before the 1969 Act, all costs incurred for this purpose had to be capitalized and then depreciated over the entire remaining life of the building. Thus, if you made changes in a building with a twenty year remaining life, you would have to depreciate the costs over the entire twenty years.

Now, however, if he meets all the tests, the taxpayer is permitted to depreciate his rehabilitation expenditures under a straight-line method for five years, regardless of the building's remaining life span.

Eligibility Requirements

To be eligible for this method, the taxpayer must have incurred his rehabilitation expenditures after July 24, 1969, and before January 1, 1975. The improvements, of course, must have a useful life of over five years to be entitled to the special amortization.

What comes under the definition of "rehabilitation expenditures?" Neither new construction nor the enlargement of an existing building is covered. But as long as a foundation and the outer walls of an existing building are retained, any work done inside the building will qualify. Moreover, new facilities related to the existing buildings—such as garages, sidewalks, parking lots—will also qualify.

This is an elected provision, which means that the taxpayer has the choice of depreciating his costs over the full useful life of the building or of using the five-year method provided by the new section. If he chooses the latter, he must make his election in the first year on which he computes his depreciation using the five year method. However, a taxpayer is permitted to file an amended return to elect this five-year provision if such a filing takes place within the normal filing period for the following year's return. Thus, for a 1972 calendar year taxpayer, he would have to file his amended return by April 15, 1974.

How does he make the election? He attaches to his tax return an income statement with a description of the property, the expenditures he has incurred, and—most important—the income of the property's occupants. He needs a certification from each occupant showing what his adjusted income was for the preceding year. Adjusted income, in this case, is gross income less business expenses only.

There are minimum and maximum limits on the expenditures that are eligible for the five-year method. The aggregate unit cost cannot exceed a ceiling of $15,000. There is also a minimum of $3,000 that must be spent over a consecutive two-year period for eligibility.

This can be made clear through a simple example. Let us say that an investor's rehabilitation expenditures per unit are:

$$
\begin{array}{ll}
1972: & \$\ 1,000 \\
1973: & \$\ 1,700 \\
1974: & \$13,000
\end{array}
$$

In 1972 he is obviously not eligible for the five-year method since he is below the $3,000 minimum. In 1973 he does not quite make it—his total of $2,700 is still below the minimum. But in 1974 he qualifies with a total of $15,700. This means he can depreciate the maximum amount of $15,000 under the five-year method, and the remaining $700 under normal depreciation methods.

RECAPTURED EXCESS DEPRECIATION

For ordinary residential property, whether old or new, there is partial recapture. If the property is held for a year or less, the entire depreciation—accelerated or straight-line—is recaptured as ordinary income. If the property is sold within 100 months, that is, within a period of eight and one-third years, all of the excess depreciation over straight-line will be recaptured. However, if the property is held longer than eight and one-third years, then for each additional full month, one percent of the excess depreciation is not recaptured. This means that if residential property is held for 200 months—sixteen and two-thirds years—there will be no recapture at all.

How do these recapture provisions affect the five-year depreciation method for the rehabilitation of low-income housing? Here is an example:

Assume that a taxpayer makes a $10,000 rehabilitation improvement in low-income housing—an improvement that will normally have a ten-year useful life. But the taxpayer makes the five-year method election, then sells the property in the fourth year after having taken three years—$6,000—of the five-year amortization deductions. Since he held the property less than 100 months, all excess depreciation over straight line will be recaptured. Normal depreciation over a ten-year period would be $3,000. However, he has taken $6,000. The difference between the two—$3,000—will be recaptured as ordinary income.

The Rules for Qualified Property

There is one major exception to this—qualified housing projects. These include not only federal projects, but also state and local voluntary-assistance housing projects. For these projects, the pre-1969 Tax Reform Act rules apply. That is, if the property is held for one year or less, all of the depreciation, straight-line or accelerated, is recaptured. If the property is held from the twelfth month to the twentieth month, 100 percent of the excess depreciation over straight line is recaptured. Then, if the property is held longer than twenty months, one percent for each full month is not recaptured. Thus, if a qualified housing project is held for ten years, the taxpayer will suffer no depreciation recapture when he sells the property.

To qualify, the properties or projects must be constructed or acquired before January 1, 1975; the mortgage must be insured under FHA or similar state rules; and the owner's rate of return must be restricted.

TAX DEFERMENT THROUGH THE SALE OF THE PROPERTY

This tax benefit is contained in Section 1039, added to the Internal Revenue Code by the 1969 Tax Reform Act. Basically, it provides that if an owner of a federally qualified project sells it to a limited group—either the tenants or a managing company formed by them—he can elect to defer current taxes on his gain, *provided* he reinvests the sale proceeds in another qualified project within a specific replacement period. The purpose of this new section is to encourage owners to sell their projects to the occupants at the lower prices made possible by the deferral of taxes on the gain from the sale.

The philosophy of the section is similar to that of Section 1033 covering involuntary conversions, such as fires or similar unforeseen conditions. This section provides that if a taxpayer sells his property to the occupants and reinvests the proceeds in another federal project, and the sale proceeds are less than the cost of the replacement project, then no gain is realized on the first sale and there is a carry-over of "cost basis" from the old property to the new.

The maximum selling price of federal projects to the occupants is determined by three factors: the cash originally invested by the owner in the project, the outstanding mortgage liability on the project, and the taxes on a gain that the owner would realize if it were a taxable transaction. These three factors are added up to produce a maximum selling price, which must first be approved by HUD.

To be eligible for the tax deferral, the taxpayer must acquire the replacement project within a two-year period, beginning one year before the sale and ending one year after the sale. To cite an example, if a taxpayer in 1972 sells a project for $60,000 and makes a $10,000 gain, he must reinvest the $60,000 by the end of 1973 in order to get the tax deferral.

As with rehabilitation expenditures, Code Section 1039 is an elective provision. In some situations, a taxpayer may choose not to elect the new provision. For example, if he has losses for that year, he might want to offset them with the gain from the sale of the project.

Simultaneous Carry-Over

In addition to tax deferral on the gain, there is the additional benefit, under Section 1039, of a simultaneous deferral of the ordinary depreciation recapture element in Section 1250. If the sale proceeds exceed the replacement cost, part of the gain will be subjected to tax, and it may be taxed as ordinary income under Section 1250. On the other hand, if the replacement cost exceeds the sales proceeds, there is a complete deferral of not only the Section 1231 capital gain, but also the Section 1250 ordinary income. Moreover, with proper reinvestment, not only will the cost basis be carried over to the new property but the holding period for purposes of computing ordinary recapture income will be carried over as well.

Here is a brief example of how it would work. In this case, a project with a cost basis of $70,000 is sold for $130,000, or a $60,000 gain. Of the $130,000, $125,000—or less than the total amount realized on the sale—is reinvested in a qualified federal project. Perhaps $20,000 of the sale price of $130,000 is subject to Section 1250, but because $125,000 has been reinvested, only $5,000 is immediately taxable. That $5,000 will be taxed as ordinary income, but $15,000 of the 1250 element will be carried over into the replacement project. The longer the taxpayer holds the replacement property, the smaller the 1250 element will become—and eventually it might be completely wiped out.

These then, are the three basic tax benefits offered by investment in public housing today: accelerated depreciation on rehabilitation expenditures, a softer impact from recapture, and deferment of tax on the sale of qualified projects.

DISCUSSION

Question: Is the 6 percent return allowed by the FHA based on book value or property value?

Mr. Kerr: It's based on your investment. Normally, you would invest 10 percent in the project, since 90 percent is insured by the FHA. You are limited to a 6 percent return on your 10 percent investment.

Question: With hundreds of properties being abandoned in New York City, for example, how confident do you feel in an investment in low-cost housing which one would have to hold for sixteen and two-thirds years to completely avoid recapture of excess depreciation?

Mr. Kerr: I think public housing is a safe investment for two important reasons. You have the economic benefits you had before the 1969 Tax Reform Act—that is, the 1 percent subsidy. But you also have in addition the benefits of the new tax provisions permitting accelerated depreciation, the deferral of tax on gains, and the softer recapture impact.

Moreover, because of the FHA rules, this type of property cannot be milked of its resale value. You do not gain anything, for example, by cutting down on maintenance expenditures, because you are still limited to 6 percent return on your investment. So the more you spend on the project, the more valuable it will be at the end of 20 years, when you do not need FHA approval to refinance or resell it.

In my estimation, this combination of factors makes these projects valuable not only from a tax standpoint now, but from the standpoint of a good economic investment.

Question: When building Section 236 housing, which fees are initially deductible and which are not?

Mr. Kerr: Basically, the FHA costs, legal fees, and construction points. There is mixed opinion as to whether construction interests and construction points can be deducted immediately or during the construction period. Most of the tax practitioners that I know have taken the position that construction mortgage points and interest charges are deductible over the construction period, which might be eighteen months. Others believe, however, that construction points and interest charges must be capitalized and amortized over the entire life of the project.

My own personal belief is that they can be amortized over the construction period—that is a position I have taken over the twelve years that I have been practicing tax law.

Question: Does the FHA supervise the maintenance of the property?

Mr. Kerr: Yes, they do. They keep a close eye on the property to make sure that it is being managed properly. And if they decide that you are not managing the project competently, they can terminate your management contract and enter into a contract with another group.

Question: I have a question about the economic soundness of investing in low-income housing. In such housing the tenants may not take care of the property, with the result that repair expenses will be high. And in a less desirable neighborhood, there may also be a high rate of vandalism. Do these possiblities affect the soundness of the investment from an economic standpoint?

Mr. Kerr: My feeling is that the after-tax benefits that the investor receives are so high that they cover these risks. And whatever is left over after the management fee is paid and after the investor receives his 6 percent is placed in a reserve fund which is usually sufficient to handle the kinds of problems you mentioned.

COMMENTARY

As with all material on real estate investment, this chapter should be read while keeping in mind the general provisions of the 1969 Tax Reform Act that affect this form of tax shelter.

GUIDELINES ON LIMITED PARTNERSHIPS

In addition, the reader should pay particular attention to the IRS guidelines on limited partnerships—discussed in the question and answer section of Mr. Cohen's chapter. Mr. Kerr mentions that, in certain situations involving low rental and rehabilitation properties, profits are limited to 6 percent. In this case, the investor would find it wise to investigate the advantages of having a corporation as the general partner that would receive a management fee, pay salaries, and provide a pension trust. With this arrangement, it may be possible to take both the salaries and the pension fund off the top—to some extent, at least—before arriving at the allowable 6 percent profit. If so, the developer might be better off than if he had "a piece of the action" subject to heavy capital gains tax and depreciation recapture plus minimum tax. This is demonstrated by one recent arrangement in which the pension contribution matched the salary of the manager. Because the salary was protected by the maximum tax ceiling, while the matching contributions were untaxed, the aggregate tax of the management fee, plus pension contributions, ended up at a low 20 percent average. This compares with a possible 60 percent capital gains burden, plus minimum tax on accelerated depreciation and ordinary income tax not sheltered by the maximum ceiling upon depreciation recapture.

17

REAL ESTATE: WHAT ABOUT INVESTMENT TRUSTS?

Samuel J. Gorlitz

Although real estate investment trusts (REITs) do provide substantial tax benefits for the investor, it is undeniable that oil investment or direct investment in real estate can provide even more. Why then, are real estate investment trusts riding a wave of remarkable popularity that has surged steadily since this form of investment was made possible by Congress in 1960? Indeed, during the past decade, REITs have largely supplanted individual public syndica-

MR. GORLITZ IS PRESIDENT OF INVESTOR SERVICE MANAGEMENT, INC. AND SERVES AS INVESTMENT ADVISOR TO THE FEDERAL REALTY INVESTMENT TRUST.

tions in real estate. Obviously, real estate investment trusts must be doing something right. What are the reasons behind their success?

One factor is investor confidence. REITs are rapidly institutionalizing real estate investment by buying from individual entrepreneurs for public companies with managers subject to all the fiduciary standards expected of public companies.

Moreover, REITs combine the liquidity of the stock market with the growth potential and built-in stability of real property. The typical investor looks upon REITs as real estate versions of stock mutual funds, because they possess the same kind of diversification and liquidity that have made mutual funds such a powerful force in the securities business. In fact, many REITs have public offerings which stay open almost continuously, so that underwriters and selected dealers sell its new shares at the same time that trading is maintained in the Over-the-Counter market.

Real estate investment trusts offer definite advantages over the limited partnership arrangement that traditionally has been the most popular vehicle for real estate investment. The investor's shares in a trust are readily marketable, the trust can minimize risk by investing in a diverse assortment of properties, and no one investor must assume unlimited liability.

THE TAX ADVANTAGES

Although as a tax shelter the REIT may not be as strong as such higher-risk investments as oil, it is definitely superior to the corporation formed for real estate investment. The corporation is a taxable entity, while the trust is not, so long as it complies with the various rules of the Internal Revenue Code. Thus, in the manner of stock mutual funds, REITs provide for the pass-through of depreciation and other tax advantages directly to stockholders. The corporation, on the other hand, is subject to double taxation.

The basic tax shelter for the REIT investor consists of the deferral of his federal income taxes until he sells his shares—a deferral that is accomplished by treating cash dividends as return of capital. This, in turn, reduces the tax-basis of the investment, so that when the investor sells his shares he pays taxes on the gain—determined by subtracting the tax-basis from the sale proceeds—at long-term capital gains rates. However, no losses in excess of income resulting from depreciation or operations can be passed on to offset other income as can be done with other types of real estate investment.

A LOOK AT THE LEGAL REQUIREMENTS

In order to qualify for favored tax treatment, an REIT must meet the following requirements:

1. It must be a bona fide trust, managed by trustees, with at least 100 shareholders, and transferable shares.

2. The trust must hold property as a passive investment, not for sale to a customer.

3. It must distribute at least 90 percent of its ordinary income to its shareholders, and at least 75 percent of this income must be derived from rents, interest secured on mortgages, and gains from real property or other real estate investment trusts. Not more than 30 percent of its gross income can come from the sale of stocks or securities held for less than six months or from real estate held for less than four years.

4. The trust's properties must be managed by an independent contractor, since the trust itself cannot be in the business of actually managing real estate.

5. Real estate investment trusts are not allowed to derive income from rendering services. For example, a trust cannot operate washing machines and dryers in an apartment building, but it can lease the right to do so to a firm that will operate those machines.

THE THREE "HIDDEN ASSETS"

The potential investor who wishes to evaluate a particular real estate investment trust will find his task complicated by the way in which standard evaluations are made. Because REIT shares are sold and traded as securities rather than as real estate, evaluations of REITs is usually based entirely on the cash dividends being paid, and the market value of REIT stock is established by the expected percentage of yield. For example, Federal Realty Investment Trust had been at this writing selling at five dollars per share, at which price its then current cash dividend of forty-two cents per share amounted to a tax-sheltered yield of 8.5 percent. A rise in the stock price may usually be expected only with an increase in the cash dividend, so long as the percentage cash yield remains relatively constant as a price determinant. If interest rates drop, and investors anticipate a cash yield of 6 percent, a forty-two cents yield would dictate a seven dollar stock price. On the other hand, a rise in the expected cash yield to 10 percent would dictate a stock price of four dollars and twenty cents.

This simplistic approach to value may be valid for some of the newer mortgage trusts, since they are really short-term lenders whose entire income is from interest and fees. But the "cash yield" approach to value does not take into account three "hidden assets" of REITs whose portfolios include the ownership of real properties. What are these assets?

The First Hidden Asset

First, the leverage provided by mortgage loans. This leverage generally makes it possible to buy or build a shopping center, office building, or apartment house with a cash input of only one-third or less of the total value. For example, in its acquisition of Wildwood Shopping Center for $2 million, Federal Realty Investment Trust needed only $250,000 in cash, while an insurance company supplied the balance in a combination land sale, leaseback, and leasehold mortgage.

The Second Hidden Asset

The second hidden asset is the fact that mortgage payments include amortization, with the result that the trust's mortgage debt is being reduced continually at an increasing rate. Moreover, the pay-down has no immediate effect on cash flow, since most large commercial properties are serviced with constant monthly payments until they are entirely repaid—regardless of how drastically they may have already been reduced. As the interest portion of the constant payment is reduced, the portion applied to principal repayment increases, just as in a home mortgage.

To illustrate again from Federal Realty's experience, mortgages originally placed as long ago as 1965 on its properties totalled some $10 million. By 1971, those mortgages had been reduced by about $2 million. By 1976, they will be further reduced by another $2 million. Measured against Federal Realty's total equity cash input of about $5 million, this paydown of $2 million represents in itself a growth of over 40 percent in equity value, with another 40 percent coming in the next five years regardless of economic conditions. But this hidden asset has had no impact on the market value of Federal Realty stock, because the mortgages continue to demand servicing in monthly payments exactly equal to the original amount. How can this asset be evaluated by means of the "cash yield" approach when even appraisers find it difficult to put a current dollar figure on the future value of a mortgage debt being reduced at an increasing rate?

In the days before high mortgage interest rates, insurance companies would occasionally "recast" mortgages to spread out the repayment period, thereby reducing mortgage amortization payments and leaving more residual cash flow. But this makes sense only when current interest rates are roughly equal to the rate on the mortgage to be recast. There is nothing to be gained by recasting a 6 percent mortgage at the cost of increasing its rate to 9 or 10 percent —even if the result is to cut down the size of the monthly mortgage servicing burden.

The Third Hidden Asset

The final hidden asset of REITs stems from the fact that in computing book balue on financial statements, real properties are valued at cost. Investors have learned that book value results in a constantly decreasing valuation of real property—regardless of its economic value—as cost figures are reduced annually by depreciation allowances. The only alternative measure of value for the investor is actual cost, but in the present period of rapidly rising real estate values, even this type of valuation ignores increases in value over cost.

Federal Realty, for example, might be negotiating to sell one of its properties for twice its actual cost. When the sale is completed, an additional amount of cash would become available for investment. The resulting increased cash flow could sharply raise Federal Realty's cash dividends and hence the price of its stock. But that increased stock value must await the actual sale of the property and reinvestment of the profit in order to raise the cash dividend rate. The increased value of the property cannot be reflected anywhere in Federal Realty's financial statement until the sale is made. Until then, the only thing that affects the stock value is a change in the cash flow.

Thus, the potential investor who is comparing real estate investment trusts should not confine himself to looking at the liquidity, diversification, income stability, and tax-shelter advantages of each trust. He should also try to evaluate—as well as he can—the hidden assets: mortgage leverage, the debt reduction made possible by this leverage, and increased value of individual properties held by the trust.

DISCUSSION

Question: When properties are being exchanged for shares in a trust, can this be made tax free to the transferring parties?

Mr. Gorlitz: Properties owned by a corporation can in some cases be exchanged for trust shares in a tax-free transaction, and of course real estate investment trusts can merge without tax consequences. Where property is held by a large limited partnership, however, those shares are personal property rather than real property, and cannot be exchanged on a tax-free basis.

Question: Would you say, then, that the holder of a piece of property could form a corporation as a real estate investment trust and then merge?

Mr. Gorlitz: Yes, that can be done. But remember that in order to qualify, the real estate investment trust must have at least one hundred shareholders.

Question: It seems to me that if you have, for example, two syndicated properties with fifty shareholders each, they could form a trust. Of course, you would have to let a decent interval go by in order to avoid any serious question of step transaction. Does that sound feasible?

Mr. Gorlitz: Yes, it does. As a matter of fact, I know of several syndicates that are doing that. But the formation of any such entity requires careful consultation with tax attorneys to assure the desired result.

Question: Do the tax-shelter benefits flow through the investment trust to the shareholders?

Mr. Gorlitz: Yes, so long as the trust meets the various criteria I mentioned earlier. But if it fails to meet these qualifying criteria, then it will be taxed as a corporation and thus be subject to double taxation. The rules are not too difficult to live with, and I know of no REIT that has been disqualified.

COMMENTARY

Although real estate trusts are too new to be appraised with certainty, they would seem to provide diversification in real estate investment with an optimum of business and tax efficiency. As the author points out, real estate trusts do have one disadvantage over directly owned real estate: depreciation in excess of income cannot be used to offset other income.

Perhaps the investor can most effectively evaluate real estate trusts by checking the prices at which shares in them are being traded.

18

CATTLE: SHOULD IT BE FEEDING OR BREEDING?

Richard S. Bright

Someone once said that between the gleam in a bull's eye and a cut of prime beef at the Waldorf lies a vast and complicated business. To explain such a business in a brief chapter is not easy. However, certain basic aspects can be described to help an investor decide whether or not the cattle business is for him, and in what part of the business he should invest.

A potential investor in the cattle business has three basic options: he can put his money into cattle feeding, cattle breeding, and/or ranch land. Each investment has its own particular economic and tax advantages and disadvantages.

MR. BRIGHT IS EXECUTIVE VICE PRESIDENT OF OPPENHEIMER INDUSTRIES, INC.

CATTLE FEEDING

An investment in cattle feeding accomplishes one major purpose: it defers income from one year to the next. Thus, it is useful for an investor who has made a large income in one year and wants to defer it to reduce the tax bite.

Cattle feeding investments—as is true of all forms of agricultural investment—have phenomenal leverage. Indeed, the investor can invest in the feeder business for as little as 5 percent down, provided he agrees to prepay the feedlot operator a portion of the maintenance or feed bill and the interest on a 95 percent nonrecourse mortgage.

How does the feeding business work? In simplified form, it goes like this: steer calves from commercial breeder herds are weighed when they reach the feedlot—at this point, they weigh approximately 600 pounds. After being fed for a period of four to six months, they grow to approximately 1,000 pounds. They are then sold to a packinghouse, where they are slaughtered for beef.

The risks involved in the feeder business are great, although not as much so as in the past. Until 1967, the feedlot operator was at the mercy of meat packinghouses—he had to take the packer's offer or move his cattle from the pens, which usually cost him more than selling at the packer's price.

Using The Stop-Loss

Now that cattle are traded on the futures market, the investor can hedge. With regard to hedging live cattle, after adjusting for quality and location of feeder animals, and determining the estimated "end product" cost or breakeven, one can utilize the Futures Commodity contract, provided the price for the projected marketing period is at a trading level agreeable to the cattle owner.

The mechanics include simply placing a sell order through brokers for contracts—each contract is equivalent to 40,000 pounds of live cattle, or approximately 40 cattle—sufficient to cover the number of animals intended to be hedged. When the cattle are ready for sale, the short position is offset by a contract purchase order, and the cattle are sold in location, rather than physically delivered to fulfill specifications of the contract.

Margin requirements are an initial $600 per contract which must be maintained at $400 at all times—in case the market moves during the contract term to the detriment of the short position. Approximately $1 per head is the brokerage cost for each round turn transaction, that is, an executed sell-and-buy order.

On the other hand, if an individual is in the commodities business and knows the futures market, he might be better off taking all the risk, all the profit, and all the losses. A word of caution, however: he should be careful not to hedge himself a loss, since he runs the danger of having the economic motive for his investment questioned by the IRS.

How does an investor actually invest in the feeder business? After purchasing the feeder cattle, he makes a weight-gain contract with the feed-lot operator which obligates him to pay the operator for the weight that the cattle have gained after 150 days. When the cattle are sold at the end of the feeding cycle, the proceeds the investor receives are entirely ordinary income. Since these are steered (castrated) animals, there is no way they can breed, so they will never qualify for capital gain. In essence, then, investment in feeder cattle merely shifts ordinary income from one year to the next.

CATTLE BREEDING

The major advantage of investing in cattle breeding is the tremendous flexibility it provides for the investor in adjusting his tax deductions to suit his requirements. Before describing how this can be done, however, a brief rundown on the basics of cattle breeding might be useful.

The investor will usually put his money into a commercial breeding herd—such herds constitute 99 percent of the breeding herds in the U.S., with the remaining one percent composed of registered herds. Although the female stock in a commercial breeding herd are pedigreed thoroughbreds, they are not registered. The bulls with which they breed are registered, however, and are intended to upgrade the female stock. The most common breed in a commercial herd is the Hereford, with Angus second. Although other breeds—such as Charolais, Devon, Brangus—have their attributes, Hereford is probably the best all-around range animal for breeding purposes.

When calves are born, the males are usually steered and subsequently sold to a feed-lot operator. The females are held as replacements in the herd. As commercial breeding herds usually produce an 80 to 85 percent calf crop every year, 15 to 20 percent of the herd will be culled to get rid of the non-reproducing females.

Negotiating a Deal

Where does the investor come into this picture? He makes a deal with a rancher similar to that he might make with a feed-lot operator. Again, there is high leverage—he can borrow up to 90 percent on a non-recourse basis. Here too, he must agree to pay interest in advance as well as prepay a portion of the feed bill. Similarly, the cattle are weighed at the beginning of the contract year— usually the fall —and then a year later, when the rancher is paid for the weight they gain.

When a female begins to reproduce, however, the goal is not weight-gain but calving. Therefore one pays the rancher for the weight of the calf crop he produces, rather than for the maintenance of the cow. In fact, if the cow does not produce a calf, the investor pays the rancher nothing for that cow.

At the end of the year, when the calf crop has been produced, the investor has the options that provide the previously-mentioned flexibility for tax purposes. He can sell half of his calf crop, all of it, or none of it, depending on what he wants to achieve. This enables him to adjust his tax deductions to meet his specific requirements.

Here is an example: assume that an investor spends $10,000 to buy and maintain 100 cows in a commercial herd. In that year, he gets a write off of from $12,000 to $13,000. The following year, these cows deliver 85 calves. If he keeps the entire crop, he will have a deduction of around $20,000 to $25,000, and an equivalent cash contribution. If he keeps half of his crop, he will have half the deduction. And he can adjust this in any way that he wants, by selling one-third of his crop, two-thirds, or whatever number he prefers.

Qualifying for Capital Gains

Keep in mind, however, that when he sells these calves, he does not qualify for capital gains—only ordinary income. To qualify for capital gains, he must hold his stock for at least two years and establish his intention as a breeder. It requires at least 2½ years for a calf to prove itself as a breeder. Therefore the investor who holds calves for two years and a day and asks for capital gains treatment is going to leave his motives open to question. He is better off taking one of two courses: selling his calves after six months for ordinary income, or putting them back in the herd, holding them for at least three years, and selling them for capital gains.

Culls, however—that is, animals not fit for breeding—can be sold for capital gains after one year.

What protection does the investor have if a cow dies? One source of protection is a Lloyds of London insurance policy. However, since this is 3 percent deductible with a 3 percent premium, he must lose over 6 percent of his herd before the policy pays off. Preferable is an agreement with the rancher that he will give him guarantee against losses over 3 percent. If the investor starts with 100 cows and only 90 show up at the scales a year later, the rancher must replace seven of the missing cows. Since the national death rate in commercial breeding herds averages 3 percent, he is covered for abnormal losses.

Aside from its tax advantages, how profitable is cattle breeding? Although commercial breeding was for many years a money losing proposition, it has recently turned around. The chances are the investor can now sell his calf for more than it cost him to raise it.

When to Get Out

Another advantage of investing in commercial breeding herds is the ease with which one can get out of the business if he wishes. He can sell his animals any day of the week. However, the best times to get out of the breeding business—or into it, for that matter—are in the fall, when the cattle are rounded up from summer grazing pastures, or the spring, before the cattle are put out to summer ranges. Once they are on the summer ranges, it is difficult to round them up and separate the individual's cattle from the herd.

Dealing directly with a rancher is not the only way in which one can invest in a commercial breeding herd. An alternative is to deal with a firm specializing in the management of cattle investment programs. Despite this indirect approach, each investor has his own brand, registered in the state in which his cattle are located. Thus, if an investor bought 100 head of cattle, he might have 30 in Colorado, 30 in Florida, 30 in Kansas, and 10 in Montana.

RANCH LAND

Investing in grazing land is still another way in which an investor can get into the cattle business. Like feeder cattle and breeding herds, ranch land has tremendous leverage—but less flexibility than either of the other two.

Typically, an investor might buy half of a 50,000-acre ranch from an owner who wants to get some capital out of his land. The investor would put up 5 percent equity, the remainder being in the form of a mortgage. The rancher would then lease back the half that he sold and continue to operate the ranch.

The investor then improves the ranch: he puts down some fertilizer, clears some brush, puts up some fencing. Thus, the rancher knows that if his co-owner defaults on the mortgage, he will still get back a better ranch than he started with. Moreover, the investor has put in a substantial amount in deductible maintenance and improvement costs.

Fencing—an important, expensive asset on a ranch—can be

depreciated over ten years, although five years is generally acceptable if the fencing is not new. A large part of a dollar investment can be recouped with this depreciation. Over a period of years, the investor can pay his loan, improve the ranch, and eventually sell it for a capital gain.

However, anyone investing in ranch land must be prepared to sacrifice a great deal of flexibility. One simply cannot dispose of 25,000 acres of grazing land as easily as he can dispose of a 100 head of cattle. This means that an investor should be ready to stick with this grazing land for a period of years.

THE NEW TAX LAWS AND THE CATTLE BUSINESS

The effect of the Tax Reform Act of 1969 will be slight on the average investor who puts $30,000 to $40,000 into the cattle business. In the case of the investor who puts in $1,000,000, it is a different story. The salient changes are these:

1. Excess deductions account.

Under this change, an investor is allowed to take as big a deduction as he pleases in the cattle business, providing he stays within the limits of the hobby law. But when he disposes of his assets, anything in excess of $25,000 a year will be taxed at ordinary rates. For example, let us assume that the investor has been taking deductions of $100,000 a year. When he sells, $75,000 of that would be taxed at ordinary rates and $25,000 would be capital gains.

2. Recapture of depreciation.

Before 1969, livestock was excluded from depreciation recapture. It is now included.

3. Hobby losses.

The investor must now show a profit for two out of five years. Also, the holding period to qualify for capital gains has been extended to one year after the animal has been bred. Thus, he must prove himself a breeder by actually breeding the animal. This means that he would have to hold on to a calf crop for at least two to two and one-half years. On the other hand, if he bought a herd of cows and sold it, he would have to wait two years to qualify for capital gains.

COMMENTARY

STOP-LOSS PROVISIONS

In discussing stop-loss provisions, Mr. Bright failed to mention the advantages of a limited partnership which would allocate losses under IRC-704 to the investor up to the stop-loss level and then to the general partner. This conversely should give the general partner a larger share of the gains above a certain level, keeping in mind the ground rules on limited partnership discussed at the end of the chapter by Mr. Cohen.

DEDUCTIBILITY OF LOSS

In considering deductibility of loss, the investor should not overlook the excess deduction account provisions of Section IRC-1251 and the hobby loss provisions in IRC-183.

RECAPTURE OF DEPRECIATION

The investor should also remember that on the sale of cattle originally purchased, there is a complete recaptutre of all depreciation under IRC-1245, not just the excess depreciation as in the case of real property. This does not apply, however, to the sale of calves or grown steers bred by the investor rather than purchased, since in that case there is no basis for depreciation.

CAPITAL GAIN TREATMENT

Cattle and horses must be held for twenty-four months from the date of acquisition to qualify for long-term capital gain treatment.

EXCESS DEDUCTIONS ACCOUNT

It is possible to avoid the burden of the excess deductions account by giving away the appreciated livestock in years when the gift in any one year is not more than 25 percent of the aggregate potential gain before the commencement of the gifts. Thus, the Excess Deductions Account load can be avoided by giving away no more than 25 percent of the gain each year for four years. In addition to avoiding the EDA by distributing the gifts over a period of years, the investor can avoid inclusion of the cattle in his taxable estate.

19

CATTLE: NEW BREED IN THE PASTURE

Alexander S. Bowers

Until recently, the taxpayer who decided to invest in cattle as a tax shelter had little choice but to put his money into either Hereford or Angus cattle—the two most popular breeds in the United States. But in the past few years, a new breed has appeared in the pasture: the Charolais. In many ways this new breed is definitely superior to both Hereford and Angus.

In the first place, Charolais cattle are anywhere from 25 to 100 pounds heavier than other breeds at weaning time—which is the point when they are sold to feedlots. Since they are sold by the pound, they bring in more dollars.

MR. BOWERS IS PRESIDENT AND A DIRECTOR OF THE STEWART CAPITAL CORPORATION.

Charolais cattle have a faster rate of weight gain than other breeds. They put on more weight per day of age from calfhood to maturity. Hardy, adaptable, and prolific, they produce healthy, fast-gaining calves in a wide range of growing conditions. Pink eye and cancer eye are practically unknown in Charolais. They are ideal for crossbreeding for hybrid beef production.

What is the Charolais breed? It is a purebred developed in France, where more than 200 years of selection have gone into making more efficient beef production. The breed is acclaimed around the world as a superb butcher's beef. It has higher carcass cutouts of boneless trimmed retail cuts. The meat is tender, it is leaner, and it does not have as much fat cover as the English breeds. The Charolais averages greater rib eye area and more length of loin in the carcass. This means more dollars to the rancher, to the feeder, and to the butcher.

Our firm, Stewart Capital Corporation, owns an interest in Stewart-Wade Farms, one of the leading purebred Charolais operations in the country. We have a show herd which we take on the road each year. In 1969, we won 62 percent of the classes that we entered.

TAX DISADVANTAGES OF PUREBRED CATTLE

The preceding facts have not been cited to support the virtues of a purebred cattle operation as a tax-shelter investment. Such an operation is far too risky for the tax-shelter investor. There are several reasons for this high risk:

Too much depends on chance. For example, weather plays a large role. If we hold a sale of purebred cattle and it turns out to be a rainy day, our cattle will sell for a lot less than if it is a nice sunny day. Most of the people who come to ranches such as ours to buy purebred cattle are not really in the purebred cattle business. They are retired people with nice farms that they like to stock with purebred cattle. If it is a rainy, nasty day, they won't bother to come to the sale.

There are very few capable purebred breeders in the United States. A purebred cattle operation requires primarily a geneticist, someone who really knows the genetics of breeding, mating cows with certain bulls, and bringing out the best characteristics.

Most purebred deals are partnerships, and they are very difficult to dissolve.

The purebred ventures offered today sell cattle at highly inflated prices. In their prospectuses, they project the sale of large quantities of offspring at sufficiently high prices to justify the inflated charges. But it does not work that way. If one is selling ten head of extremely good cattle, he might get good prices for them. However, if he is selling 10,000 head of purebreds a year, the money is simply not there. That volume will not bring the kinds of prices that are projected in most of these deals.

TAX ADVANTAGES OF COMMERCIAL RANGE CATTLE

There *is* money to be made in the cattle business. It is made at the bottom, in commercial range cattle that sell for a little more than their weight as slaughter animals.

And yet even this business is essentially uneconomic. A straight commercial cow-calf operation produces the steer calves that go to the feedlots and the heifers used as replacements in the large breeding herds all across the country. But a cow has an 85 percent chance of producing one calf per year—and it is a calf worth less than the mother.

For this reason, Congress, aware of both the need for commercial beef operations and of its poor economics, established certain tax advantages for the investor. However, the tax advantages alone still do not make the business sufficiently economic. So how does one make money raising cattle?

THE CROSSBREEDING APPROACH

At Stewart-Wade, we think the answer lies in producing a calf that is worth more than its mother. For some years, we have been crossbreeding commercial cows with purebred Charolais bulls and experimenting with various breeds. We have come up with some very effective combinations which produce calves that, when weaned, weigh almost as much as their mothers. Such calves are almost ready to go to market, and we are convinced that eventually we can wean them, then send them straight to market without any grass feeding. It will take years to accomplish this, but it can be done.

As a result of its successful experimentation, Stewart-Wade currently manages over 10,000 head of cattle on 40,000 acres of owned or leased land. We have one of the largest purebred Charolais bull herds in the world, numbering over 400.

THE CHAROLAIS CREDENTIALS

There is ample data to show that Charolais cattle are superior to other breeds. Take carcass data, for example

Figure 1. Charolais leads all the way, with larger rib eye, less fat cover, higher carcass weight per day of age, higher percentage of salable beef.

Figure 2 compares the amount of feed required to put 100 pounds of gain on a Charolais-sired steer or a British breedsired steer. It can easily be seen that the Charolais is a more efficient animal in that it puts on the same amount of weight with less feed.

Figure 3 shows that $87 more retail meat is available from the Charolais carcass than from a Hereford carcass.

Figure 4 is a tenderness score based on the number of pounds of pressure required to cut through the core of the meat. On an Angus, 15.8 pounds are required, on a Hereford 16.4 pounds, on a Charolais 15.5 pounds. The results show that Charolais beef is more tender than that of other breeds.

Fig. 1

CARCASS DATA — 1968 NATIONAL BEEF SHOW

Breed Averages and Comparisons

	No. Cattle	DIVISION II (Performance Tested Individuals)				DIVISION III (Progeny Pens of Five)			
		Ribeye Area Sq. In. Avg.	Fat Cover Inches Avg.	Carcass Wt. Per Day of Age Avg.	% Total Salable Meat Avg.	Ribeye Area Sq. In. Avg.	Fat Cover Inches Avg.	Carcass Wt. Per Day of Age Avg.	% Total Salable Meat Avg.
Charolais	9	13.03	0.31	1.60	67.47	12.2	0.34	1.50	66.12
Charolais Crossbreds	37	12.85	0.38	1.60	66.25	12.51	0.43	1.55	66.09
Angus	11	11.24	0.610	1.42	63.85	10.8	0.41	1.47	64.38
Herefords	16	11.19	0.56	1.42	64.96	10.26	0.52	1.33	64.61
Other Breeds	6	11.55	0.40	1.31	65.64	—	—	—	—
Crossbreds (other than Charolais)	10	10.54	0.40	1.25	65.64	10.40	0.51	1.05	64.96
All Charolais, Charolais-Crosses	46	12.88	0.37	1.60	66.49	12.48	0.42	1.54	66.09
All Other Cattle	43	11.10	0.51	1.36	64.96	10.39	0.50	1.30	64.63

Fig. 2

Efficiency of gains of crossbred calves from Charolais sires as compared to crossbred calves from British sires.	Feed per 100 pounds gain	
	Charolais sires	British sires
England (Milk Market Board)	9.5–21.5% more efficient	——
Florida (Report No. 1)	823	890
Florida (Report No. 2)	1057	1106
Missouri (heifers only)	808	821
Kansas*	722	1156
Average	853	993

Efficiency of gains of crossbred calves from Charolais sires as compared to purebred British calves.	Feed per 100 pounds gain	
	Charolais sires	Pure British
Florida	1057	1073
Missouri (heifers only)	808	817
Ohio	777	840
Kansas*	794	1102
Average	837	958

*Fed a similar ration but the two groups were fed at different locations.

Fig. 3

CHAROLAIS CARCASS EVALUATION DEMONSTRATION
Ohio Valley Charolais Association Field Day
June 12, 1965—Supervised by Ohio State University

Birth dates April 10, 1964		Hereford 1	1/2% Charolais & Hereford 2	3/4% Charolais & Hereford 3
Slaughter Weight		955.	1175.	1175.
Carcass Weight		554.	690.	716.
Dressing Percentage		58.01	58.72	60.94
Carcass Wt./day age		1.31	1.62	1.74
Rib Eye Area Sq. in.		10.8	13.9	14.3
Rib Eye/100 lb. Carcass		1.95	2.01	2.00
Fat Thickness		.70	.50	.25
Carcass Grade		Choice	Choice	Choice
Weight of Left Side		281	353	372

Retail Cuts*	Price**	Wt.	Value	Wt.	Value	Wt.	Value
Chuck Roasts	.73	35.5	25.91	51.5	37.59	51.7	37.74
Standing Rib Roasts	1.09	11.5	12.53	15.3	16.68	14.5	15.81
Rib Steaks	1.25	6.3	7.88	8.7	10.87	9.3	11.62
Short Ribs	.45	9.7	4.36	10.0	4.50	11.7	5.26
Boneless Brisket	.59	6.9	4.07	10.7	6.31	10.2	6.02
Boneless Shank	.59	7.1	4.18	8.0	4.72	9.4	5.55
Full Round Steak	1.19	26.6	31.65	34.9	41.53	36.8	43.79
Steaks for Cubing	1.39	7.9	10.98	13.0	18.07	12.4	17.24
Boneless Rump Roast	1.35	6.0	8.10	10.7	14.45	12.8	17.28
Sirloin Steak	1.35	13.2	17.82	13.3	17.95	19.5	26.32
Sirloin Tip Roast	1.39	3.3	4.59	4.9	6.81	4.3	5.98
Porterhouse, T-Bone Club Steaks	1.55	13.0	20.15	17.3	26.81	19.25	29.83
Flank Steak	1.23	1.0	1.23	1.8	2.21	1.9	2.34
Kidney	.35	0.8	0.28	0.9	0.32	1.0	0.35
Lean Trimmings	.59	47.9	28.26	69.67	41.10	69.40	40.94
Total Fat Trim	.045	62.35	2.81	50.65	2.28	52.20	2.35
Total Bone Removed	.015	21.65	0.32	31.65	0.47	36.05	0.54
TOTAL VALUE OF SIDE			$185.12		$252.67		$268.96
VALUE/100 carcass wt.			$ 65.88		$ 71.58		$ 72.30
TOTAL SALABLE BEEF CUTS			$196.70 70%		$270.67 76.67%		$284.15 76.38%

*Method of cutting designed for present a variety of normal retail cuts. No attempt has been made to merchandise the beef for its highest value. Cutting data obtained from left side.

**Retail prices taken from those used at local supermarket on day of cutting.

Fig. 4

Here is how the steer and heifer carcasses from 72 Angus cows over a 3 year period did:

Breed of bull bred to:

	Angus	Hereford	Charolais
Slaughter weight (lbs.)	835	884	914
Carcass weight (lbs.)	539	570	565
Carcass grade (pts.)	11.8	11.4	11.5
Loin eye area (sq. in.)	11.0	10.8	12.3
Fat thickness (inches)	.64	.71	.39
% Fat	23.8	24.2	18.7
% Bone	11.9	12.2	13.0
% Retail Yield*	64.2	63.4	67.8
Marbling score (pts.)	6.95	6.43	6.56
Pounds required to cut thru core of meat	15.8	16.4	15.5

*This is based on % of carcass weight rather than live weight.

Here is how all steer and heifer progeny from the 72 Hereford cows did in carcass in 3 years.

Breed of bull bred to:

	Hereford	Angus	Charolais
Slaughter weight (lbs.)	875	847	951
Carcass weight (lbs.)	527	553	599
Carcass grade (pts.)	10.4	11.1	11.0
Loin eye area (sq. in.)	10.2	10.6	12.0
Fat thickness (inches)	.61	.68	.42
% Fat	21.7	23.1	19.2
% Bone	13.1	12.4	13.4
% Retail Yield	65.0	64.5	67.3
Marbling score (pts.)	5.53	6.14	5.43
Pounds required to cut thru core of meat	16.7	17.0	16.6

FLEXIBILITY FOR THE INVESTOR

How does the investor interested in tax shelter fit into the Stewart-Wade program? At a herd owner's request, we purchase quality Florida range cattle at cost. We crossbreed the cows with our purebred Charolais bulls and wean heavier than average calves. As a result, our herd owners' calves sell for more than other breeds, and each successive generation sells for more than the one before. Thus, our herd owners are creating a valuable capital asset by using income dollars. The longer they are in the program, the more profitable their investment will be. But they can get out of it at anytime, should their situation change.

It is also a highly flexible program, because the investor can hold varying numbers of calves from year to year. One year he can hold all of his female calves to enlarge his herd, and the next year, if he needs less deduction, he simply sells off some of his calves.

Another technique the tax-shelter investor can use is to place steers on feedlots. The primary usefulness of feeding programs is to defer taxable income from one year to the next. But they have other uses, too.

For example, assume that an individual has an unusually high income in one year, which he does not expect to have in future years. He decides that a cattle breeding program is the investment that he should make. He then must ask himself where he will get the funds in future years to maintain his breeding herd.

One answer would be to take enough money to maintain his breeding herd for, say, the next four years and put it in feeder cattle. He would then have a deduction equal to his original investment in the breeding herd, plus all of the cattle he put on feed.

The following year, he would take one quarter of his steers off the feedlot and sell them. The proceeds would go to maintain his breeding herd, and the deduction should equal the income resulting from the sale of the feeders. Each succeeding year would reduce his number of cattle on feed in order to maintain his breeding herd. By the fourth or fifth year, the breeding herd should be self-sustaining.

Feeder cattle can also be utilized in this way for other types of investments. If, for example, the investor has a real estate development on which he will have to do more developing next year, but he wants to fund it this year and get the deduction, he can put that money in feeder cattle. If he has drilled an oil well and knows he will have to complete it next year, but wants the deduction this year, he can roll that money over into the next year using feeder cattle. The deduction for completing the oil well in the second year will offset the income from the feeder cattle.

DISCUSSION

(The participants in the following discussion included Mr. Bowers and Mr. Richard Bright of Oppenheimer Industries.)

Question: What is the cost of a young Charolais bull?

Mr. Bowers: That is like asking how much a car costs. One can buy a Charolais bull from $200 or $300 up to $100,000. It would depend on the quality he is looking for. Our average bull cost is around $1,500. Pretty good Charolais range bulls can be bought for $750.

Question: Do you ever consider managing a herd on the investor's own ranch?

Mr. Bowers: Yes, if he has a big enough operation so that we can manage it efficiently and economically. It would have to be in the area where our management is currently located, or it would have to be large enough to support hiring management for that area.

Question: Would you care to comment on that, Mr. Bright?

Mr. Bright: We will manage a ranch if it can sustain 800 head or more. In other words, that is where it becomes economical for us to go in. We manage about 100 ranches right now.

Question: Do you identify the individual cattle by registered number?

Mr. Bowers: Yes. The cows are all mortgaged, so that they have to be branded, and we get warehouse receipts on all the cows. If a herd owner has 100 cows on one of our ranches in Florida, they have their brand numbers on them. It's an (S—W) and then a number.

Question: I have a question for Mr. Bright. If Charolais cattle have all the advantages that Mr. Bowers claims for them, why is Oppenheimer Industries not switching to Charolais just as fast as they can?

Mr. Bright: We have a different philosophy on what our clients want. Our clients are not in this business basically to make money. True, they do want to make some profit, but they could make more money in a day being a doctor or a stock broker than they will in the cattle business in a week. For this reason, we have stressed the ability to get in and out of the cattle business easily. So naturally we picked the breed that is the most popular and the most marketable. If in twenty years Charolais becomes a more popular breed that is more marketable, then we certainly will get into it.

I would say 90 percent of our herds are Herefords. The reason is that probably 90 percent of the cattle in this country are Herefords. So they are easier to buy and easier to sell.

Also, we like uniformity. Our typical client is unsophisticated in the technical aspects of the cattle business. When he visits his cattle, he wants to see some pretty cows. When first generation crossbreds are developed, it is only natural that one sees specks of black and white and so on. In Florida we started to cross Hereford with Brahma and we came up with a Braford. The Braford is a relatively good animal from a technical point of view, but it is the ugliest looking thing you have ever seen, and our clients were dismayed when they saw these animals. So, we crossed the Brahma with the Angus and they came out all black. Our client did not see speckles here and there, and he was happier.

Question: Anything to add to that, Mr. Bowers?

Mr. Bowers: We are not in love with the way cattle look. If we find one that performs better, we will switch to that. That is one of the reasons we experiment with so many different breeds.

Question: How will the 1969 Tax Reform Act affect cattle investment as a tax shelter?

Mr. Bowers: I think that if an investment is moderate there are still many tax advantages left. Fortunately, Congress has realized the necessity for some sort of subsidy to the beef industry.

More specifically, if the EDA is avoided by creating losses of only $25,000 per year or under, there is considerable benefit left. One can still convert ordinary income to capital gains. Although there is some recapture on depreciation when purchased animals are sold, the investor has the use of this money for a number of years. He writes it off in the beginning and then, when he sells these animals, he will have to report some ordinary income which formerly was capital gains. But it is just a moderate change.

Mr. Bright: May I inject this point. In commercial herds, such as those in which we are dealing, depreciation is a smaller part of the deduction than maintenance and interest costs. Depreciation is related to the cash dollar that is put in and is a small part of the total deduction.

When one gets into prize registered herds, which we do not advise, it becomes a different ball game. Then the investor's depreciation is a larger part of his tax deduction and, therefore, he has a recapture problem.

In commercial herds also, if he stays in the program for an extended period of time, by the time he decides to liquidate his herd he will have sold his originally purchased animals—the only ones he can depreciate—as culls. Since, in most cases, he will get less for these culls than what he paid for them, depreciation recapture will not actually affect his program.

Question: What about the new "hobby loss" section in the Code?

Mr. Bright: One should, of course, show a profit in two out of five years. If he does take losses for five years running, the onus is on him to prove to the IRS that he is in this for the intention of making a profit.

To show a profit, one can first sell his calves. Then if he still does not have enough income to generate a profit, he can withhold some of his maintenance for that year.

Mr. Bright: There has been a hobby loss provision in the tax law for about fifteen years, and in 1969 they just changed it around a bit. I think that even if the investor does not take this profit two years out of five or two years out of seven, it will be sufficient for him to prove that the sale of his animals would create a profit at that point in time. In my opinion, the hobby loss provision will be a rarely-used device.

A famous case is the Elsworth case in Hartford. The investor took $50,000 a year for four years, and the fifth year he brought his losses down to $48,000, just so that he would not be $50,000 or above. He won the case. So, it is still a grey area.

Question: If an investor goes to you for advice about purchasing a ranch and starting his own cattle operation, can you give him some assurance that the IRS will accept this as a trade or business?

Mr. Bright: If he buys a ranch in the middle of Aspen, Colorado, builds himself a $100,000 house and has five head of cattle on his land, we would not even get involved in it. However, if he says to us, I would like to buy a ranch that will sustain 500 head with the potential capacity for 800 head, we certainly would get involved in it and there is no question in my mind that he could prove that he did go into the cattle business for trade or business.

COMMENTARY

There is little doubt that Charolais cattle deserve serious consideration from the investor looking for a tax shelter in this area. This is a superb breed. It is important, however, that he be mindful of the tax aspects of cattle investment discussed in Mr. Bright's chapter and its following comments.

20

FARM LAND: A FERTILE FIELD FOR INVESTORS

Herbert G. E. Fick

To say that agriculture is a dynamic industry would perhaps seem an overstatement in view of the dizzying technological achievements in so many other areas of American enterprise.

And yet, despite our dwindling farm population, farming remains the nation's biggest business and its biggest buyer and supplier.

Behind this seeming contradiction is the dramatic increase in farm productivity brought about by the development of modern agricultural methods. We are now able to feed and clothe our entire population with only about 5 percent of our total workforce in farm

MR. FICK IS VICE-CHAIRMAN, BOARD OF DIRECTORS AND DIRECTOR, INTERNATIONAL SERVICES OF DOANE AGRICULTURAL SERVICE, INC.

occupations. In 1950, farms used less than 3 million tons of plant nutrients—in 1970 they used nearly 14.8 million. In 1950, each farm worker supplied 15 persons with food—in 1970, each farm worker supplied 45 persons.

Our farms have grown bigger, more specialized. Computerized records and accounts are common in large farm operations. Farms have more efficient machinery, more effective fertilizer, more effective chemical controls, and improved hybrid seeds. In just a few years, they have gone from two-row equipment to twelve-row equipment. They have moved from the old two-bottom tractor plow to the eight-bottom plow, enabling one man to do the work that formerly took four.

Just a few years ago, a yield of 100 bushels of corn per acre was considered outstanding. Now, yields are sometimes hitting 250 bushels per acre, and the time is not too far off when even this figure will be doubled.

ECONOMIC ADVANTAGES OF LAND INVESTMENT

These striking developments in agriculture are of great significance to the investor who is looking for a tax shelter that will be a sound economic investment as well. As the land is able to produce more, it becomes worth more and thus becomes a better investment. This, coupled with the increased demand for agricultural land for all types of urban development—highways, reservoirs, expanding metropolitan areas, recreational sites—creates a strong market for land.

Naturally, there is no way to increase our supply of land— it is fixed. Yet, by the year 2000, our population will have increased by 100 million people, four-fifths of whom will live in cities. At the present city density ratio of 3,100 people per square mile, another 80 million in city population would create a continuous city eight miles wide, running from the Atlantic coast to the Pacific.

With all of these factors working together, the appreciation potential of farm land is great—assuming, of course, that in the long run the general economy does not decline. Historically, the location value of agricultural land has always increased. This cannot be said of urban investments. Just to cite one example, an investor might buy some urban property and twenty years later find that the neighborhood has deteriorated to the point where he not only has paper depreciation but actual physical and economic depreciation—which is not at all what he had in mind when he made his original investment.

No Slump in Land Prices

But the price trend of agricultural land is almost constantly upward. According to a recent U.S. Agricultural Department survey, the national average increase in land prices was 4.0 percent for the twelve months ending March 1, 1970, the smallest rate advance in 7 years. Since 1933, land prices have almost continuously climbed, with a small decline during only three of those years. Figure 1 reflects the average value of land and buildings per acre as of March 1, from 1950 to 1968. In 1950, it was something under $70 an acre; by 1968 the price had increased to $180, and by 1970 to about $193 per acre.

This period has seen increases in the cost of farm production, but not corresponding increases in farm product prices, leading some economists to conclude that land prices were in danger of imminent decline. However, advances in technology and the increased demand for land has kept land prices moving upward, with no indications that the trend will be reversed.

Other economists have suggested that farm land prices are too high in relation to the rate of return on the land. To rebut this opinion, Professor L.H. Simeral of the University of Illinois recently made the following observations:

It is said that farm land is too high because the average rate of return is less than the interest rate on farm mortgages. So we find people saying that farm land would not pay for itself at these prices.

But why should farm land pay for itself when the buyer borrows to buy it? We do not expect to be able to borrow money to buy a bond and have the interest pay for the bond, nor do we expect to borrow from the bank to buy corporation stock and wait for

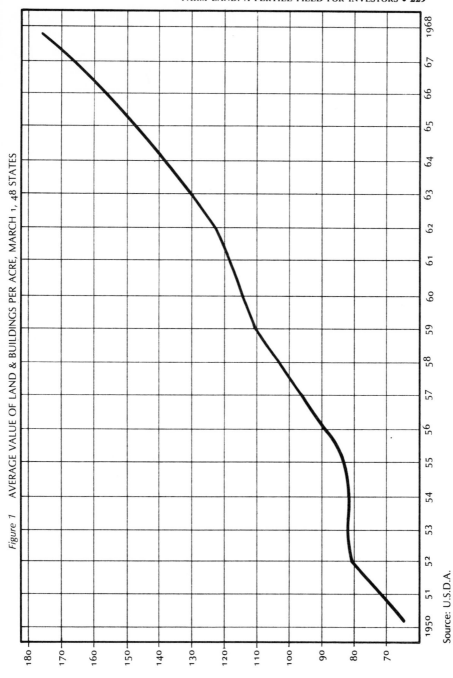

Figure 1   AVERAGE VALUE OF LAND & BUILDINGS PER ACRE, MARCH 1, 48 STATES

Source: U.S.D.A.

the dividend to pay for the interest and principal of the bank loan.

Many bonds now yield 5 to 6 percent. This is more than most farm land will make at present prices. But the people who buy farm land are not fools. They have good reason to expect that at least half of the return from the bonds will be lost through inflation. That brings the real return on bonds down to or below the return on land.

Dividends on corporate stock may range from zero to 5 percent, but many return between 3 and 4 percent. Well-managed land does equally well or better.

FIGURING THE RETURN ON LAND

It is impossible, of course, to guarantee that a farm-land investment will give the investor a certain return—earnings on farm land vary greatly. One of the many factors involved is the productivity of the land itself. Figure 2 gives a comprehensive picture of the earnings from Illinois farms with different Soil Production Ratings. The table was prepared by the University of Illinois from income and expense records kept on Illinois farms.

The land with the highest soil rating of 76 to 100 and an average value of $800 per acre returned a rent dividend of 3.72 percent, plus an appreciation in land of 6.38 percent—making a total for the year of income and growth appreciation of 10.10 percent.

Land with a rating of 56 to 75—not quite so productive—and a value of $600 per acre had a total income and growth appreciation of 10.78 percent.

Compare this with the rating of common stocks in 127 industries. The over-all average total for income and appreciation was 9.69 percent, indicating that if one is willing to wait for the appreciation of agricultural land, it is at least an equally good investment and perhaps better.

The next table, Figure 3, reflecting the returns from farm land

Figure 2
LAND VERSUS COMMON STOCKS

Net rents on crop share leases, dividends and appreciation in value of
Illinois farm land and industrial stocks, 1964–67

Type Of Investment	Value On Mar. 1, 1967 Acre or Share	Net Rent or Dividend	Appreciation In Value	Yearly Income & Growth
		Percent of 1967 value/acre or share		
Farm Land: a/				
S.P.R., 76–100	$800	3.72	6.38	10.10
S.P.R., 56–75	600	4.40	6.38	10.78
S.P.R., 5–55	400	4.74	6.38	11.12
Common Stocks b/	279	3.06	6.63	9.69

a/ Farm land with different soil productivity ratings. Values on Mar. 1, 1967
are estimated.
b/ Moody's Industrial Common Stock averages; a composite of 127 industries.

Source: University of Illinois

Figure 3
VALUE OF FARM REAL ESTATE: ANNUAL COMPOUND RATE OF INCREASE

Region	10-year period 1958–68	5-year periods	
		1958–63	1963–68
	Percent	Percent	Percent
NORTHEAST	5.5	4.4	6.6
LAKE STATES	4.1	2.7	5.6
CORN BELT.	4.8	2.2	7.6
NORTHERN PLAINS . . .	5.3	3.8	6.6
APPALACHIAN	5.7	5.0	6.4
SOUTHEAST	6.8	6.2	7.4
DELTA STATES	7.9	5.9	9.9
SOUTHERN PLAINS. . . .	6.6	7.0	6.1
MOUNTAIN.	4.6	4.6	4.6
PACIFIC	5.7	5.5	5.9
48 STATES	5.5	4.4	6.6

Source: U.S.D.A.

in different areas of the country, gives an investor a rough idea of what land earnings to expect in these areas.

Keep in mind that the return an investor gets on his actual investment in farm land is sharply enhanced by the leverage factor. Let us say, for example, that he goes into the deal with 25 percent equity. Even an appreciation of only 5 percent on the total investment is actually 20 percent on the equity—and when realized, the gain is taxable at capital gain rates.

The gain, of course, will not be realized overnight—farm land is a relatively long-term investment. Though farm land possesses a limited inherent liquidity, it cannot be turned over as rapidly as stocks and bonds. Farm land traditionally has had a stable but unspectacular rate of annual return—the greatest return is through appreciation. Thus, the investor must be willing to hold his land over the long term in order to recover his principal.

When he is ready to sell his property, however, he will always find a market for it. Land priced at fair market value is definitely a marketable commodity. Active, successful farmers are always ready to add land to their existing operations. In fact, farmers purchase nearly two-thirds of all farm transfers. In addition, more and more investors—both corporations and individuals—are turning to land as an attractive investment medium.

TAX ADVANTAGES OF FARM LAND

Though land investment should never be regarded strictly as a tax shelter, there are good opportunities to shelter income through sound investment and sound management.

For example, assume that the investor has purchased a farm or ranch property. He now has depreciable assets: buildings, fences, wells, breeding livestock. His property probably requires some improvements—perhaps bulldozing of hedgerows, inprovement of pastures, fertilizing, liming, fence repairs, building improvements. All of these can be expensed. And within certain limits the investor can deduct as ordinary business expenses the money he spends on soil and water conservation, such as filling gulleys, collecting water, retarding runoff, and preventing flood damage. For any one year, these expenses can be deducted up to 25 percent of the farm's gross income, according to Section 175 of the Internal Revenue Code. Expenditures exceeding 25 percent of gross income from farming can be carried forward for future years, within the limitation of 25 percent of gross income from farming in each such year. However, the 1969 Tax Reform Act added Sec. 1252, which subjects these deductions to total recapture if the land is sold within five years and partial recapture if sold within ten years.

In order to qualify for these soil and water conservation expense deductions, the investor must be engaged in the "business of farming," and the land must be used in farming.

What if he has raw or uncleared land that is not being used for farming? Within the limitations set up under Section 181 of the Code, he can deduct expenditures incurred to make the land suitable for farming use. Land-clearing expenses are limited to the lesser of $5,000 or 25 percent of the taxable income derived from farming during the taxable year. In this case, there is no carry-over, and the expense excess must be capitalized. These limitations restrict the tax advantages of buying raw or uncleared land. In addition, IRC Section 1252 imposes the same recapture provisions on land clearing as it does to soil and water conservation.

Depreciation from capital assets, soil and water conservation expenses, land clearing expenses and other expenses is deductible and can provide a write-off against ordinary income. If and when the property is ultimately sold, the gain from appreciation and a lower tax basis comes back as a capital gain. On pre-1970 depreciation, recapture can be avoided by holding the property for at least ten years, in accordance with Section 1250. However, Section 1250 was amended in 1969 to stipulate that all post-1970 depreciation in excess of straight line is recaptured.

There is another important tax advantage in farm-land investment: the "farmer" can use a cash basis for reporting his income.

It works this way: when the farmer is on a cash basis, he reports as income only those commodities that he has actually sold, and reports as expenses those he has actually paid in the taxable year. Originally, this method was allowed to farmers because it made tax computations simpler for them. But it also provides useful flexibility that an outside investor can exploit in conjunction with his other income to achieve tax savings. Crops can be stored and held into a new crop year; seed and fertilizer can be purchased in advance for the next year; and large, depreciable items, such as machinery, equipment, or storage structures, can be purchased to help in adjusting total income.

SELECTING THE RIGHT PROPERTY

If farm land property is wisely selected and efficiently managed, it can provide income, depreciation, substantially increased value, and a great deal of pleasure. On the other hand, if it is done wrong, a farm land investment can be an over-priced, money-losing, time-consuming disaster. Investing successfully in farm land boils down to a simple maxim: buy it right and run it right.

Purchasing farm land is very different from purchasing something like common stock. No matter where the stock is purchased, it is for the same price. But land prices vary extremely according to the locality. The man who buys farm land at $850 per acre in central Illinois may be unaware that he could purchase equally productive land in Mississippi or Louisiana for as low as $400 per acre. The west Texas rancher who buys land at $1,200 per animal unit may not be aware that he can buy equally productive property in Oklahoma at $800 per animal unit or in Arkansas for $500 per animal unit. He has always ranched in west Texas and he wants to continue ranching there. Thus, he does not care about prices in other areas.

Since the tax-shelter investor, however, is an absentee owner, he can take advantage of the fact that there are better land buys in some areas than in others. He will get a better return on his money and have a greater opportunity for appreciation. Farm land in certain areas of the country is underpriced in relation to its capability for production and appreciation. And then there are individual situations—such as estate liquidations and forced sales—that make exceptional purchases possible. In some cases, a property may have been allowed to erode. Do not shy away from such land—it may seem like an unattractive investment, yet it is often the best buy in the area. The few dollars spent on improvements—and they are deductible dollars—can substantially increase the property's value and the ultimate long-term capital gain. However, caution is advisable when the investor is considering eroded land. A thorough analysis of the soil's responsiveness is called for, since in some cases the soil is too far gone to respond to treatment.

FACTS ON FINANCING

Financing for farm land purchases has been affected by the recent tight-money situation just as have other forms of investment. However, farm land purchasers do have one financing source not generally available to other investors: "seller financing."

If the down payment on a farm land purchase is 30 percent or less, the seller can reduce and postpone his tax on the capital gains he derives from the sale. For this reason, about one out of two land sellers prefer to sell on the installment basis. Not only does this increase the financing available, but the seller will usually carry back the balance of the purchase price at a lower interest than the commercial rate.

In addition to seller financing, farm land has the traditional commercial credit sources such as life insurance companies and banks, plus the Federal Land Banks. The Federal Land Banks make long-term farm loans with repayment in annual, semi-annual, quarterly, or monthly installments. Loans are made through local Federal Land Bank Associations, which own all the capital stock of the Land Bank. Funds for making loans are obtained by the sale of bonds to the investing public.

The amount loaned is based on the normal value of the farm and may be used for any agricultural purpose or other requirement of the owner of the property. Loans are made on part-time, as well as full-time farms. Loans are also made on forest properties.

Loans from commercial sources average between 60 and 70 percent of the purchase price, with reasonable repayment terms at the going rate of interest.

MANAGING THE PROPERTY

Besides being absentee owners, most urban investors in farm land have had no experience in modern farming and ranch management techniques. When land is purchased strictly as an investment, the investor should hire competent professional management to operate his property.

A professional farm management company will manage the property and do the economic and tax accounting necessary. It will usually procure tenants to operate the property on a crop-share or a livestock-share basis. To find out about professional farm managers, the investor might consult the American Society of Farm Managers and Rural Appraisers, (470 Colorado Boulevard, Denver, Colorado 80222), or one of the thirty-one state societies of farm management and appraisal. The total membership in these groups approximates 2,000 people involved in professional farm management and appraisal work.

The management company, in consultation with the property's tenant or operator, plans the development and operation of the investor's farm. The company will also collect rents, pay bills, and send periodic reports to the owner, which include a record of the crop-land acreage and production and complete monthly or quarterly financial records.

SUMMING UP THE ADVANTAGES

Investment in farm land, then, is attractive in a number of ways. The demand for land is increasing, while the supply is decreasing, giving the investment a strong appreciation potential. The investor has an opportunity to select land that is underpriced in relation to its potential productivity. There is the advantage of leverage. And not least, of course, investment in farm land provides a useful tax shelter.

COMMENTARY

FEDERAL LAND BANK

By making loans at reasonable interest rates, the Federal Land Bank provides favorable leverage for the investor wishing to put money into farm lands. The land must be used as a farm to qualify for such a loan, but later on it can be shifted in whole or part to residential, commercial, or industrial property.

PROBLEMS OF FARM INVESTMENT

The investor should keep in mind a number of common problems afflicting investment in farm lands:

1. Relative lack of liquidity.
2. The excess deduction account.
3. The hobby loss provision.
4. Excess depreciation recapture provisions.
5. Increasing local real estate taxes.
6. The threat of zoning limitations.
7. Heavier taxes on any capital gains.
8. Excess interest provisions in highly leveraged situations.
9. The difficulty of finding good professional management for the farm, unless it is a very large joint operation.

21

TAX SHELTER OPPORTUNITIES IN AGRIBUSINESS

Peter C. Reid

Despite some limitations imposed by the 1969 Tax Reform Act, investment in agricultural operations can still provide an effective tax shelter by turning taxable income into productive assets. Such an investment, however, is subject to a maxim which all farmers know well: as ye sow, so shall ye reap. Just as a farmer must plant his seeds with care, so must an investor place his money wisely and cautiously. His chances of reaping benefits are slim unless he is sophisticated enough to sidestep the pitfalls that await him.

MR. REID IS THE EDITOR OF THIS BOOK.

The aim of a sound tax shelter investment in an agricultural program should be two-fold:

1. To attain as close to 100 percent writeoffs as possible.

2. To build a solid asset which can either be retained for its returns or disposed of for capital gains.

The investor cannot achieve these objectives, of course, if he approaches a program purely as a tax gimmick. He must give as much attention to the program's economic soundness as he does to its tax benefits. Only then can he make a profit as well as achieve tax savings.

The best tax shelters are usually not easy to understand; in fact, according to agribusiness expert John Train, the more comprehensible a tax shelter is, the less effective it will be, because it will become popular, too much money will be available, and good deals will be hard to get. This brief chapter cannot hope to delve into the abstruse details of an intricate agricultural tax shelter program. It can, however, present some basic guidelines for the investor to follow —while leaving the technical complexities to his tax advisors.

CRITERIA FOR A SOUND INVESTMENT

Is Agribusiness the Right Investment For Him?

As a tax shelter, investment in agricultural operations is most useful to those who are in at least the 50 percent tax bracket and particularly if they have unearned income. An example might be a successful architect planning to retire in five years. He is making $150,000 a year from his profession, plus $30,000 from other sources. This puts him in a painfully high tax bracket. He can ease the pain, however, by investing his money in an agricultural operation. Assume that he invests in an orchard. During the five years it takes the trees to mature, he can use his investment losses to shelter his other income, while delaying any cash flow from the investment until after his retirement, when he will be in a much lower tax bracket.

Does the Program Sell Limited Partnerships?

In agriculture, as in many other forms of investment, a limited partnership format is the most effective way to pass tax benefits through to the investor. In addition, this type of program limits the investor's liability.

Does the Program Provide Maximum Writeoffs Without Gimmicks?

The investor who desires to write off most or all of his investment should seek a program that is designed to relieve him of paying any capital costs of the program, since they are non-deductible. One organization created such a format for a large-scale tree-crop program. As general partner, this organization purchased the land, planted it, then sold it to a pension fund at cost. It then leased the land back for fifty years at 8 percent, with an option to buy at a fair percentage of the estimated market value when the trees matured. The general partner then conveyed the lease to a limited partnership and sold the program to individual investors who agreed to put up some $20 million to pay the costs of operating the groves over a period of years. Thus, the investors enjoyed all the losses until the trees matured—and when income began to flow, they shared the profits.

Although the investor should seek maximum writeoff of his investment, he should firmly resist the temptation of gimmicky deals involving pre-paid interest and other early writeoffs. At first glance, such programs seem attractive because they give the investor tremendous immediate writeoffs. But the investor who gets more writeoffs than he pays for will establish a "negative basis" and sooner or later will have to pay taxes on his excess writeoffs.

Rather than establish such a negative basis, the investor would be wiser to take his writeoffs as he makes his actual investments. Then, when the loss situation becomes an income situation, he will have the cash to pay his taxes. Agricultural shelters are ideal for using this investment approach. After the high initial costs of starting an agricultural operation, the operating costs are fairly even from year to year. This means the investor puts in approximately the same amount of money each year, takes his writeoff, and continues to build his equity in a productive asset with growing capital value.

The way such a program works is illustrated by the breakdown of a tree-crop program in Figure 1. The projections clearly indicate the high degree of tax salvage available to a limited partner, showing that for the first six years of the program he can expect to enjoy the benefit of tax deductions at least equivalent to his cash contributions. Meanwhile, the capital value of his interest is steadily mounting, until at the end of a 10-year program it is equivalent to his cash outlay.

Are the Agricultural Operations Professionally Managed?

It is traditional to consider two major risk factors in agriculture: the weather and the market conditions. However, investors often overlook a third major factor and one that often determines how much return—if any—the investor gets for his money. That factor is the skill with which the operation is managed.

In order to run an agricultural operation profitably, management must first have the incentive to do so. When evaluating tax shelter programs in agriculture, the investor should ask himself if the deal is structured so that the promoter has a selfish interest in trying to make it profitable. In too many agricultural programs, the promoter buys the land, plants it, then sells it to a limited partnership at a big profit, while retaining the management contract, and the packing and processing rights. Having taken his profit out of the deal immediately, he may be less than dedicated in his management of the operation. It is the investors who may suffer as they see a large portion of their investment go down the drain, leaving them with no capital value in exchange for their money.

To avoid this kind of situation, the investor should look for a program in which the promoter does not make a profit until the operation itself is profitable. From the investor's standpoint, the ideal arrangement is one in which the promoter does not take his profit off the top, but shares in the net profits after the *investor* has made money. This type of program provides the promoter with the incen-

ANALYSIS OF MINIMUM LIMITED PARTNERSHIP PARTICIPATION
(2% Interest)

Year	Cash Investment	Estimated Operating Loss Deductions	Estimated Investment Credit	Estimated After-Tax Investment Cost				Estimated Funds Available For Cash Distribution	Est. Market Value of Ltd. Partner's Interest (A)
				77% Bracket	70% Bracket	65% Bracket	60% Bracket		
1968	$ 6,000	$ 6,445	$ 688	$ 350	$ 800	$ 1,123	$ 1,445		$ 10,000
1969	16,000	16,026	832	2,828	3,950	4,751	5,552		20,000
1970	18,000	19,800		2,754	4,140	5,130	6,120		30,000
1971	18,000	20,300		2,369	3,790	4,805	5,820		40,000
1972	18,000	19,535		2,958	4,325	5,302	6,279		50,000
1973	14,000	15,934		1,731	2,846	3,643	4,440		60,000
1974	6,000	8,266			214	627	1,040		
TOTAL	$ 96,000	$106,306	$1,520	$12,990	$20,065	$25,381	$30,696		
1975								$ 1,000	$ 70,000
1976								6,000	80,000
1977								10,000	90,000
1978								14,000	100,000
Thereafter				Historical Price Levels				15,600	100,000

(A) See Footnotes (A) and (C) on Exhibit C-1.

INVESTMENT RATIO'S

		Bracket			
		77%	70%	65%	60%
1. Estimated Market Value of Ltd. Partner's Interest x After-Tax Investment Cost	1974	4.6	3.0	2.4	2.0
	1979	7.7	5.0	3.9	3.3
2. Estimated 1979 Distribution ÷ After-Tax Investment Cost		1.20	.78	.61	.51
3. Estimated 1979 Distribution as a % of Pre-Tax Investment Cost		16.3%			

tive to staff the operation with first-class management people.

Evaluating an agricultural operation itself is not easy for the uninitiated investor. As a general rule, however, he should look for a large, vertically integrated operation. The larger an agricultural operation, the more substantial are the economies it can effect. Just as important is vertical integration. Any fresh produce operation involves a number of important steps such as planting, harvesting, packing, and marketing. Poor management of any one of these steps can turn a potentially profitable operation into a losing venture. Only if all the steps are controlled by one highly skilled management team can the investor be confident that his money with be well utilized. Such a team should consist not only of knowledgable growers—preferably second or third generation farmers of a given commodity —but of first-class financial people, experienced marketing and processing managers, and top people in any other relevant function.

With this kind of team, all steps in the operation can be properly coordinated to maximize its profitability. In addition to devising large-scale economies, such a team can develop innovative practices to beat the competition.

To cite an example, one creative management team in a vertically integrated citrus grove operation has developed a unique method of storing fresh oranges that provides extraordinary marketing flexibility. Traditionally, oranges grown in this particular area have been picked, packed, and shipped immediately to their markets in the spring months. Since most oranges are harvested during the same months, the produce floods the market and drives prices down. With its new storage techniques, the vertically integrated operation can extend its marketing season through the summer, enabling it to ship a substantial portion of its crop when the market is in short supply.

Moreover, the harvesting season itself can be extended. Formerly in this area, oranges had to be picked before the summer months, because if they were left on the tree, they turned green again, robbing them of market value. Now, however, they can be harvested during the summer and stored in a cool environment where they regain their classic color. Spreading out the harvesting season also means that less harvesting equipment and labor is needed.

This is but one example of the kinds of profitable innovations that can be developed by a vertically integrated agricultural operation in which one management team controls all the important steps. Agricultural operations are not known for their sophisticated management practices. This gives the edge to the program that is managed with the same skill and expertise as a successful industrial enterprise.

Can the Investor Get Out of the Deal Successfully?

The investor must always think in terms of the long haul—he must not be so beguiled by short-term tax benefits that he ignores the problems he may face five or ten years from now. He must be constantly aware of exactly what he is committing himself to—before he actually puts in his money.

Basically, there are two types of agricultural programs in which he can invest. One is a tax deferral program, giving him a writeoff in one year and income the following year. Such a program might involve cattle feeding or row vegetables like tomatoes. The investor who puts his money into this kind of program can continue his investment from year to year or discontinue it at any point as he chooses.

Other agricultural programs can be classified as actual tax shelters. The investor puts his money into a long-term operation, such as the start-up and development of an orchard or the development of raw land into an irrigated potato farm over a period of years. He may commit himself to a five-year program in which he makes an investment each year, writes it off, but gets no income. He is, however, building a productive asset. At the end of five years, when the orchard matures, or the farm is fully developed and the cash flow turns positive, he can incorporate, sell his interest, and take his capital gain.

SOME SPECIFIC CROPS

The investor looking for tax benefits in agriculture has a wide variety of possible crops into which to put his money. With the exception of the distinction already pointed out between tax deferral investments and tax shelter investments, almost all of the agricultural crops provide basically similar tax benefits. However, the development of new citrus groves has lost its favored position as an agricultural tax shelter because of changes imposed by the 1969 Tax Reform Act. According to the Act, the first four years of development expense for any citrus grove planted after January 1, 1970, must be capitalized rather than written off as was possible before the Act. The reasoning behind the change: tax incentives had stimulated overplanting of citrus groves, glutting the market and driving prices down. In order to inhibit further planting, Congress decided to remove the incentives. However, an investor can still find tax shelter opportunities in citrus groves. Typically, a citrus grove does not begin to generate a net profit income until eight years after planting. By putting his money into a grove planted before 1970, the investor can still enjoy substantial losses until the grove fully matures.

Almond groves: As a tax shelter, almond groves were recently hit by the same 1969 tax change that took away the tax benefits of citrus groves.

Row vegetables: Investment in such vegetables as tomatoes, cucumbers, bell peppers, string beans, and squash provides tax deferral benefits similar to those of cattle feeding. With the market and climate risks that are present, the investor probably has more of a chance to make or lose money in row vegetables than in cattle feeding.

Potatoes: Investment in potatoes can provide basically the same benefits that were formerly provided by investment in citrus groves—with the major difference being a shorter cycle. In one large-scale Idaho potato operation, the investor commits himself to a four-year development program. He invests in the summer, then sells the crop after the first of the year. The proceeds are plowed into new planting each year.

Christmas trees: Although this crop can provide tax benefits, it has some risks as an economic investment. It is a specialized crop with major marketing problems, and the investor would probably be wiser to stick to basic, broadly marketed commodities such as fruit and vegetable crops.

Vineyards: The growing taste for wine by Americans may make vineyards an attractive investment both for tax benefits and economic returns. As a tax shelter, vineyards provide the same benefits as were formerly provided by citrus groves, and since there is a shortage of wine grapes in California, the government is unlikely to remove the tax incentives from this crop. Once they are planted, vineyards take five years to mature, thus giving the investor substantial writeoffs during that period.

THE EXCESS DEDUCTIONS ACCOUNT

In addition to zeroing in on citrus groves as a tax shelter, the 1969 Tax Reform Act aimed a blow at all agricultural tax shelters with its Excess Deductions Account (EDA). The EDA is applicable to any investor whose nonfarm adjusted gross exceeds $50,000 and whose farm net loss exceeds $25,000. He must then record his excess farm net loss in his EDA, after deducting any farm net income he might have. If he makes any gains from the sale or exchange of farm recapture property, that part of the gain equal to his EDA balance is taxed as ordinary income rather than capital gains.

Thus, although there is no direct restriction on the amount of farm losses an investor can take, his losses in excess of $25,000 will be recaptured if he disposes of farm property. For example, if his EDA balance at the end of the year is $50,000 and he has sold farm recapture property for $80,000, $50,000 of that gain will be taxed as ordinary income and $30,000 at capital gains rates. His EDA balance, however, will be reduced to zero for the following year.

Despite these recapture provisions imposed by the 1969 Act, there are several mitigating factors for the tax shelter investor. First, he can take losses of up to $25,000 before he is affected by the EDA. Second, even if he does take greater losses, he need not worry about the EDA unless he actually disposes of his property. In effect, then, the EDA does not deter a taxpayer from enjoying immediate tax savings from agricultural losses.

COMMENTARY

What this chapter says about limited partnerships is quite sound, but the investor should keep in mind the ground rules of this arrangement that are discussed at the end of the chapter by Mr. Cohen.

22

PENSIONS AS TAX SHELTERS

David G. Lewis

Tax-favored treatment of qualified private pension plans can substantially benefit executive-stockholders of a closely-held corporation. All contributions to such a plan are deductible (within certain limits) by the employer. Benefits are taxed to an employee only when he receives them after retirement. Moreover, they can qualify under certain conditions for favorable tax treatment at the time of receipt. If a trust is established to fund the plan, it is exempt from income tax on its earnings whether they be capital gains, dividends, interest, royalties, or some types of real estate rentals. There is, in addition, the possibility of an estate tax advantage: a death benefit paid under

---

MR. LEWIS IS A PRACTICING ATTORNEY.

a qualified pension plan is not includable in the employee's gross estate for federal estate tax purposes to the extent that it is attributable to employer contributions—if it is paid to someone other than the employee's estate and if the employee did not receive any part of the proceeds before his death.

By adopting a qualified pension plan, executive-stockholders can achieve the following:

1. Defer income to years in which they will have less income and will therefore be taxed at lower rates.

2. Permit earnings on contributions to be free of taxes until paid to the participant.

3. Permit lower tax rates on lump-sum distribution to participants at retirement.

4. Reduce corporate income taxes.

5. Avoid accumulated earnings tax problems for the corporation.

6. Decrease the net worth of the business and the value of its stock for gift and estate tax purposes.

Without a qualified pension plan, the corporation would have to pay out profits as additional salary, or dividends which would be taxed, to the executive-stockholders as ordinary income at higher rates. But when some of these profits are put into a qualified pension plan, they can be paid to the executive-stockholders in the form of pensions in later years when the executives are in lower income tax brackets.

A word of caution is necessary: to qualify for tax-favored treatment, a plan cannot discriminate in favor of officers, stockholders, supervisory, or high-paid employees either by its terms or in its operation.

PENSION PLANS IN GENERAL

A pension plan is a systematic method of accumulating funds to provide deferred compensation to an employee at retirement. The plan may provide for either a fixed and determinable amount to be contributed by the employer regularly, or for a fixed and determinable benefit that an employee will receive at retirement.

To find out how the benefits of a qualified pension plan can be utilized in an executive-stockholder's estate plan, we must first examine the various pension programs that are available.

Suppose a client owns all of his corporation's stock and draws a salary of $3,000 a month. He is 55 years old, and wants to retire at age 65 on a monthly income of $2,000, with the option of taking a cash payment at retirement of $320,000. For ease of computation, we will disregard any other employees of the corporation.

It costs about $160 at age 65 to buy a commercial life annuity paying $1.00 per month. To find how much he must have at age 65 to provide a monthly pension of $2,000, he must multiply $160 by $2,000. The result is $320,000. He has ten years (age 55 to 65) in which to accumulate this amount—therefore he must put aside $32,000 a year as his pension deposit. However, since he will invest the money, he will put aside each year $32,000 less a certain amount that will be gained by earnings compounded annually.

> *Example:* To have $320,000 in 10 years:
>
> 3% interest—Put aside about $27,000
> 4% interest—Put aside about $25,600
> 5% interest—Put aside about $24,230

Obviously, one of the best ways to reduce funding costs is to increase a plan's earnings on its investments.

The actual determination of the contributions to be made is directly related to the benefits desired. Of the many possible benefit arrangements, the most common are:

- Fixed benefit
- Unit benefit
- Money-purchase benefit

FIXED BENEFIT PLAN

Under a fixed benefit plan, the employee receives annually a definite percentage of his compensation, usually his average compensation during his entire employment, or an average of his compensation during a stated number of years before retirement.

Example: The employee will receive an annual pension equal to 40 percent of his average compensation during the last 10 years of employment.

The compensation is the primary factor; the number of years of service of the employee does not enter into the computation of his benefits. However, the plan may require a minimum length of service before an employee becomes eligible to participate.

A formula producing a uniform relationship to the total compensation or the "basic or regular rate of compensation" may be satisfactory, provided it is neither manipulated nor operated to result in a discrimination in favor of the executives, managers, or other highly paid employees.

Example: A fixed benefit plan would operate in the following manner for Mr. Paul, a 55-year old executive. He has 10 years until retirement. His annual salary is $48,000. If his corporation chooses to set up a pension plan, a fixed-benefit-80 percent offset plan can be used to allow the company to put close to $37,000 a year into his account. The total cash in his account at age 65 will be about $461,400.

If Mr. Paul wants to continue working after age 65, the amount accumulated in the fund can remain intact. He may therefore defer the taxation of this accumulated amount until he actually retires. If he were to die before retirement, the entire amount accumulated would pass free of federal estate tax.

UNIT BENEFIT PLAN

Under a unit benefit plan, the participant receives a unit of pension for each year of credited service. As a general rule, unit benefit plans granting past service credit on "actual" compensation during the past service period are adequate. Such plans may also be adequate if the past service credits are based on compensation "as of the effective date of the plan," provided this compensation is reasonable in line with that of prior years. The average of compensation for the five years before the inception of the plan would provide one reasonable basis for comparison.

The annual unit of benefit can be expressed as a percentage of compensation or as a stated dollar amount. The dollar unit includes the situation where an eligible employee is entitled to receive an annual pension which is the product of the stated dollar amount multiplied by credited years of service under the plan.

Example: If the annual unit of credit is $30 and the employee has 30 years of credited service, he would be entitled to a pension of $900 per year.

The percentage unit benefit includes the situation where an employee earns a pension benefit each year which is expressed as a percentage of compensation. For example, in a one percent unit benefit plan, an employee with 25 years of credited service would be entitled to 25 percent of his compensation as an annual pension.

Usually a percentage is applied to compensation up to a stated amount and then a larger percentage is applied to compensation in excess of that amount.

Example: The plan provides a pension of one percent of the first $6,600 of annual compensation plus $1\frac{1}{2}$ percent on any excess. Under such a formula, an employee with 40 years of credited service and an annual compensation base of $10,000 would be entitled to an annual pension of $4,680 computed as follows:

$$40\% \ (40 \times 1\%) \times 6,600 \quad = \$2,640$$
$$60\% \ (40 \times 1\frac{1}{2}\%) \times 3,400 \ = \underline{\ \ 2,040}$$

Annual pension $4,680

Here is a comparison of a unit benefit plan with a fixed benefit plan, assuming both employees are age 55.(Fig. 1)

The contribution and cash value at retirement for Employee A remain the same under either the fixed benefit or the unit benefit plan. But the company gets a substantial cost reduction for Employee B, who had only 10 years of service. Reason: in a fixed benefit

Figure 1
Fixed Benefit

Employee	Salary	Pension	Annual Pension Contribution	Cash Value at Retirement
A	$48,000	$36,912	$37,000	$461,400
B	24,000	17,712	17,800	221,400
			$54,800	

Unit Benefit

Using a 2% unit benefit plan for each year of service (offset with Social Security), we get the following results:

Employee	Years of Service to Retirement	Benefit Rate	Annual Pension Contribution	Cash Value at Retirement
A	40 × 2% =	80% offset with Social Security	$37,000	$461,400
B	10 × 2% =	20% offset with Social Security	3,300	41,400
			$40,300	

plan, the compensation is the primary factor; the number of years of service of the employee does not enter into the computation of his benefits. In the unit benefit plan, the years of service of the employee do enter into the computation of his pension benefit.

MONEY PURCHASE PLAN

A money purchase plan provides for a stipulated annual contribution by the employer, such as 10 percent or 25 percent of the annual compensation of each covered employee. No specific benefit is formulated in advance as under the fixed benefit plan or the unit benefit plan. Instead, each employee will receive whatever benefits the total contributions, plus the earnings thereon, will purchase at retirement. A simple money purchase plan, therefore, recognizes no element of past service. The benefits of each employee will vary substantially with age, compensation, and years of service under the plan. This contrasts with both the fixed benefit and the unit benefit plan, under which the contributions vary according to the amounts required actuarially to provide proportionately equal benefits, or units of benefits, for all employees.

Keep in mind that under a money purchase arrangement, the employer usually contributes a level amount or a stipulated percentage of the participants' compensation. However, the employer's contribution can also be fixed at a specific dollar amount for each participant, e.g., $5 or $10 for each full week worked during the year. The money is either held in trust or by an insurer. The employer contributions plus the earnings thereon are available, at retirement age, to pay whatever pension the accumulated sum can support. For example, in a 25 percent money purchase plan, the employer would annually contribute 25 percent of each participant's compensation. Assuming annual compensation of $10,000, and 20 years to retirement age, the employer would contribute $50,000 for the participant's pension. This amount plus its share of fund earnings would then be available at retirement to provide the participant's pension.

How does the money purchase plan meet the requirement that benefits be definitely determinable? Given the participant's length of service to retirement, his annual compensation, the rate of employer contributions, and an assumed earnings rate, the expected pension benefit meets the test of determinability.

In the fixed benefit plan and the unit benefit plan, the pension was expressed as a stated amount or stated rate of benefit. The employer then was required to make contributions in an amount actuarially determined, which would be sufficient to pay the pension benefit. In the money purchase plan, the rate or amount of employer contribution is stated; the pension plan benefit ultimately payable to a participant will depend upon the number of his years of participating employment after the effective date of the plan and his variations in compensation during such period.

Example: Let us compare a 25 percent money purchase arrangement and a fixed benefit plan for the 55-year -old executive. Assume interest at 4 percent compounded annually.

	Age	Age at Retirement	Salary	Annual Contribution	Cash Value at Retirement
Fixed benefit	55	65	$48,000	$37,000	$461,000
Money purchase	55	65	$48,000	$12,000	$149,800

It is obvious that under the fixed benefit plan, the company will be able to accumulate substantially more dollars for its executive-stockholder.

Now, assume that the executive is 35 years old instead of 55.

	Age	Age at Retirement	Salary	Annual Contribution	Cash Value at Retirement
Fixed benefit	35	65	$48,000	$ 7,910	$461,400
Money purchase	35	65	$48,000	$12,000	$699,900

This example makes it clear that a money purchase plan favors the younger employee over the older employee.

Thus, the type of pension plan selected by a corporation will determine how much will be available for its executives at retirement, and how much can be accumulated free of estate tax should he die before his actual retirement.

COMPARING PENSION PLANS AND PROFIT-SHARING PLANS

Assume an executive-stockholder is 25, and owns all the stock of the corporation. He makes $36,000 a year and wants a pension at age 65 of $2,000 a month or a lump-sum payment of $320,000. In that case, all he need place into the pension plan account would be about $3,240 a year, assuming a 4 percent rate compounded annually. While he needs the $320,000 at age 65, he has 40 years in which to accumulate it.

The next chart shows the maximum amount of money a corporation can put into a pension plan, assuming a pension of $2,000 a month at age 65 or a lump-sum payment of $320,000, and an interest rate of 4 percent. It assumes different ages at which the plan is started and it compares the amount that can be contributed each year under a profit-sharing plan. The executive earns $36,000 a year.

Age	Pension Plan	Profit-Sharing Plan
25	$ 3,040	$5,400
35	5,140	5,400
45	9,690	5,400
55	24,030	5,400

The maximum deduction for an employee in a profit-sharing plan with a $36,000 salary is $5,400. The age of the employee does not matter, since the Code limits deductions for such plans to 15 percent of salary.

As a general rule, if the executive-stockholders are about 45 or older, they should be looking at pension plans. And if they have a profit-sharing plan that was installed when they were younger, they should consider changing to a pension plan.

Let us take this case: the corporation has a profit-sharing plan to which it is contributing 15 percent of the employee's compensation —the maximum deductible amount. The chart below shows what happens if the corporation changes to a pension program, using the same total corporate payments.

CHANGE FROM PROFIT-SHARING TO PENSION PLAN

			Profit-Sharing Plan		Pension Plan	
Employee	Age	Salary	Corporate Payment to Plan	% To Total Payment	Corporate Payment to Plan	% To Total Payment
President	55	$48,000	$ 7,200	37	$ 13,418	67
All other		85,200	12,780		6,562	
Total			$19,980		$19,980	

Now consider a company that has both a pension plan and a profit-sharing plan. When there are two plans, the deduction is limited to 25 percent of covered payroll. If it has a pension plan only, there is no such limitation. This is the result where the profit-sharing plan is suspended and the pension plan formula revised upward:

	Salary	Contributions Present Plan	Contributions New Plan
President	$100,000	$ 25,000	$ 45,000
12 Associates	482,000	121,000	132,000
All others	117,000	58,500	61,200
		$204,500	$238,200

Before suspending the profit-sharing plan, the company may want to amend it to provide for earmarked investments. That is, the participants can select, within certain limits, the investments to be held for their account. In the case just discussed, the plan's trust—as an investment—can insure the company's president, its key man. The trust pays the premiums from its earnings. On the president's death, the profit-sharing trust would have on hand the amounts accumulated plus the insurance proceeds. The trust then buys the president's stock from his estate and holds it as a trust investment. Each of the 12 associates elects to have some of the stock credited to his account. When each retires, leaves the company's service, or dies, he or his beneficiary will receive the stock as a distribution from the trust. This arrangement accomplishes three objectives:

1. The president's estate has a market for the closely held stock.

2. The profit-sharing trust acquires a good investment.

3. Each associate acquires for himself or his family an interest in the business.

LIMITATIONS FOR SUBCHAPTER S CORPORATIONS

The Tax Reform Act of 1969 imposed Keogh-type restrictions on plans adopted by small business corporations electing partnership-type taxation under Subchapter S. No change was made in the allowable contribution amounts if the corporation does not make the election. Here are the contribution limitations for Subchapter S corporations for years after December 31, 1970:

1. The maximum amount that can be contributed to a plan on behalf of a shareholder-employee is the lesser of 10 percent of the compensation received or accrued by him from the corporation during the taxable year, or $2,500. If any greater amount is contributed on his behalf, he must include such excess amount as gross income in that taxable year. A shareholder-employee is one who owns more than 5 percent of the corporation's stock.

2. Forfeitures attributable to contributions deductible for any taxable year begun after December 31, 1970, may not be allocated to any shareholder-employee.

3. If a Subchapter S Corporation terminates its election, it cannot carry forward any excess contributions (not deducted) from a year when it was an electing small business corporation.

TREATMENT OF LUMP-SUM PAYMENTS

One advantage of a qualified plan is the special tax treatment afforded a lump-sum payment of an employee's share at his retirement, death, or other separation from service. Any contributions made by the employer for tax years beginning before 1970 qualify for long-term capital gain treatment. Employer contributions for taxable years beginning after 1969 are treated as ordinary income on payout. But when received in a lump sum they are eligible for a special seven-year averaging procedure. Under this special method, the tax is determined by first subtracting the capital gains portion of the lump-sum distribution. Also subtracted is the amount received by the employee as compensation from the same employer during the distribution year—if he has reached age 59½, has become disabled, or has died. Then, only 1/7th of the lump-sum amount is added to the remaining taxable income—and the tax calculated. The difference between the tax with the 1/7th lump-sum amount and without such 1/7th lump-sum amount is then multiplied by seven. Any amount attributable to employer contributions for plan years prior to 1970 still get long-term capital gain treatment, as will the earnings on any contributions made to the plan. The favorable tax treatment of lump-sum distributions at retirement is the reason why many executives, especially those in the higher income tax brackets, elect such distribution. Before making such an election, however, the employee should realize that the amount he receives will—to the extent that it is still held by him at his death—be subject to federal estate tax.

FITTING THE PENSION INTO THE EXECUTIVE'S ESTATE PLAN

Strictly from the standpoint of estate taxes, an employee might be better off electing an option, if available, to receive his retirement benefit over a period of years—such as for life, with 20 years guaranteed—or under a joint and survivor annuity arrangement. Any balance distributable at his death would still be entitled to the estate tax exemption to the extent it is attributable to the employer's contribution. Such balance, if payable in a lump sum at death, will be entitled to capital gains treatment.

A death benefit from a qualified plan can, as we have seen, escape federal estate tax in the employee's estate. Another consideration—often overlooked—is the effect of the death benefit in the beneficiary's estate. The benefit—to the extent it is not consumed by the beneficiary—will be included in his or her gross estate. In many cases, therefore, it makes sense for the executive to name as beneficiary someone other than his wife.

Suppose a husband has left his wife $2 million in a marital deduction trust—an amount equal to the maximum marital deduction his estate could take. If he names his wife beneficiary of the death benefit under a qualified pension or profit-sharing plan, the proceeds will be added to the marital deduction property received and her own property in forming her gross estate.

A basic goal in estate planning is to skip generations, where possible, so as to reduce the number of times the same property will be subject to federal estate tax. Where the executive's estate is substantial, his wife's estate plan must therefore be considered before he designates the beneficiary of his death benefit. He can name his children as beneficiaries, or he can name a living trust as beneficiary.

The trust can provide generous and flexible benefits for his wife and children, with remainders payable to grandchildren. The trust can be drawn so that no part of the principal will be included in the gross estates of the wife or the children. Thus, the death benefit can escape tax in the estates of the executive, his wife, and his children. (Although this is possible at this writing, proposals by the Treasury Department would eliminate the advantages of generation skipping permitted under the present law.)

In addition to the tax savings available through an *inter vivos* trust are the advantages of trust administration of the death benefits as compared with the direct payment of death benefits. The use of a trust vehicle may be advisable because a lump-sum payment of death benefits carries with it the risk of dissipation by the widow or other beneficiary. A trust can protect both the fund and the beneficiary. The proceeds can be administered by a trustee chosen by the executive, and according to a plan which can be perfectly integrated with his basic estate plan.

The trustee can also be authorized to lend money to the executor and to buy assets from the executor, thereby helping the estate get the liquid funds it needs to pay debts, taxes, and expenses. By naming an *inter vivos* trust as beneficiary of his death benefit proceeds, the employee can control the devolution of the proceeds in any manner and over any term permitted by law, while making available a liquid fund.

In many cases, therefore, naming an *inter vivos* trust as beneficiary of the death benefit is an advantageous step. Such a trust can be created with a nominal *corpus*. It should be authorized to receive death benefits and other property that may be designated by the grantor, and should contain all the necessary administrative and dispositive provisions.

Income tax, as well as other considerations, may indicate the desirability of using more than one *inter vivos* trust. The executive-stockholder may want to name a separate trust for each separate group of beneficiaries. Income tax economies may be effected both with respect to the receipt of the death benefit payments and the income thereafter earned by the trust. If there is more than one trust, and the trustees of each trust are designated to receive a portion of the death benefits, the resulting aggregate income tax to the several trusts may be smaller than if received entirely by one trust.

Earlier, we saw that liquidity problems of the executive's

estate can be solved by authorizing the trustee to deal with the estate. He may be given the power to purchase assets from the estate, to make loans to it, to pay its charges, or to perform any combination of these. The use of a trust provides many practical advantages for an estate holding non-liquid assets.

However, the authority given the trustee for the benefit of the estate may result in a holding that the proceeds were receivable by the executor and therefore are includable in the gross estate for federal estate tax purposes. It has been established that proceeds received by a third party are to be imputed to the estate of the decedent where it is *mandatory* that the beneficiary apply them to charges against the estate.

Therefore, the executive-stockholder should confer on the trustee only a *discretion* to pay such charges, so the proceeds should not be deemed receivable by the executor. Thus, no tax consequence should flow from an authority to make loans to the executor or to purchase property of the decedent so long as the trustee has *no legal obligation to do so*. It is not likely that a discretionary use of employee death benefits to make a bona fide loan with adequate interest or a bona fide purchase at a fair price could be construed to impute the proceeds under a qualified plan to the executor.

THREE IMPORTANT ASPECTS OF PENSION PLANS

Executive-stockholders interested in setting up a pension plan often ask about three particular aspects of such plans: voluntary contributions, life insurance payments, and investments and loans by the trust. Here are the facts on each of these areas.

Voluntary Contributions

The IRS permits an employee to make a voluntary contribution to a pension or profit-sharing plan up to a maximum of 10 percent of his compensation. The trust can provide for 10 percent of the aggregate of his compensation. This means that if there is any year in which he was a participant but did not contribute, he can make an additional voluntary contribution in a future year, up to the maximum of 10 percent of his aggregate compensation while he is a plan participant. Although he does not receive a deduction for this contribution, any earnings on this amount are tax-free while it remains in the trust. Moreover, he may take out his voluntary contribution at any time without penalty. Indeed, a recent revenue ruling was that the participant can also withdraw any increment earned on the voluntary contribution while it was in the trust. This increment would be taxed at the time of withdrawal, but not the voluntary contribution itself.

Life Insurance Payments

Payments for life insurance under a pension or profit-sharing plan can be made from either employer or employee contributions. If they are made from employer contributions, the participant must report as taxable income the pure insurance cost. The amount, which is less than the actual cost of a policy, is determined by the participant's age and the policy's face amount. The IRS permits the use of a term cost based on tables set out by them in Revenue Ruling 55–747.

If the employee authorizes the use of his contributions to pay premiums, he will not have to pick up the cost of the insurance as taxable income. However, the proceeds paid to his beneficiary would then become taxable in his estate. It is only when employer contributions are used to purchase the insurance that the proceeds are excluded from the decedent's estate under Section 2039 (c) of the Internal Revenue Code.

Investments and Loans by the Trust

A trust can invest in any type of securities, funds, mortgages, or other means of earning interest or dividends on its money, all of which is exempt from tax while the fund is building up in the trust. However, if the trust engages in a business other than through owning stock of a corporation, then it is taxable as any other business entity. In addition, earnings from rent on real property are taxable to the extent that there is a mortgage on the property owned by the trust.

For example, if 30 percent of the purchase price is paid in cash and the balance is secured by a mortgage from the trust, 70 percent of the earnings are taxable to the trust. Such earnings, of course, are net after deduction of rental property expenses, including depreciation.

A trust may also lend money at interest. However, if it lends money to the corporation that established it or to stockholders of that corporation, the loan must be adequately secured. If it is not, such a loan would be prohibited under Section 5.03 of the Internal Revenue Code and would result in the trust losing its qualification. Internal Revenue requires that this type of loan meet rigid standards. For example, the general assets of the corporation are not considered adequate security. However, the pledge of specific property valued in excess of the loan is acceptable, as are the accommodation endorsements of those officers of the company who are financially able to meet the indebtedness. Thus, the unconditional guarantee of the stockholders would be adequate if their financial ability to meet the loan is demonstrated.

COMMENTARY

Pension and profit-sharing plans are often essential elements of tax sheltering, particularly if the investor is willing to wait longer to get a larger shelter. Freedom from estate taxes is a bonus shelter. Mr. Lewis's excellent chapter might be even more useful with the following supplementary comments:

1. Pension plans can be financed by sheltering earnings of past and future years, since a contribution can be made even in a year without profit and thus create a carry-back or carry-forward so that taxes of other years go toward the creation of tax-sheltered capital.

2. The amount contributable in a pension plan, particularly for men over 40, rapidly becomes much larger than that available either under a profit-sharing plan or a combination of both types of plans. A profit-sharing plan is limited to 15 percent of compensation and a combination plan to 25 percent. Maximum contributions are made where the group of professionals or executives are put into their own service corporation. This might become a personal holding company, making it necessary to use up as much of the income as is reasonable in salaries under the 50 percent ceiling plus tax-free pension contributions.

3. The advantages of a pension or profit-sharing plan for a corporation with only one or a few employees should be stressed.

4. The cash flow advantages of contributions in kind, such as land constituting a parking lot outside a company plant, should also be considered.

5. It is possible to exchange a lump sum credited at

termination for a variable annuity contract without coming under the seven-year averaging provisions. The taking of this annuity can be deferred. It may even be possible to have the executive control the investments made by the company issuing the variable annuity. This procedure creates minimum taxes, optimum inflation hedges, and maximizes the estate tax exemption potentials.

6. An alternative providing greater selectivity of participants and benefits with considerably lower costs may be found in nonqualified, insured salary continuance plans. Also, particularly for older executives, group ordinary insurance programs for a special class have recently been developed, and approved by the IRS.

23

THE PROS AND CONS OF EQUIPMENT LEASING

By Arthur R. Spector

As a tax shelter—or perhaps tax deferral device would be a more apt term—equipment leasing has some definite advantages over other forms of investment. But no tax shelter is perfect, and like all similar devices, this one has its pitfalls and problems.

Despite them, however, equipment leasing has grown greatly in recent years. Companies that were little more than start-ups a few years ago are now large organizations—examples are Leaseco and Capital Equipment Leasing Corporation. Banks, too, are getting into the equipment leasing business. They are permitted, under the regulations of the Controller of the Currency, to engage in direct leasing,

MR. SPECTOR IS VICE CHAIRMAN OF CAPITAL RESOURCES, INC. AND PARTNER, EWING & COHEN ATTORNEYS AT LAW.

so that an individual or corporation can go to a bank and lease equipment just as he would from any large leasing company. To give but one example of how banks are making use of this permission, the First Pennsylvania Bank and Trust Company during 1969–70 boosted its direct lease financing business from $8 million to $24 million.

The growth of equipment leasing is based on advantages for both the lessee and the lessor.

ADVANTAGES TO THE LESSEE

1. Equipment leasing can make his balance sheet look better. When a businessman borrows money to finance the purchase of an asset, his balance sheet will show no net change, since the asset on one side and the liability to the bank on the other will cancel each other out; however, he may not want an additional liability on his balance sheet, and if he leases the equipment instead of borrowing it, his accountant may not require him to show a liability. This, of course, will improve the balance sheet picture on the liability side.

2. Equipment leasing is useful when the individual or corporation for one reason or another has limited bank borrowing ability.

3. It can be cheaper to lease than to buy. For example, in one well-publicized equipment leasing deal, United Airlines leased a number of Boeing aircraft at a net interest cost of 3.76 percent a year for fifteen years. If they had borrowed to buy the aircraft, they probably would have had to pay 6 percent for their money. I have been informed that a major airlines recently made a comprehensive study of the net cost to them of leasing as opposed to buying. The study convinced them that leasing was the less expensive way for them to acquire a fleet of aircraft.

4. In addition to freeing cash to finance business growth, equipment leasing can generate cash for investing in other tax shelters. A doctor, for example, often owns valuable equipment, but lacks the cash to invest in such tax shelters as real estate or oil. To obtain that cash, he can sell his equipment to a leasing company and then lease it back from them. Anyone doing this, however, should be aware that sell-and-leaseback transactions are vulnerable to recapture of ordinary income. If he has used an accelerated method of depreciation and sells his equipment for a price in excess of his adjusted basis—that is, the original cost minus depreciation—a portion of the gain will be treated as ordinary income, not capital gains. For example, he may have paid $100,000 for his equipment, depreciated it to $30,000, and sold it for $60,000. He must then pay ordinary income tax on his excess depreciation.

ADVANTAGES FOR THE LESSOR

1. The lessor usually knows precisely what his income will be during the term of the lease. This is not true of such tax shelters as real estate investment, where you can project potential income but cannot be sure you will have the tenants to turn the projection into reality.

2. The lessor does not have to worry too much about what salvage value his equipment will have at the end of the lease, because he usually will have already recovered his investment from the lease itself. Anything he can sell the equipment for at the end of the lease is additional profit.

3. Typically, equipment leasing transactions are structured as limited partnerships, permitting the tax consequences of any losses to be passed on to the individual partners. This, of course, is tremendously important, because in the early years of an equipment lease, large tax losses are incurred.

4. Equipment leasing deals can be highly leveraged, permitting the lessor to take depreciation on the full cost of the equipment, not just the amount that he has actually invested in cash. Thus, if equipment has been purchased for $100,000, but only $20,000 invested in cash and the balance borrowed, the lessor can still take depreciation on the full $100,000.

5. In an equipment leasing deal, the partnership may be able to arrange a non-recourse loan to buy the equipment. This means that even though the partnership borrows the money, it has no obligation itself to pay back the loan. The lending institution has recourse only to the rental payments from the lessee—or, in the case of default, to the sale of the equipment for repayment of the loan. Thus, the investor is protected from being personally liable for the loan.

6. During the first few years of its term, an equipment lease provides the lessor with large tax losses. This, of course, is the basic feature that makes equipment leasing a tax shelter device, and it is worth describing in terms of an actual example. Let us say that the lessor has bought a piece of equipment for $100,000. He invested $20,000 in cash and borrowed the rest from a bank at 7 percent interest. To repay the loan, he will make level payments of $11,150 a year for ten years.

He has negotiated a ten-year lease of the equipment specifying rental payments of $13,150 a year, for a total of $131,500. This means the lessor will have a yearly cash return of $2,000 over the term of the lease.

What tax losses will this arrangement provide? First, the lessor can use an accelerated method of depreciation on the equipment. Let us say that he chooses the double declining balance method. If the equipment has a useful life of ten years, he can take 20 percent depreciation—or $20,000 worth—in the first year of the lease. He will also make interest payments of $5,400 in the first year. These two large deductible items will give him net tax savings of $12,250.

In the second year, his tax savings will go down, but will still be impressive: with a depreciation deduction of $16,000 and an interest deduction of $5,000, he ends up with a net tax loss of $7,850. Thus, after two years, he has achieved a net tax savings of $20,100 and has already recovered his cash investment.

THE PROBLEMS BEGIN

It would be pleasant to report that the lessor continues to receive substantial tax losses as the lease goes on, but unfortunately this is not the case. Herein lies the major problem of equipment leasing as a tax shelter—and it is a problem for which there is no really effective solution.

To continue with our example, the lessor's tax losses diminish with each successive year of the lease. There are two reasons: First, he must deduct less for depreciation and second, as he continues to pay back the bank, his deductible interest payments shrink while his principal payments grow. In this case, his net tax loss would drop to $4,200 in the third year and $1,150 in the fourth. The fifth year would be the crossover point, because in that year his income will exceed his tax savings by $1,400. In the sixth year, the difference will be $3,600, and by the ninth year, he will make $5,500 in excess of his tax savings. Keep in mind that the net cash return on his lease is only $2,000 a year—therefore, if he is in the maximum tax bracket, in this ninth year he will have to pay the maximum tax on $5,500 of income. His tax, then, will be $2,250, leaving him $250 out of pocket.

In this particular deal, the lessor will still come out ahead overall. But there have been many equipment leasing deals with less pleasant results, where the substantial tax savings of the first few years have been completely wiped out by the end of the lease.

IS THERE A SOLUTION?

The most obvious solution to the problem, of course, is for the investor to get out of the deal at the end of the fourth or fifth year when the tax savings vanish. However, this is not only difficult to do, but the tax consequences of doing it can be as bad as those of staying in. There is very little free tranferability of interests in equipment leasing partnerships. When the investor tries to sell his partnership interest, he will find very few buyers knocking at his door. Who wants a deal that will produce no cash flow, and yet cause a taxable event? Probably only tax-exempt organizations, who might buy the partnership interest in the hopes of selling the equipment for a profit when the lease is up.

What if the lessor does find a buyer for his partnership interest? Then his problem will be the tax consequences of the sale. He will have to pay tax on the amount he realizes over the adjusted basis of the partnership interest. That amount will include not only any cash or property he may receive on the sale, but also any liabilities from which he is discharged. Since most of his repayments to the bank in the early years have been interest payments, he will still have very large indebtedness at the time of sale. And a gain arising from the discharge of liabilities will not put any cash in his pocket with which to pay the tax.

Moreover, the lessor selling his partnership will find that, under Section 1245 of the Internal Revenue Code, his gain will be treated for tax purposes as ordinary income, not capital gain.

Although an installment sale might seem a likely way out of this, it is not. The lessor will still have Section 1245 to contend with, even though the tax may be deferred. But more importantly, a share of partnership liabilities over adjusted basis would probably be treated as a payment in the year of sale, and under installment sale provisions the seller cannot receive more than 30 percent in the first year. If he treats the share of partnership liabilities over basis as a payment because he has been discharged from them, he will have difficulty meeting the 30 percent test.

How About Pyramiding?

Another frequently suggested answer to the crossover problem is pyramiding. That is, when his tax savings on an equipment leasing deal begin to dwindle, the investor simply joins a new partnership. Ideally, he could continue this constant turnover until he retires.

This system would work, however, only if equipment leasing can survive as a viable tax shelter. Already it has been hurt by the elimination of the investment tax credit in the 1969 Tax Reform Act. In the future, it may be hurt by further changes in the tax laws, such as a disallowance of the accelerated depreciation that is so important to equipment leasing. Thus, the investor who resorts to pyramiding may find in a few years that there are no more equipment syndicates to invest in. This possibility makes the pyramiding approach a rather precarious solution to the crossover problem.

Another possibility is to invest in equipment leasing a few years before retirement, assuming the investor will then drop into a much lower tax bracket. If he is in the highest tax bracket and at retirement would drop into, let us say, a 25 percent bracket, he will be getting his major deductions when he needs them most. Then, when the lease reaches the crossover point, he will not be hurt badly because he will be in a much lower bracket. On the other hand, many executives covered by deferred compensation plans may not drop into a significantly lower bracket at retirement.

Some experts have suggested that the best solution to the crossover problem is to give the property away, either to relatives or to a charitable organization. In this way, they argue, the investor would avoid having to report any gain.

This is not, however, as clearcut as it might seem. Under the Internal Revenue Code, there are substantial questions as to whether the gift of property subject to a liability in excess of the donor's basis is a taxable event. The donor will have a very low basis and a very high liability; therefore, even an outright gift could be considered a gain. Here again, Section 1245 can be troublesome—even though the investor makes a gift of his property, his gain will be treated as ordinary income.

What about contributing the property to a corporation? Though this solution is sometimes suggested, it looks less than attractive if one is familiar with Section 351 of the Code. This specifies that in a free transfer of property to a controlled corporation there will be a tax on the amount by which the liabilities exceed the basis in the property. Once again, the lessor would face the situation of having a taxable event but no dollars.

In some cases it may be possible to combine other property with the partnership interest in the equipment leasing syndicate, and then transfer the whole package to the corporation. In this way the investor can increase his basis to equal his liabilities. This solution, of course, is not for everybody.

SOLUTION: STAY IN FOR THE DURATION

Upon analyzing the drawbacks of getting out of an equipment leasing deal, it becomes fairly clear that the investor who contemplates such a deal should plan to stay in it for the full run of the lease. He is more likely to end up in the black with this approach than by trying to avoid the problems of the later years of the lease.

The crossover problem is not the only one with which an investor in equipment leasing may be faced. Another is careful scrutiny harassment by the IRS. Equipment leasing syndicates are carefully set up as limited partnerships so they will not be treated as taxable corporations. But at least one equipment leasing syndicate has been challenged recently by the IRS, which contends that it should be taxable as a corporation. The likelihood is that the syndicate will eventually win its case. However, the case should be warning to those considering equipment leasing deals that the IRS may not willingly accept their partnership status.

IRS agents are also on the lookout for ostensible equipment leasing deals that are actually conditional sales. An example would be the company that leases a $20,000 piece of equipment for five years under an agreement that it can buy the equipment for one dollar at the end of the lease. Obviously, this is a conditional sale and will be taxed as such. In a bona fide leasing deal, the partnership owns the property at the end of the lease term. If the lessee has the right to buy it, the sale must be made at the fair market value for which the lessor can sell it to anybody else.

TAX SHELTER—WITH PROBLEMS

Equipment leasing deals can be a useful tax shelter, but the investor must be aware of the serious problems and pitfalls that can wipe out whatever tax savings he achieves in the early years of a lease. Before selecting an equipment leasing deal, the investor must carefully project exactly what the tax consequences for him will be, not just during the first few years, but throughout the complete term of the lease.

DISCUSSION

Question: How binding are the leases in an equipment leasing deal?

Mr. Spector: The leases are non-cancellable for the initial term, so that unless the lessee goes bankrupt, he can be sure he will get that amount of money for the term.

This means the lessor has no real risk in the property. The lessee will return to him all of his investment, amortize his debt, provide him with a return. His only real risk is in receiving the payment.

Question: If the lessee does not pay, do you sue?

Mr. Spector: Yes, but that is not a very effective remedy. In such cases, the lending institution gets first crack at the money. It will first get any payments it can from the lessee, and it can keep those payments until its debt and any penalties or accrued interest have been satisfied. Then it can, if necessary, sell the equipment and keep the proceeds to satisfy the debt. The lessor will get only whatever is left over after that.

Question: What happens if one leases a piece of equipment and a few years later more advanced equipment is introduced that makes the leased equipment obsolete?

Mr. Spector: If that happens, the lessee will be very upset. Despite that, however, he is still legally obligated to pay the rentals throughout the term of the lease. What he might do is sublease the equipment to another organization, continue to make payments to the lessor as required, and acquire the more advanced equipment.

Question: How did the 1969 Tax Reform Act affect equipment leasing as a tax shelter?

Mr. Spector: A number of important provisions in the Tax Reform Act affected equipment leasing as a tax shelter.

For 1970 and 1971 only, "excess investment interest" is a tax preference item. To the extent that an investor's "investment interest expense" exceeds "net investment income" there will be a preference. It should be noted that net investment income includes rent not derived from a trade or business; the Act provides that property which is subject to a net lease entered into after October 9, 1960 shall be treated as property held for investment and not as property used in a trade or business. This Reform Act section may not be as troublesome as might first appear, however. In the first place, the excess investment interest simply is not going to be that large. Secondly, certain leases may not be "net leases" within the meaning of the section. In a computer lease or airplane lease where the lessor provides maintenance services one may not be within the definition of a "net lease" for these purposes.

Another tax preference item affecting equipment leasing is accelerated depreciation on personal property subject to a net lease which is in excess of the deduction allowable if the taxpayer had used straight line depreciation from the inception of the lease.

Next, beginning in 1972, there will be a limit on the deductibility of "investment interest" which is comparable to "investment interest expense". Property subject to a net lease will be deemed to be held for investment and a limitation placed on the deductibility of the investment interest.

Finally, the investment tax credit was repealed in the 1969 Tax Reform Act. This, of course, was one of the major advantages of equipment leasing as a tax shelter, and its elimination is a serious blow.

COMMENTARY

RECAPTURE OF DEPRECIATION

A major problem of equipment leasing is that under IRC-1245 *all* depreciation—not just excess depreciation— is subject to recapture on sale. This offsets the fact that, unlike real estate investment, equipment leasing permits the use of double declining depreciation.

SALVAGE VALUE

The investor should be aware that the IRS may declare a high salvage value on the equipment which must be subtracted before depreciation is determined. This is mitigated if the property is used in trade or business, since a 20 percent additional deduction may be taken under IRC-179.

PROFIT POTENTIAL

The key to successful equipment leasing lies in how much rent can be collected and how much the equipment can be sold for eventually. This means that when the investor is considering a specific equipment leasing deal, he must make a complete analysis of the ultimate tax effects and have an extremely accurate idea of how profitable the leasing operation will be in a business sense.

24

CURACAO: PORTRAIT OF A CARIBBEAN TAX HAVEN

Neil A. Martin

For years, when business organizations sought a tax shelter in the Caribbean, they inevitably turned to the Bahamas. Like Switzerland, the Bahamas offered the freedom from income tax, privacy, and accommodating governmental attitude so important to companies wanting to establish a financial subsidiary.

Recently, however, a new name has been added to the list of Caribbean tax havens. Curacao, with its favorable tax climate, strategic location, strong currency, and sophisticated banking, financial,

MR. MARTIN IS A FREE-LANCE WRITER ON BUSINESS AND FINANCE.

and legal services, is now a popular retreat for foreign-owned finance and investment companies. Over the years, more than 1,500 such companies have been incorporated in Curacao, nearly 100 alone in 1970. The majority are finance holding companies, but they also include about 85 mutual funds of all varieties, some 225 patent-holding companies, and a number of Free Zone, ocean shipping, and aviation companies. They pay about $6 million yearly into the government kitty.

HOW CURACAO BECAME AN INVESTMENT CENTER

Curacao's recent growth as an investment center has been due largely to the establishment of financing subsidiaries by big international companies. The first to try was Siemens Ag., the West German electronics firm, which started to float a $25 million bond in May, 1967, but withdrew at the last minute because of poor market conditions. Five months later, Royal Dutch/Shell was more successful—it established a finance subsidiary to raise $50 million in the Euro-dollar market. Since then, by one count, more than a billion dollars has been raised on the Euro-dollar market by such subsidiaries, most of them American-owned firms seeking ways around current U. S. restrictions on overseas investment.

Moreover, in 1969, just before world stock markets began their 18-month nose-dives, a number of U. S. companies, such as Tenneco, Walter Kidde, Leasco Data Processing, Giffen Industries, and Tyco Labs, obtained nearly $1 billion in the Euro-Bond market through Curacao. In addition, several European firms—Swiss Aluminium, Courtaulds, Siemens, Watney Mann, and Redlands Holdings among them—used the same route to tap the market for more than $325 million. Things slowed down a bit in 1970 due largely to unfavorable interest rates on the European continent and a bear stock market on Wall Street, but the issuing of three debt issues in early 1971 (General Mills, Hamersley Iron, G. U. S. International) signaled the return of the finance subsidiaries to Curacao. "Business has picked up again," says A. A. G. Smeets, a prominent notary whose Handelskade (Commerce St.) office has registered more than

600 of these companies in the last three decades. The importance of Curacao as a financing center assumes even more significance when it is noted that island-based companies accounted for nearly half of all Euro-dollar bonds issued by international companies.

Scores of off-shore mutual funds, investing in everything from other funds to Japanese and Australian securities, have been set up in Curacao. Some of the more recent newcomers include First Security Capital and Income Fund, Pacific Seaboard Fund, The Fund of Hedge Funds, and the Convertible Bond Fund. While assets of Curacao mutuals may vary from as little as $5 million or $10 million dollars to $90 million or more, the combined portfolios of all the funds operating on the island is believed to range between $750-$800 million.

Although Curacao has been a Johnny-come-lately on the financial scene compared with such long-entrenched tax havens as Switzerland, Liechtenstein, Luxembourg, and the Bahamas, the Dutch retreat has, nevertheless, certain advantages over these centers. As a result, business is rapidly swinging its way. "If we continue as we have in the last two or three years," says Ernst F. Blase, manager of Pierson, Heldring & Pierson, investment bankers, "we certainly have a chance to become a second Switzerland."

SOME BASIC FACTS ABOUT CURACAO

Surrounded by the deep blue waters of the Caribbean and cooled by the year-round northeast trade winds, Curacao is the largest member (pop. 138,000) of the Netherlands Antilles. This group of semi-independent Dutch islands is in turn part of the Netherlands Commonwealth, along with Surinam on the South American mainland and Holland itself. The territory of the Netherlands Antilles (N. A.) consists of two island groupings—the so-called "ABC" islands (Aruba, Bonaire, and Curacao) and, 500 miles away, the second and smaller group of Leeward Islands, St. Maarten, St. Eustatius, and Saba. The latter group lies about 100 miles east of Puerto Rico.

With a population of 200,000 its only natural resource, the

economy of the N. A. depends largely on tourism and the processing of basic materials for export. Shell and Standard Oil operate large refineries in Curacao and Aruba, respectively, and government officials have recently been trying to diversify the economy by attracting new investment to absorb excess labor. A number of well-known U.S. and foreign firms have recently set up shop in Curacao and the other islands, including Texas Instruments, Solitron Devices, Continental Grain, International Salt, and Pot Distiller (a German-run producer).

CURACAO'S FINANCIAL INCENTIVES FOR INVESTORS

While these government efforts have so far enjoyed only limited success, Curacao continues to grow with the business it knows best—sheltering investment companies, patent-holding firms, and other N.A. corporations. Under tax laws drawn up in 1940 and modified only slightly in subsequent years, Curacao offers some of the most liberal financial incentives for foreign-owned corporations to be found anywhere in the world. N.A. corporations not actively engaged in local business are exempt from foreign exchange controls and are free to dispose of their capital and profits derived from foreign sources. A stable currency, covered 100 percent by gold, guarantees easy convertibility whenever needed. No statutory minimum capital is required of companies wishing to set up a fund-raising holding company, as is the case in Switzerland and other tax havens. Borrowing flexibility is also assured by the absence of limitations on the size of bonds being issued (in Luxembourg, for example, the bond debt of a financial company is limited to ten times the nominal share capital). Another advantage is that directors, officers, or shareholders can reside outside Curacao.

THE TAX LURES OFFERED BY CURACAO

By far the biggest incentives, however, are offered by Curacao's tax structure. For financial holding companies, the benefits are immediately apparent. There is no capital tax, no withholding tax on interest paid to non-resident holders of bonds, and no estate tax for non-residents. Although a corporate income tax is levied, the special rates are low: 2.4 percent on net income up to $53,000 and 3 percent on net over that amount. Interest payments are deductible from taxable income.

A big boost to Curacao's attractiveness as a tax haven came in 1963, when the U.S.-Netherlands tax treaty was extended to the Netherlands Antilles. This meant that U.S. finance companies, which more often than not ship the proceeds of their bonds sales back to their U.S. parent or fellow subsidiaries, are exempt from U.S. withholding tax on interest and royalties from U.S. sources—a benefit the Bahamas cannot offer. And dividends from U.S. sources are subject to a reduced U.S. withholding tax of only 15 percent, while interest income of the Curacao finance subsidiary is taxed at a 24 to 30 percent sliding tax rate.

The Netherlands Antilles, however, has introduced one requirement aimed at ensuring that the financial company generate some income for tax purposes; namely, that the net fiscal income derived by the company by means of financing with a bond shall not be less than one percent of the face value of the issue. For all practical purposes, this means that the difference for the Curacao subsidiary between in-coming and out-going interest must be at least one percent. This requirement has brought complaints by some companies that they are being forced to charge affiliates or subsidiaries at least one percent more than the rate they themselves pay on the Eurobond market.

However, this inconvenience is more than compensated for by the absence of sales taxes, surtaxes, and most other kinds of levies, except for a stamp tax which is assessed on the face value of the stock certificate at the rate of 4 percent per 1,000. Moreover, the tax position of these holding and investment companies is guaranteed for at least ten years from incorporation.

HOW TO ESTABLISH A HOLDING COMPANY

In addition to offering tax advantages, holding companies are inexpensive to establish, are easily dissolved, and leave few tracks. N.A. law defines an investment company as "a corporation which exclusively or almost exclusively has the following objective: aquiring, holding, administering, and alienating securities."

To set up such a company five simple steps must be followed: 1) obtain a "deed of incorporation" through one of Curacao's seven local notaries (notaries are not to be confused with U.S. notary publics—in Curacao, a notary is an attorney of long-standing and is appointed to his position by the Netherlands Crown); 2) secure a "no objection" from the Justice Department; 3) get a business license from the Department of Social and Economic Affairs; 4) receive an exemption from the Exchange Control Board; and, 5) keep at least one managing director in residence locally.

To meet the last requirement, most Curacao investment companies retain management companies such as Curacao International Trust Co., Antillian Management Corp. (AMACO), Trust Co. of the Algemene Bank Nederland, or Pierson, Heldring & Pierson, to represent them in Curacao, while most of the important investment and policy decisions are made by the parent company back home.

Since the incorporation process involves mostly paperwork, investment companies can be established within a few days if necessary, although slow government processing makes the normal waiting period from four to six weeks.

CURACAO'S DEPENDABLE DISCRETION

Still another point in Curacao's favor is the Swiss-like secrecy with which these dealings can be accomplished. Most of the notaries and trust managers refrain from discussing the details of even those transactions that have been advertised publicly. Although all companies incorporated are on file with the Commercial Register of the Chamber of Commerce and Industry in Curacao, holding company registrations show only the authorized capital and names of three local managing directors, usually a trust company and two individuals. The names of the companies do not reveal who the owners are and no official statistics are kept on the nationality of the holding companies.

Furthermore, courts are reluctant to order banks and trust companies to open their records in tax disputes and, in the case of funds, shares are not required to be registered with the government. By contrast, the Bahamas, because it is a part of the Sterling Area, is forced to keep track of capital movements, including dividends, interest, and profits, and requires that at least five shareholders be registered with the Exchange Control. In Curacao, Europeans can invest in a Curacao fund, receive bearer shares, and dispose of them as they see fit without worrying about reporting to the government. "We have better anonymity here than in the Bahamas," says Peter C. Poot, managing director of Algemene Bank Nederland's Trust Company.

CURACAO'S "GO-SLOW" POLICY

Not surprisingly, government officials and businessmen are publicly cautious about Curacao's past growth and future potential, lest success spoil the island's image. "We don't want the Antilles to become another Bahamas, and we avoid people who are merely tax dodgers or attempting to funnel 'hot money' into the island," notes Dr. J. A. Schiltkamp, a prominent notary who has incorporated about 400 investment companies over the years. Adds Algemene Bank's Mr. Poot: "The government watches the funds very closely to guard against any attempts by Americans to invest illegally. Nobody here wants to kill a good thing (the U.S. Tax Treaty) and Curacao can't afford to antagonize the U.S. Treasury or I.R.S."

Consequently, the government has adopted a "go-slow" policy, particularly in permitting the growth of foreign banks in the N.A. Remembering the experience of the Bahamas, where paper banks were set up one day and disposed of the next, N.A. officials are determined this kind of thing will never happen there. They also want to protect the businesses of local banks. So far, only two foreign banks have been chartered for business in the N.A. Besides the aforementioned Bank of America, The Bank of Nova Scotia was permitted to establish a branch at Philipsburg, St. Maarten, earlier in 1969. "We want to wait and see how things work out before permitting any other foreign banks to come into the islands," says J. G. Blikslager, director of the central bank of the Netherlands Antilles.

The phenomena of foreign branches is so new to the N.A. that the government had to draw up a banking act to cover the situation. The act includes temporary provisions now applied to the foreign banks: no branches on more than one island; no lowering of paid-in capital; no participation in other N.A. banks or credit institutions; and, no merging or regrouping.

MUTUAL FUNDS IN CURACAO

Funds are also watched closely, not so much for illegal U.S. investment by U.S. citizens, but for buying by local citizens. In the early 1960's, Antillians were able to purchase fund shares, but the promotional activities of an Investors Overseas Service (I.O.S.) fund soured the deal for the rest. I.O.S. was said to have used a hard-sell approach, even to the point of a door-to-door campaign. This rankled the government, which refused to grant I.O.S. an exemption for exchange controls, thus effectively ending its operations there in 1964.

The central bank and some government officials would like to see local mutual sales resume, but in an orderly fashion. "We don't want any Barnum-and-Bailey type promotion," says one high-ranking official. A ruling on this matter may be forthcoming in the near future.

Whether there would be much of a market in the N.A. for sales of fund shares is questionable. With the exception of a few wealthy private individuals and families, sources of local capital are scarce. Per capita income in the N.A. is only slightly over $1,000, savings total about $325,000, and the total assets of the Antilles commercial banks are about $146 million. Moreover, with Curacao's offshore mutuals' portfolios expanding every year, there would seem little need for them to look to the N.A. for customers.

Most of the funds' portfolios are invested in U.S. securities. Like Nassau, Curacao is in the same time zone as New York, where the money is invested and managed. Air and phone contacts are generally good. Thus supervision from Willemstad, where the funds' managers are located, is little more than a formality, with the real brain work being done in New York.

Fees for the New York advisor generally are based on a percentage of the monthly increase in fund assets over the Dow Jones averages increase. In Curacao, fund managers may simply charge a flat fee for their services or a percentage of the growth in assets. "It depends on how much work is involved," notes one fund manager. "If we have to do everything, the cost will be higher," he adds. Like most offshore mutuals, the Curacao funds are aimed at permitting foreigners without substantial savings or financial connections to invest directly in Wall Street. Both the U.S. treasury and the S.E.C. encourage such investments as a means of helping to correct the balance-of-payments deficit. In 1968, for example, foreigners invested $2 billion in U.S. securities, up from $500 million in 1967. A major inducement to foreigners to invest in Curacao is the Foreign Investors Tax Act of 1966, which for the first time exempted foreigners from U.S. taxes on trading profits and capital gains. Offshore funds on the island also enjoy a low withholding tax rate of 15 percent (instead of the usual 30 percent) on U.S.-source-dividends, which when combined with a 15 percent N.A. profit tax can result in a 4 to 5 percent total tax savings on dividends for funds compared with the general tax schedule.

A Variety of Funds

Curacao has all three types of funds—hedge, holding, and captive. The Fund of Hedge Funds, for example, established in 1968, has diversified its holdings among a number of U.S. funds which specialize in hedging (short selling) and leveraging (borrowing) in order to achieve capital appreciation and minimize the impact of general dips and rises in the market. As its name implies, The Convertible Bond Fund was set up in 1968 to invest in Euro-dollar bonds and debentures issued or backed by U.S. companies for long-term capital appreciation.

Two more recent and rather unusual funds appeared in 1969: the Pacific Seaboard Fund and the First Security Capital and Income Fund. The first, capitalized at $2 million, has most of its portfolio outside Wall Street, mainly in countries with a window on the Pacific such as Japan, Australia, and Canada. The latter, on the other hand, is a "dual invest" fund that seeks long-term growth of both capital and income from capital shares worth $16 million, while maintaining current income to pay interest due on $24 million worth of 7 percent debentures. Hence, the investor is given a choice of whether to go for short-term return or long-term capital appreciation.

There are some other new wrinkles being devised by innovative money-managers. One involves what is essentially a combination finance company and mutual fund. Under a setup currently being experimented with by several U.S. companies in Curacao, the finance company floats bonds on the Euro-dollar market. The fund part of the combine uses proceeds as capital and offers bonds in amounts larger than its own capital, on a five-year basis. The theory is that at the end of five years, if the market is good, the fund will have achieved a considerable non-taxable capital gains profit and can pay back its finance partner.

"It is complete speculation," cautions one local investment advisor. "A wrong decision or unexpected turn in the market could bring the whole thing down like a house of cards."

CURACAO'S REAL ESTATE POSSIBILITIES

Encouraged by the success of Greater American Corp. in the Bahamas, a number of investment companies are hungrily eyeing real estate as a new field to conquer in Curacao. Although no real estate investment companies have been cleared for business yet, one local trust manager says that he has four such companies in the process of registrations. The companies would invest largely in U.S.

plates such a deal should plan to stay in it for the full run of the lease. He is more likely to end up in the black with this approach than by trying to avoid the problems of the later years of the lease.

The crossover problem is not the only one with which an investor in equipment leasing may be faced. Another is careful scrutiny harassment by the IRS. Equipment leasing syndicates are carefully set up as limited partnerships so they will not be treated as taxable corporations. But at least one equipment leasing syndicate has been challenged recently by the IRS, which contends that it should be taxable as a corporation. The likelihood is that the syndicate will eventually win its case. However, the case should be warning to those considering equipment leasing deals that the IRS may not willingly accept their partnership status.

IRS agents are also on the lookout for ostensible equipment leasing deals that are actually conditional sales. An example would be the company that leases a $20,000 piece of equipment for five years under an agreement that it can buy the equipment for one dollar at the end of the lease. Obviously, this is a conditional sale and will be taxed as such. In a bona fide leasing deal, the partnership owns the property at the end of the lease term. If the lessee has the right to buy it, the sale must be made at the fair market value for which the lessor can sell it to anybody else.

TAX SHELTER—WITH PROBLEMS

Equipment leasing deals can be a useful tax shelter, but the investor must be aware of the serious problems and pitfalls that can wipe out whatever tax savings he achieves in the early years of a lease. Before selecting an equipment leasing deal, the investor must carefully project exactly what the tax consequences for him will be, not just during the first few years, but throughout the complete term of the lease.

DISCUSSION

Question: How binding are the leases in an equipment leasing deal?

Mr. Spector: The leases are non-cancellable for the initial term, so that unless the lessee goes bankrupt, he can be sure he will get that amount of money for the term.

This means the lessor has no real risk in the property. The lessee will return to him all of his investment, amortize his debt, provide him with a return. His only real risk is in receiving the payment.

Question: If the lessee does not pay, do you sue?

Mr. Spector: Yes, but that is not a very effective remedy. In such cases, the lending institution gets first crack at the money. It will first get any payments it can from the lessee, and it can keep those payments until its debt and any penalties or accrued interest have been satisfied. Then it can, if necessary, sell the equipment and keep the proceeds to satisfy the debt. The lessor will get only whatever is left over after that.

Question: What happens if one leases a piece of equipment and a few years later more advanced equipment is introduced that makes the leased equipment obsolete?

Mr. Spector: If that happens, the lessee will be very upset. Despite that, however, he is still legally obligated to pay the rentals throughout the term of the lease. What he might do is sublease the equipment to another organization, continue to make payments to the lessor as required, and acquire the more advanced equipment.

Question: How did the 1969 Tax Reform Act affect equipment leasing as a tax shelter?

Mr. Spector: A number of important provisions in the Tax Reform Act affected equipment leasing as a tax shelter.

For 1970 and 1971 only, "excess investment interest" is a tax preference item. To the extent that an investor's "investment interest expense" exceeds "net investment income" there will be a preference. It should be noted that net investment income includes rent not derived from a trade or business; the Act provides real estate, but also perhaps in South America and Europe. If the companies perchance invest in Holland or Surinam, net profit (including capital gains) derived from such property would be entirely tax-exempt.

And finally, Nomura Securities, Japan's largest brokerage house, and Pierson, Heldring & Pierson in Curacao, have joined together in a unique approach to financing part of the construction program of Pioneer Electronic Corp., Japan's leading producer of stereophonic systems and components. They offered a "Curacao depositary receipt," or CRD. American and European depositary receipts—certificates showing stock ownership without actual possession of the shares—have been used for some years by foreign companies to avoid unfavorable taxes in markets where their shares are to be listed. But this was the first time someone had offered depositary receipts out of Curacao. The reason: the stamp tax on a CDR, which can be listed on the Amsterdam exchange, is only four per mille of the face value of each certificate, whereas if the shares were offered outright in Holland they would be assessed two per mille of their actual market value, meaning a higher premium for the Dutch investor. "We were amazed that nobody saw the possibility before of issuing CDR's" comments Pierson's Mr. Blase. "It's clearly laid down in black and white in the statutes for anyone to see."

In this booming tax haven, reading between the lines as well as the black-and-white is all part of the game.

COMMENTARY

Though this article is basically sound, the investor should be sure to consult a tax expert on certain specific provisions of the Internal Revenue Code that may affect investment in Curacao. They are:

1. The interest equalization tax (IRC-4911 - 4920).

2. Subpart F (IRC-951 - 964).

3. Foreign personal holding company (IRC-551 - 558).

4. Tax on sale of stock in foreign corporation (IRC-1248).

5. The advantages of such stock being held in an offshore trust should be considered (see Chapter 9). The extreme tax shelters of Puerto Rican exempt corporations, particularly when held by such trusts, also should be considered.

APPENDIX

PREPAID INSURANCE RESERVE—ACCOUNTING FOR THE SURRENDER CHARGE

In the first year that a life insurance policy is put in force, the full reserve behind the policy is reduced by a surrender charge. This is an amount that the life insurance company would keep to cover its start-up costs if the life insurance policy pays another premium, a fraction of this surrender charge is released and picked up in the cash value or surrender value of the policy. After all the surrender charge is released, the cash value is equal to the full reserve behind the policy.

A typical way to calculate this surrender charge is the way one major company does it. Its surrender charge is calculated at $16 per original face thousand of insurance, no matter what the type of insurance. In policy years 2 through 9, as each renewing premium is paid, $2 per thousand of this $16 surrender charge is released and picked up in the cash value. Thus, at the beginning of the 10th year when all the surrender charge has been released, the cash value is up to the full reserve.

For this reason it is suggested that a corporation on an accrual accounting basis could set up this surrender charge as a prepaid insurance reserve and then expense it out of the reserve at the rate of one-eighth per year for years 2 through 9 as the released surrender charge is picked up in the cash value on the books of the corporation.

The only event that would prevent the full surrender charge from being recovered by the corporation would be the surrender of the policy during the first 9 years. If this should happen, any remaining balance in the prepaid insurance reserve *for such policy only* would be expensed in that year. To further explain this procedure, here is how it is explained in the master rate-book of the referred-to insurance company:

"In the first year of an insurance policy there is acquisition expense for doctor's fees, taxes, commissions and other expenses connected with putting it on the books. This expense must be charged against the regular policy reserve in establishing the cash value in the first year. However, if the policy stays on the books, this acquisition expense is recovered and credited back over the next years in *additional* cash value reserves. By the 9th policy year the cash value is up to the regular policy reserve. In the 10th and subsequent years the cash value increases at a normal rate.

"An example of how this shows up on a 20-Pay Life policy at age 20 is as follows:

Policy year	(1) Policy reserve increase	(2) Acquisition charged	(3) Expense credited	(4) (1) − (2) + (3) Cash value increase
1	$ 202.50	$ 160.00	$ -------	$ 42,50
2	207.10	--------	20.00	227.10
3	211.90	--------	20.00	231.80
4	216.60	--------	20.00	236.60
5	221.80	--------	20.00	241.80
6	227.10	--------	20.00	247.10
7	232.30	--------	20.00	252.30
8	237.80	--------	20.00	257.80
9	243.30	--------	20.00	263.30
10	248.90	--------	-------	248.90
Totals	$2,249.20	$ 160.00	$ 160.00	$2,249.20

Comment

The accounting fraternity has an opinion issued late in 1970 which states that it *is not* in agreement with the idea that the early year's "expense" of owning a life insurance contract could be reserved and spread as an expense over the life expectancy of the insured. This is a logical opinion because such an approach is a marshmallow. The tables say that Mr. X, the insured, should live 21.7 years. But no one knows if Mr. X, in particular will prove to be that average man.

However, the establishment of the prepaid insurance reserve described above is purely mechanical and is exactly the way the life insurance company sets up its surrender charge.

INDEX